DATE DUE		
- 4 APR 2005			

TRINIDAD VILLAGE

TRINIDAD
VILLAGE

MELVILLE J. HERSKOVITS

AND

FRANCES S. HERSKOVITS

OCTAGON BOOKS

A DIVISION OF FARRAR, STRAUS AND GIROUX

New York   1976

Reprinted 1964
by special arrangement with Alfred A. Knopf, Inc.

Second Octagon printing 1976

OCTAGON BOOKS
A DIVISION OF FARRAR, STRAUS & GIROUX, INC.
19 Union Square West
New York, N.Y. 10003

LIBRARY OF CONGRESS CATALOG CARD NUMBER: 64-24843
ISBN 0-374-93876-8

Manufactured by Braun-Brumfield, Inc.
Ann Arbor, Michigan
Printed in the United States of America

FOR

JEAN

THE YOUNGEST MEMBER OF
THE FIELD PARTY

PREFACE

IN 1929, returning from field-work among the Bush Negroes of Dutch Guiana, we spent several days in Port-of-Spain, Trinidad, waiting for a ship to take us to the United States. In a local newspaper we came upon a letter from an aroused citizen expressing indignation at certain practices then being carried on near the capital by Negroes who were worshippers of Shango. We forthwith promised ourselves to come back to Trinidad after we had finished the field-work in West Africa that had been arranged for the following year, and investigate this Shango worship and the ways of life of the people who carried it on. For we knew it could derive only from the Yoruban peoples of Nigeria, and must represent an important body of direct African cultural retentions.

Ten years were to pass before we found ourselves in Trinidad, ready to undertake the study we had outlined in our minds on the basis of the letter in the *Trinidad Guardian*. Because Shango worship was so near the capital, we thought it evident that this cult, and the African ways of life we assumed to be associated with it, would be met in greatest purity in the districts remote from this center of European contact. The choice of a community removed from Port-of-Spain was thus the first requisite; the second, that it be small enough so that we might come to know it well.

Contrary to all our expectations, however, the remote community where we worked proved to be without Shango worship — without, indeed, any more Africanisms than would be found in almost any rural Negro community in southern United States. Yet the materials it eventually yielded, as if casting a sudden flare against indistinct masses, silhouetted for us in clear outline the means whereby transitions from African custom to ways of life preponderantly European had been achieved by Africans and their descendants. The Shouters sect, for example, revealed how African worship, as exemplified in present-day Trinidad in the Shango cult that we were able later to study in Port-of-Spain, had been shaped and reinterpreted to fit into the pattern of European worship. The institution of "keepers," the form of Trinidad common-law marriage that resembles extra-legal Negro matings in all the New World, was seen to be a reconciliation of European monogamic institutions and African relationship groupings based on broader definitions of kinship and plural marriage. The transformation of Sankey and Moody hymns into "shouts" was found to represent a parallel point of transition in musical style.

Materials of this nature, projected against the background of our earlier work in Negro cultures elsewhere, led us to the formulation of the theoretical postulates that are stated in the early pages of this book and are documented from the comparative materials in the final chapter. These, we believe, are applicable to the processes of change in human civilization everywhere. We call attention here specifically to the concepts of cultural focus, of cultural retention, and to the mechanisms of readaptation and reinterpretation of custom that permit a people to retain the inner meanings of traditionally sanctioned modes of behavior while adopting new outer institutional forms.

These hypotheses of cultural dynamics led us in turn to recognize the specific historical sequences that eventuated in the culture we were studying, and in similar institutions and value-systems found elsewhere among New World Negro peoples. One such sequence was made up of the events that stripped away from New World Negro societies the larger aspects of African culture, leaving as the distinctive characteristics of their ways of life only the more intimate elements in African custom. Another was the sequence that set up the divergent drives through which the Toco Negroes, and those living in similar situations elsewhere in the New World, are at once held by the force of a learned tradition that springs from African sources, and driven by the desire to acquire for themselves the benefits that arise from ability to manipulate European culture.

From a less theoretical point of view, our materials will, we hope, prove of use to those who are charged with the solution of more immediate problems, both in the Caribbean and in the United States. As far as we know, this study is unique in that it constitutes the only attempt thus far made to present a systematic, rounded view of all phases of life of any Negro community in the English-speaking portion of the Caribbean area. Those charged with facilitating adjustments of an inter-racial character, or with ameliorating the position of underprivileged Negro groups, have understandably devoted their efforts to immediate political and economic questions. We believe that the implications of the picture of Toco life given in this book indicate the need to take into account traditional sanctions no less than overt institutions.

We realize, of course, that changes have occurred in Trinidad since 1939. However, correspondence with friends on the Island has made it clear that, although the war and the establishment of American bases have somewhat altered the picture, no fundamental changes in the life of the rural Negroes has taken place.

Our field-work was made possible by a grant from the Car-

viii   *Preface*

negie Corporation of New York, and assistance for working
up our data was provided by the Graduate School of Northwestern University. In Trinidad itself, we count ourselves
fortunate in having had the fullest cooperation of the Colonial Government, then headed by His Excellency, Sir
Hubert Young, who showed sympathy towards the ethnological approach, and deep understanding of the aims of our
research. Our friends, Mr. Edward MacEchrane and Mr.
James A. Bain, were sparing of no effort in helping us resolve some of the practical problems of getting settled to
carry on our work. In Toco we were the recipients of many
courtesies from Mrs. Albert Monsegui, and of the aid of
Sergeant Dash, head of the police detachment there. The
many villagers who came to be our friends, and to whom
we owe whatever insight these pages may hold, we must
leave unnamed, as is their wish. The freedom with which
men and women described their beliefs, their aspirations
and discontents, contained an implicit awareness that we
would not make light of the realities of the situation of
village life, nor of colonial attitudes. Dr. Richard A.
Waterman has kindly permitted us to use the transcription
he made of the Sankey hymn included in this work. Mr.
Charles S. Espinet, of Port-of-Spain, has been helpful in
clarifying for us the picture of war-time economic conditions in the Island, and has secured for us the cooperation
of Mr. Conrad S. Bennett, a native of Toco, and photog-
rapher for the *Trinidad Guardian,* who made photographs
from which some of our illustrations are taken. To all these,
we wish to express our deepest gratitude.

MELVILLE J. HERSKOVITS
FRANCES S. HERSKOVITS

Evanston, Illinois,
September 10, 1946.

CONTENTS

ILLUSTRATIONS

TRINIDAD VILLAGE

CHAPTER I

TOCO

TOCO IS A SETTLEMENT at the extreme northeastern part of the island of Trinidad, situated almost exactly at the juncture of the Atlantic Ocean and the Caribbean Sea. Across a twenty-mile strait northward, dark on the horizon, is Tobago, famous as the scene of Robinson Crusoe's adventures. For Toco it is more important as the birthplace of many inhabitants of the village.

The population of Toco is almost entirely Negro. There are a few Chinese and a few whites, but Toco is far removed, in terms of island distances, from the southern and western portions of Trinidad, where most of the British Indians live, and from the capital in the northwest, where the majority of the whites are found. Nor is Toco touched by the industrialization of southern Trinidad, where the oil-fields and refineries are located, or by the commercial preoccupations of Port-of-Spain, the capital, and of the trading centers in the interior parts of the Island.

The life of the Toco Negroes parallels that of Negroes in many other West Indian islands, and in the rural sections of southern United States. Despite the differences in physical setting and prevailing social and political regimes, the ways of life of all these groups have been influenced by historical and economic factors so alike that the societies they constitute have comparable institutions. In all these regions, the bearers of one body of tradition have

3

had to adapt it to the patterns of another, dominant culture, with the resulting effect of variable, yet recognizably similar attitudes and reactions.

The system of slavery, of which the present order in Toco like that elsewhere in the West Indies and in rural southern United States is the immediate descendant, did provide for the minimum physical requirements of the slave, and to that degree afforded him at least bare subsistence. But it deprived him of psychological security by rendering meaningless traditional African institutions and their validating sanctions. Only in a few areas of the New World was aboriginal tradition able to reassert itself as a functioning reality — that is, after escape from slavery through uprisings or by its abolition.

Such a restoration of earlier patterns may be seen in the peasant life of Haiti, for example, in the interior of Dutch Guiana, or among the Maroon communities in northwestern Jamaica. But in most cases where the estates or the plantation system carried over from slavery times, the freed Negro found employment as landless laborer or sharecropper. There was no possibility for wider relationship groupings to function, no mechanism was available to meet pressing economic needs, and supernatural sanctions had to be sought in terms of reinterpretations of a new religious system.

In northeastern Trinidad, the life of the Negroes presents such an adjustment, one that may be thought of as a kind of disordered orientation. It has the integration of any long-established body of custom; yet as one talks to the people, and observes their ways of life, tensions of a particular kind soon become apparent. These tensions are manifested most clearly in uncertainties arising from the prevalent economic insecurity, and from frustrations bred of the social and legal proscriptions of culturally sanctioned traditions of family life and worship. It will be our task to describe the customs of Toco, their derivation, their effect on the life of the people, and the compensations to them which have given this society continuity and a measure of adjustment.

2

Students of human societies, almost since the inception of their disciplines, have been concerned with the problem of law in history. Lacking the laboratory controls of the exact sciences they have been baffled by the challenge of accurate prediction. Hypothesis has bravely followed hypothesis — that society evolved in stages, that human social behavior is actuated by the operation of a group mind, that material elements in culture are more changeable than ideas and values, that the quality of a culture is determined by the circumstance of rural or urban setting. But none of these hypotheses has been found to have more than a limited validity, for the exceptions established for each were so numerous as to negate its value as a universal.

The materials from Toco, when considered in terms of the historic past and the functioning present, form a representative segment of the range of New World Negro cultures that together give us a veritable historical and social laboratory. These materials suggest that attempts to determine valid laws of social change have not been successful because they have not adequately distinguished the two different kinds of drives that, working together, fashion any civilization. There are first of all the forces that, without reference to cultural form as such, are constantly at work to maintain the balance between stability and change in every culture or, where different cultures are in close and continous contact, to accelerate change. Then there are the unique historical sequences of events which, in any given instance, determine particular reactions in specific situations, and through this the particular forms that the institutions, beliefs, and values in a given culture will take at a given moment in its history.

In the analysis of this Toco culture, it will be necessary to keep in mind both kinds of forces if we are to understand the culture as it is to be observed. Thus, the broad underlying principle that a culture is learned, rather than determined by some element in the biological endowment of a people, and that in consequence any tradition can pass from the group that has devised it to any other that may have the opportunity to learn it, is fundamental to our approach. As regards cultures in contact, the further hypothesis is advanced that while opportunity to learn new ways accelerates borrowing, the circumstance of a particular contact will modify this process so as to make for a greater or lesser degree of acceptance of the new and retention of the old. In this process of change, it is thus assumed that acceptance of the new, or retention of the old, in responding to the total situation of contact, will be subject to the operation of the mechanism of reinterpretation.

Further, it is assumed that this borrowing — and the assumption will be documented by facts about Toco ways of life — will be selective. It will never take place evenly over the total range of a culture, but will rather be determined by the prior concerns of a borrowing people. This brings us to the concept of cultural focus: those aspects of the life of a people which hold greatest interest for them. In a stable culture, innovations are most readily accepted here, for people like to talk about the things that interest them. This talk familiarizes them with differing possibilities, and increases their receptivity to new ideas. Under contact, however, especially where pressures are applied to force change, resistance is greatest in the focal area; or, if resistance is futile, the psychological resilience afforded by the process of reinterpretation comes into play.

These are some of the mechanisms that, operative in all human cultures, have been at work in Toco. But here, as elsewhere, these general processes must be distinguished from sequences of unique historical factors that explain specific cultural forms found in a given culture. Slavery immediately comes to mind as an example of such an historical sequence. For though the institution of slavery is widespread, the forms of New World Negro slavery were quite different from those of the Graeco-Roman world; and the two had quite different influences on the patterns of life of those who lived under them.

The effect this New World system had of stripping from the aboriginal African culture of the ancestors of Toco Negroes their larger institutions, leaving the more intimate elements in the organization of living, and thus setting up a new balance between the roles of men and women, is another specific and unique historical sequence. Similar results might eventuate in other slave societies, or they might not. Here we are not dealing with a general "law," but with the forms of particular institutions, the nature of which in any given case would depend on the kind of slavery, the intensity of the repressions in the system, and other specific determinants. This is history; and the specific quality of historical factors will be further apparent in the comparison of religious Africanisms in a community such as Toco, where Protestantism prevails, with the retentions in the Trinidad Shango cult that developed in contact with Catholicism, as did the comparable African cults of Haiti, Cuba, and Brazil.

The study of Toco life thus lays bare processes that throw light on the controversial problem of law in history. It suggests that the idea of the uniqueness of historical events, and the related concept that it is impossible to establish laws concerning human social life, derive from the stress that has been put on explaining the forms of particular institutions, to the neglect of the study of the dynamics of cultural change in general. If, however, we assume that cultural forms are unique, but that the underlying processes they express are constant, a fresh attack upon the problem becomes possible.

It is apparent, furthermore, that our analysis of Toco has far wider application than a mere comprehension of Trinidad Negro society, or even of New World Negro behavior. Everywhere over the world, peoples of different cultures are in continuous contact, with results of the utmost importance for their future relationships. The processes operative in Toco are, in many instances, those that have given the Negro the place he holds today within the wider cultural spheres of the United States, the Caribbean, and Central and South America. If we are to understand these processes and to attain control over them; if we are to cope adequately with the day-to-day problems raised by the presence of minority groups of varying cultural background within majority populations; we must assess and comprehend both the general laws of cultural dynamics, and the particular historical forces that brought about change in Toco, even in so fundamental a phase of human social life as the respective roles of men and women.

3

The important place which women hold in Toco culture is one of its most distinctive aspects. In this, we at once recognize a characteristic of other Negro societies in the New World, where the significant place of women has often been remarked. We may best phrase this by regarding the women of these societies as the principal exponents of the culture; a fact that takes on the greatest significance for any understanding of the nature of the adjustments that

Negro groups have made to their varying situations not only in Toco but in all the New World.

What do we mean when we say that women are the "principal exponents" of their cultures? We mean, in short, that they are the essential bearers of tradition, the primary agents in maintaining conventionally accepted modes of behavior. This is something tangible that field research soon comes to take into account. For, over an amazingly large part of the total range of Toco culture, the women know how things are done, and by whom; they understand best why things are done, and what happens if they are not. They figure importantly in the economic life of the community, they are paramount in matters having to do with family affairs, they are predominant in the religious life, and in any concern with magical controls.

Their place does not mean that men do not count. For the most important figures in the community are men who are specialists of various kinds. But again, to turn to the insight field investigation can give, one soon discovers that men do not have much to discuss concerning the prevailing modes of life. A man, when asked to talk about what he does and how he does it, is much sooner exhausted as a source of information than a woman.

A ready explanation of this comes to mind when the life led by this society is described, as it will be in the chapters that follow, for the men have the duty of providing for their families, their economic position is low, their time for leisure is slight. One is tempted to conclude, therefore, that the women have time to concern themselves with other matters. Further probing, however, shows that this explanation does not suffice. Women, as will be seen, have no more leisure than men, for in the main they participate fully in the task of earning a living. Furthermore, one soon learns that it is not all women who hold this place, but essentially the older women. These, again, though less pressed by their round of duties than their juniors, are released to no greater degree than are old men.

The fact is that an understanding of the place of women in Toco or other Negro societies cannot be gained unless full account is taken of the present situation in the light of its historical antecedents, African no less than those sequences of events on this side of the Atlantic that gave the lives of these people their present form. In essence, we must assess the place of men and women and their customary activities in African societies, compare this with the New World scene of today, and determine what caused the change that resulted in the phenomenon that has claimed our attention.

The place of men in the African societies from which were derived the ancestors of the Negroes of Toco, the remainder of Trinidad, and the rest of the New World, is that which, broadly speaking, men have held in most integrated social units. With few exceptions, the over-all direction of affairs is in their hands, no matter what aspect of culture is considered. Larger matters in the field of economic endeavor are their responsibility; they head the extended families and are chiefs of the sib organizations; they exercise political control, filling the chieftainships and constituting the tribal and local councils; religious cults are under their direction; they are the artists and craftsmen who do the woodcarving, metal working, weaving.

The role of women, though not less important for the functioning of these cultures, may be termed a more intimate one in most of its phases. While West African and Congo women hold a high economic position, and do most of the selling in the markets, the crafts-guilds are composed principally of men; though there are wealthy women, most wealth is under the control of men. Except in the more complex African economies, indeed, woman's sphere is essentially associated with maintenance of the household.

Within the family, she is most concerned with the nuclear unit which, in these polygynous African societies, is likely to consist of herself and her children, inhabiting a hut within the compound that also houses her co-wives and their children, and the common husband.

The political sphere of women has perhaps best been summarized in an admonition to colonial officials concerning their dealings with African tribes, written many years ago by one of the ablest early observers of West African life, herself a woman, Mary Kingsley. *A propos* of dealing with the native chief, she stresses the importance of not underestimating the power of "the old woman you may see crouching behind him, or whom you may not see at all, but who is with him all the same, and says, 'Do not listen to the white man, it is bad for you.' " In West Africa and the Congo, a man rarely fails to consult his mother — or, to a lesser degree, a wife or selected wives — for advice in making the decisions he must make as a political figure or as family head. In the religious life of African peoples, women hold a comparable place. The priests who exercise the controls are almost always men. But the initiates, the devotees who carry on the rites — who, deep down within the cults, perform the essential routine and are charged with the responsibility of everyday management of affairs, who train initiates in cult dances and songs, and teach the details of sanctioned behavior within the shrines to those who are preparing to worship there — are women. To phrase the relative place of men and women in the religious life, the experience of field research may again be called on. In the main, the student finds himself discussing theology with men, ritual with women.

The extent of this contrast to a New World Negro culture such as that of Toco will later be apparent. Similarly we shall recognize the challenge of accounting for the change from a society in which men have their well defined executive powers, to one in which women exercise important controls and functions. As has been stated, the answer must be sought in an analysis of those drives that developed from the institution of slavery under which the Negroes lived during most of their existence in the New World. In essence, we are concerned with understanding how this institution suppressed certain elements in the cultural patterns that were brought from Africa, distorted others, and lifted still others to a place of unwonted importance.

In our opening paragraphs it was indicated that slavery deprived the Negro of psychological security by rendering meaningless the traditional African relationship groupings and their validating supernatural sanctions. This, however, was only a part of the process. Most of the principal aspects of the aboriginal economic system were suppressed; few African political mechanisms could survive; the organization, if not the spirit and meaning of African religion was rendered impossible; there was little time for art, and few incentives to stimulate the artist to express his aesthetic drive. In short, what slavery did to African culture was to strip it of all its formal aspects; its broader institutional structures, its principal mechanisms of control — those forms by which these African societies expressed their individuality and achieved their equilibrium.

Today, the economic destiny of New World Negro groups is determined by forces, and is under the control of persons, as far removed from these groups psychologically as they are distant geographically. In the political sphere, also, and in the realm of law, the regulations that govern behavior are not of their making; indeed, many of their codes, as will be shown, are outside the law, so that moral sanctions often run counter to regulations set up by governing bodies in which they have no word.

The broader relationship structures of Africa have, as has been stated, ceased to exist, for there is no place in a society such as Toco, or in other Negro societies like it, for functioning extended families, much less sibs. Even in the field of religion these people must seek surreptitious means of worshipping in ways of their own choosing. The church groups with the largest resources, and the best buildings, that in Toco and elsewhere in the West Indies often conduct the only schools in Negro communities, are controlled from afar, or are under immediate white supervision.

Controls of just this order in Africa are the concern of men. This means, then, that the process, under slavery, of stripping the New World societies, composed of Africans and their descendants, of these institutions, in depriving them of traditional direction of their own ways of living, had the inevitable result of emasculating their cultures. No other term is applicable to the situation that emerged on the abolition of slavery. For after generations of immediate supervision, the Negro, though now legally free, still found himself in the lowest social and economic strata of the societies of which he was an integral part, without voice in the direction of affairs, whether social or economic or political, whether he was immediately affected by the decisions made or not.

When this occurred, what then was left to these Negro societies? The answer to this question, when phrased in these terms, becomes at once apparent. Those more immediate concerns of living, the more intimate and detailed phases of the culture survived, which in aboriginal society were the affairs of women. These essentials could be, and were carried on despite the prohibitions of slavery, since they in no way constituted a challenge to the dominance of the master or to the regulation of life imposed by him. These cultural elements could be, and were handed down from one generation to the next in the slave cabin until, under freedom, they emerged, this time as distinctive aspects of Negro culture everywhere in the New World.

How this process worked out may be exemplified if we consider in greater detail a single aspect of Toco life — and the life of other Negro societies of the Americas. For this analysis, the family may be chosen. Like other aspects, Toco family life presents deviations from the canons of customary behavior sanctioned by the dominant, European-derived cultures of the peoples among whom the Negroes live; deviations that must be explained if the present forms of social and other institutions characteristic of Negro life are to be grasped in proper sociological and historical perspective.

The three levels of social structures based on kinship now found in the parts of Africa from which the ancestors of the New World Negroes came have already been mentioned; here we may describe them briefly and indicate the roles they play in African society. The first is the immediate family: a man, his wife or wives, and their children. They inhabit a compound, constitute the primary economic unit, and are the effective mechanism for perpetuating the culture, since in this unit the education of the young is carried on. Within the immediate family, however, is the nuclear group, made up of a given wife and her children, who inhabit a separate dwelling-place within the compound, in accordance with the fundamental rule of African polygyny never to place two wives in one hut. The husband has a place of his own to which his wives come, each in turn at fixed intervals to cook for him and wash his clothing, and to sleep there. Pregnancy, and sometimes the nursing period interrupt this regime, so that psychologically the center of existence for a woman and, more important, for her children is the hut where she and her children live.

A number of immediate families, headed by brothers and elder sons who live near one another, make up the extended family, the next level of kinship grouping. An extended family is often of considerable size. If the men in it are persons of consequence, each has a number of wives and many children. At times, a grouping of this sort will constitute an entire quarter of a town. Women are little concerned with relationship groupings of this order, except when as older members they serve the ancestors, or when the eldest male, the family head, must rule on a proposal of marriage, or there is financial aid to be sought, or the rites of death or of the ancestral cult must be participated in.

The sib, or clan, is even more exclusively the affair of the men, once more excepting the old women who carry out the daily rites of the ancestral cult. A sib may be a very large organization indeed, with its extended families found over the whole of the territory inhabited by a tribe. It is semi-political in nature and, insofar as it is the instrument of enforcing the totemic prohibitions and prescriptions of its forebears, has deep religious and ethical significance. It may be wealthy and powerful. This is especially true in the case of the royal sib, whose ancestors, moreover, are not far removed from the category of national deities.

All this superstructure disappeared in the New World. Only in the interior of Dutch Guiana, where live the Bush Negroes whose ancestors escaped from slavery more than three hundred years ago, are sibs found. The extended family is occasionally retained, altered, and reinterpreted as an informal, broad kinship group. Such groups, as encountered in the United States, for example, play little role in ordering the lives of the people, and they take on no institutionalized structure at all. But the immediate family, especially the nuclear grouping with a woman as its effective head, has everywhere persisted — to such a degree that students sometimes speak of the New World Negro family as "matriarchal" in character.

We shall see how, in Toco, this type of family has persisted, with the mother or, more impressively, a grandmother, as the real stabilizing agent. The lightness with which the bonds of mating can lie on the parties to a union will be indicated; and what false perspective on the thinking of the people is given by the application of legal terms such as "legitimate" and "illegitimate" to the offspring. Men do play their roles — but the roles remaining to them are those of contributors to the maintenance of the household and collaborators in bringing up the children. Only when one moves into more favored social and economic strata of Negro society does one find the man regaining in terms of white patterns some of the controls that were his under African patterns of family life.

What happened to bring about this new pattern of family structure should now be clear. The sib, the extended family — that is, those institutions where the men were paramount — were stripped from the culture the Africans brought to the New World. Impossible to maintain under slavery, to a degree that not even the tradition of their existence still survives, they withered and died. Yet, though all this was lost, little of the fundamental, basic realities in family life was changed. For when the superstructure was removed, those more intimate phases of the kinship order were left exposed, where they had always been, deep at the heart of the larger, more imposing units. And these nuclei of African family life, which had always been the concern of the women, continued to be their concern. Under slavery, and since, until the present, the deep attachments between a mother and her children continued to dominate the emotional life of the people, and to give stability to the family. As for the father, he continued to play for the nuclear group the institutionally remote, humanly somewhat secondary role that in Africa was his as the parent shared with the children of other mothers than one's own, a role that was transmuted into the more or less transitory position he holds in so many of the poorer families of New World Negro societies.

The matter may now rest at this point, since the total problem of the retentions and reinterpretations of African customs by the Toco Negroes can best wait for consideration until their culture has been described and its functioning analysed. But the assumption made here should be kept in mind as the materials in the chapters that follow are presented, since this will aid in understanding how the apparent simplicities of Toco culture are but the outer garb of a way of life that, at the core, is anything but simple.

4

Though Trinidad was discovered by Columbus in 1498, it was settled so slowly that almost three hundred years later, in 1783, the population was somewhat less than three thousand persons. Originally inhabited by Carib, Arawak, and other American Indian tribes, Spanish settlement and control, which meant the enslavement of these Indians and their deportation to the nearby South American mainland, soon destroyed all but a remnant of them, those remaining being mixed-bloods crossed with whites and runaway Negroes. So effective was their extermination that a traveller, in 1864, deemed a visit to a "pure Arawac Indian woman" worthy of special note. The last refuge of the Indians was in the northern mountains of the Island, in the vicinity of Toco, where now can be found old people who remember having seen some of them.

The policy of the Spanish crown, which closed the Island to all who were not of Spanish nationality, and the depredations of pirates operating off the Spanish Main, were the principal factors that kept Trinidad a poverty-stricken backwater of the flourishing West Indies. These were also the reasons for the late introduction of Negro slaves in any numbers, wherein Trinidad offers a striking exception to the rest of the Americas of that time. This is the more remarkable because employment of Negro slaves on the Venezuelan mainland was well-established from the early days of Spanish occupancy. The account of the Carmelite friar, Antonio Vasquez de Espinosa, who wrote at the end of the sixteenth century, gives an extended description of how Negroes were employed as pearl-divers on the nearby island of Margarita, but does not mention Negroes at all in the description of Trinidad.

In 1783, however, when Spain opened the Island to non-Spaniards — provided only they be of the Catholic faith — the population increased rapidly. The period between 1783 and 1797, the year when Britain captured the colony from the Spanish, gave this Island, never a French possession, its French character. "Encouraged by the liberal offers made under that cedula," says de Verteuil, the historian of Trinidad, "colonists began to throng from Grenada, St. Vincent, and the French islands, succeeded by a few refugees from San Domingo, with some émigrés from France, and even Canada. Their example was followed by many respectable colored families from the above-mentioned islands. . . ." Many immigrants brought their slaves — in such numbers that, with other recruits, there were over two thousand white persons, forty-five hundred free Negroes, and ten thousand slaves on the Island before 1790. The first sugar plantation was established during this immigration. By 1797 there were over a hundred and fifty of them, and twice as many specializing in coffee, cotton, and cocoa.

Little was changed when the English took over. French and Spanish residents, undisturbed, continued to dominate the life there. English became the official language, but for most of the people, particularly the Negroes, "créole," the Negro-French *patois* heard in all the West Indies, was the language most widely, if not exclusively employed, especially outside Port-of-Spain. This is apparent in the querulous comments of English tourists of the nineteenth century who, in their travels through the back country of this British possession, experienced such difficulties in making themselves understood as would be expected in foreign territory. Today, though the Island is thoroughly Anglicized, Spanish and French names abound. There is a local French group, proud of its heritage and highly self-contained, and among themselves many Negroes still speak créole.

In 1838 slavery was abolished. The slaves deserted the estates and assumed "squatter's rights" over garden plots, which by the end of the century numbered more than twenty thousand. But the estates had to be worked, and to work them the owners, especially in the southern parts of the Island, where sugar was the principal crop, began to import "Coolies" from British India as indentured workers. Today these workers may no longer be brought to the Island, but their descendants number almost one hundred and seventy-five thousand. They speak their own language, dress in the Indian manner, cultivate their irrigated rice patches, and otherwise follow the modes of life of the parts of India from which they derive. Their temples are everywhere in the southern part of Trinidad, and their religious processions are often encountered on the roads. This population constitutes one of the most picturesque elements of the Island, bulking large in the literature of tourist bureaus.

From the first, the Negroes showed no liking for these new arrivals, and this feeling was reciprocated. Charles Kingsley, in 1871, tried to explain this in the terms of his day: "The Coolie, shocked by the unfortunate awkwardness of gesture, and vulgarity of manners of the average negro, and still more of the negress, looks on them as savages; while the negro, in his turn, hates the Coolie as a hardworking interloper and despises him as a heathen." Scenes enacted two decades earlier, when a shipload of British Indians was unloaded at Port-of-Spain, as recounted by an eye-witness, testify to the fact that this antipathy existed from the time the importation of these people began. It still exists as a negative attitude, though softened by time and experience, and by the fact that the British Indians have established their position on the Island.

The question of cultural borrowing between these groups, who have been in close and continuous contact now for almost a century, immediately comes to mind in connection with our analysis. By many who do not know Trinidad well, its inevitability is taken for granted, as, indeed, the experience of cultures in contact elsewhere might suggest; for it need scarcely be pointed out that antipathy, as such, between groups in contact is no barrier to the diffusion of the customs of one to another. This has not occurred to any significant degree among the Negroes of the northern part of the Island, where British Indians are few, as will be apparent in the pages that follow.

A high-ranking police officer of wide experience in the Island stated, however, that this mutual cultural aloofness also holds for the south, where "Coolie" settlements are concentrated. Moreover, he indicated that such borrowing as had occurred had been by British Indians of Negro custom, particularly magic; for the power of the Negro obiaman, the worker of magic, is called on with some frequency by these people. An explanation of the slight degree of cultural interchange between the two groups will not be attempted, since the problem lies outside the scope of this investigation.

Trinidad has long been one of the crossroads of the earth; today it continues this role in intensified form. Its capital, Port-of-Spain, is a modern city. The economic importance of Pitch Lake, where, in earlier days, caulking materials were to be had, and later asphalt for paving the world's roads, has given way to the oil-wells and the refineries of the southeastern arm of the Island. The high bush, except in substantial government reserves, has been replaced by estates, or by individual holdings of small proprietors, who, however, are relatively few in number when contrasted to those who work the land on shares, or perform agricultural or industrial labor for wages.

The great majority of the present population is Negro, though the census does not tell how many are Negroes in the Island's total of a half million inhabitants. Negroes are predominant in the lower economic and social strata. Some, principally mixed-bloods, have achieved positions of importance in government and business, and more and more are demanding a share in the direction of affairs which has lodged historically in the hands of Europeans, or those of European descent.

Whatever his economic status, the Trinidad Negro is proud, and is jealous of his rights; if reports from early travellers are to be trusted, he has long exhibited these traits. He is eager for education, as is shown by the presence of more than two hundred fifty primary and intermediate schools, in a colony where education is compulsory in only a few centers. He is, in a word, at home in a setting with which he now identifies himself, and where he is willing to spare no effort to gain for himself control over the ordering of his life.

The origins of this Negro population, critical in any analysis of a New World Negro culture, can be indicated only in the most general terms, and then principally by reference to what is known of other areas in the Americas. That some slaves were brought early and that Negroes, both free and slave, came or were imported in considerable numbers beginning with the nineteenth century, has been stated. African tribal and place names encountered elsewhere — Yoruba, Kromanti, Ibo, Congo — appear often enough in the scant literature to assure us that the provenience of these people is no different from that of Negroes of the

United States, Jamaica, Haiti, the Antilles, or South America.

In the documentation of provenience through contemporary sources Trinidad differs from the other islands. Had the archives of the Legislative Assembly of the Colony not been destroyed by the fire of 1903, facts of this order might perhaps have been had. But, in all likelihood, they would only have supported the inference to be drawn from available evidence: that the Trinidad Negro, in greatest proportion, is only secondarily of African derivation. In 1876, there were in the Island but 4,250 Africans; in 1881, 3,035 of African birth; in 1931, only 164. Both oral and written accounts tell that he came from other West Indian islands and, in small numbers, from the nearby South American mainland, and the United States.

Some corroborative materials can be had from the study of present-day custom. The Shango cult, treated in an appendix to this work, offers testimony of importance, since this cult is derived from the Yoruba of southwestern Nigeria. Shango, in the Yoruban pantheon, is the god of thunder, and in the African mode of worship witnessed in Trinidad, he is joined by many other deities of the same derivation. Besides specific African names, the words of the ritual songs sung by the devotees are in Nago, the language of the Yoruban people. The members of this cult-group who were visited also spoke of a Rada sect, whose center was on a nearby hill. Rada is the New World term applied to groups from Dahomey, the word itself deriving from Allada, an early capital of the Dahomean kingdom, today a quiet village in the French colony.

Certainly the question of African affiliation holds but little interest for the average Trinidad Negro today. His attitude toward things African is, indeed, in striking contrast to Jamaica, Haiti, Dutch Guiana, or Brazil, where there is pride in African ancestry and in retention of

African custom. Yet the attitude of the Trinidadian is not one of distaste or shame toward things African. It is not negative at all; it is an attitude of indifference. What is important in his reactions is the positive, passionate drive to achieve the benefits in living that he observes have accrued to the Europeans, a drive that causes the illiterate Negro to make sacrifices that his children may learn to read and write; that causes him to suspect the churches under white control of withholding sacred books — parts of the Bible — that he believes give the white people their power; a drive that leads him equally to value the understanding of machinery and to scorn those who stand in the way of attaining what is generally accepted as progress.

This point need not be labored, but it must at this time be made clear. For it is another of those keys to an understanding of the reactions of the people with whom, in these pages, we will be concerned; without which it will be difficult, if not impossible to comprehend the values that underlie their behavior and the goals they strive for. That aspects of African custom have been retained by the folk of Toco and elsewhere in the Island will be apparent when this phase of our investigation is treated in our final chapter. But these retentions will be found, in by far the greatest proportion, to take the form of reinterpretations, carried on without awareness of the fact that they are African, but merely as a part of the accepted patterns of living that mark the daily round.

5

The history of Toco is not long, for the village is in that part of Trinidad which was until comparatively recent times least accessible to the more settled portions of the Island. The only access to it, indeed, was by the Tobago boat that called there on its trips to and from Port-of-Spain.

Today Sangre Grande, at the end of a broad paved highway from the capital, can be reached from Toco by an all-
weather road, a part of which is itself paved. This was
opened about twenty years ago; shortly after this the Tobago boats stopped calling. Along the northern coast this
principal road has more recently been extended westward,
so that automobile traffic is possible as far as Matelot, some
fifteen miles away — twice as far as indicated on the official
maps dated 1930.

In Toco there is no electric light, no running water, no
sewage system. A small phonograph, a bicycle, a sewing
machine are all items of luxury; there are only three or
four radios. In 1939, at the time of this research, an automobile, owned by a Chinese, could be hired when available
and in working order, and there were a few privately owned
cars, though, except in dry weather when some of the larger
"traces" are traversible, they could be used only on the
main road. It is a village where standards of living are low,
and where diversions are few.

The village, lying in the parish of St. David, is the center
of Toco ward. It contains the police controls of the ward —
a detachment of a few men under a sergeant having jurisdiction over the smaller police units stationed in the coastal
settlements of Sans Souci and Matelot to the west, and
Cumana to the south. A telephone from the police station
connects with the Island system, but the line that carries the
messages to Sangre Grande is not very efficient, and is prone
to be out of working order much of the time. There is a
postoffice, with a "bank," as the postal savings department
is termed by the Toco people, and a court of first instance,
having jurisdiction over cases in this segment of Trinidad,
sits biweekly. Earlier — and perhaps since the period of
this study — the Warden, the administrative officer of the
ward, resided in the village, but in 1939 Toco ward was
administered from Sangre Grande. The Warden would

Toco Village on Public Works Department payday

The center of Toco Village

come by car weekly or every other week to meet Public
Works Department payrolls, to pay old age pensions, or to
care for other governmental matters.

Except among the younger people, one rarely encounters
a native Tocoan. Apparently — for it is not easy to get the
facts except in the accounts of individuals — a substantial
migration to this part of Trinidad from Tobago took place
about a half-century ago. The inducements that brought
persons from across the strait — land, and opportunities
for work — also seem to have brought Trinidadians and
natives of other islands of the Antilles, especially St. Vincent, Barbados, and Grenada.

Although they have converged from these several islands,
or neighboring British Guiana on the mainland, the population is nevertheless homogeneous. All the villagers share
an agricultural tradition, a body of lore, of popular medicine, of safeguards which in nonsecular terms provide them
with some inner sense of security in the face of hostile outer
forces — all passed on by oral tradition and observation
from one generation to the next. Thus, while few men and
women beyond middle age are Toco-born, and many born
there live or have lived in other parts of the Island — the
oil-field region, or the capital — the village is nonetheless
"home," where their families await them, eager that they
return to the village to marry and live their lives.

Let us give a few instances of the background of Toco
residents. One man, a laborer, whose case can be cited, is
in his late thirties, and has been living in Toco for some
twenty years. He was born in Tobago, and lived for a time
in San Fernando, the center of southern Trinidad, before
settling in his present home. Another, owner of a small
"estate," and a fisherman who builds his own boats, was
brought directly from Tobago in 1895, when he was about
ten years of age. An elderly woman, a resident in Toco for
some forty years, herself from Barbados, is married to a

Tobagonian. A spiritual leader, head of one of the "Shouting" groups, had come from St. Vincent.

One man, born in Port-of-Spain about 1875, a resident of Toco for the preceding thirty years, was of partial American descent. His maternal grandfather had worked "in de sugar fact'ry in America," and had migrated to Trinidad "about a hundred years ago," bringing his wife and three daughters. This descendant, who in Toco earned his living as laborer and fisherman, had been partial heir to a garden in Belmont Valley Road, near the capital; the original plot the grandfather had "bought from de public." But it was entailed, and its six acres could not support the ten families that now had rights to it. Toco was home to this man, who felt that his relations with his family had improved since his leaving. "We livin' nice together now. They sen's me what they could, an' I sen's them."

The source of common traditions that have acted so effectively to unify this community of persons of diverse geographical origin is twofold. Immediately it derives from the broad similarities that underlie West Indian Negro tradition, similarities that have far more importance in ordering the way of life of the people than those customs which, in a somewhat immediate but superficial fashion, distinguish one island from another. Language is an instance of this. For though English is the speech of the British West Indies, and French that of the French islands and Haiti, créole, the Negro-French *patois* of which mention has already been made, is spoken in most of the Antilles, excepting the Bahamas, Cuba, and Jamaica. All the older people in Toco speak this dialect, and most of the younger ones understand it if they do not regularly employ it. The fishermen use it almost exclusively, and it is a favorite vehicle for comment on vacationing white families, since whites are not expected to understand it. Indeed, it was knowledge of créole, gained in Haiti, that figured no little in facilitating this field-work, especially in setting a tone of amused friendliness after comments, made as in the case of any visiting stranger, were not only understood but replied to, jokingly, in kind!

More remote than the immediate causes of cultural unity lies the African background of tradition which, under similar situations of contact in the West Indian islands, has been an effective, if unrecognized factor. As elsewhere in Trinidad, Toco folk are indifferent to this African tradition — indifferent, or in rare instances regretful that the knowledge of the ancestors had not been more carefully transmitted. One man said of the older generation, "They don' teach us. Want children to come up, learn things white people know."

Knowledge of tribal derivations is slight. One man said his father's grandmother was "Kramanti" — Kromanti, or Coromantyne, the term employed generally in the New World for the Ashanti-Fanti peoples of the Gold Coast — and that he was also "part Hibo" — Ibo, from the Niger delta country of eastern Nigeria. "People here in Toco say they're Congo, Yariba, Kromanti, and Ibo"; this statement by a woman introduced two more terms, the "Yariba" being the local term for the Yoruba tribe, and the Congo of central Africa. The same woman said that a decade before she had heard at San Fernando the names of all these and of the Gedevi, original inhabitants of the plateau of Abomey, capital of the Dahomean kingdom during the late eighteenth and nineteenth centuries. There, too, she said, were "people they calls Mandingo, like Africans. They wear pretty little caps, an' their blouse button up like a priest's." But neither Gedevi nor Mandingo are known in Toco, except in the words of songs. A Tobago woman remarked, "People in Tobago say the big people in slavery time brought plenty Congo slaves to work the estates." Her own grandmother was Kromanti, and she knew of Ibo strains in her family. Papa, the coastal principality of slaving times named Popo, is heard, and Djinea, Guinea.

Only one elderly woman who lived in the area about Toco identified herself primarily with things African. She called herself "Yarriba," and recorded a considerable number of songs in the Yoruban language, which she said she could also speak. She told of an organized group of these people on the Island, of which she, with six other women and four men, were the leaders. At New Year's they come together for seven days, when they "play" — dance — and sacrifice a sheep for the well-being of all. She fully knows she represents a dying tradition, that her efforts to transmit what she knows to her "gran" must fail, not only because there remains but little time to her, but also because, with no one about with whom to speak the language after her death, whatever she teaches the child will inevitably be poorly remembered.

It was apparent that in her was encountered a last flicker of full-fledged African tradition. She represented one of the last of the "Yarribas" described by de Verteuil in the latter half of the last century:

> "The Yarribas, or Yarrabas . . . are a fine race, tall and well proportioned; some of them with fine features, intelligent, reflective, and can appreciate the benefits of civilization and Christianity. They are laborious, usually working for day-wages on estates, but preferring job-work. The women are mostly occupied in petty trade and huckstering; some also in the culture of ground provisions. Their houses are comfortable, and kept in perfect order within. In character they are generally honest, and in disposition proud, and even haughty; so that cases are rare where a Yarriba is brought before a magistrate for theft, breach of contract, or other misdemeanour. They are besides

guided in a marked degree by the sense of association;
and the principle of combination for the common weal
has been fully sustained wherever they have settled in
any number; in fact, the whole *Yarriba* family in the
colony may be said to form a sort of social league for
mutual support and protection."

Her importance for a study of the Negro in Trinidad was as
an historic residue rather than as a cultural reality. What
she believed in and stood for is merely a gloss on Toco culture today, signficant only as helping to indicate provenience.

6

In the body of this work the culture of the Toco Negroes
will be described as it is to be observed from day to day.
This is done because the reinterpretations of African custom, as illustrative of the hypotheses advanced at the beginning of this chapter, are of such a character that their form
and significance are to be grasped only in terms of the present-day culture as a whole. For there is little question that,
in any scale of intensity of Africanisms over the New World,
Toco would be far toward the European end — almost as
far as the culture of the Negroes in rural communities of
southern United States.

We will therefore now turn from problems of theory, of
provenience, and of the working out of historical forces to
describe the life of the village as in 1939 it was to be observed in its various aspects, economic, social, and religious. After this description, we will seek to discern the
elements of African tradition that are here to be found in
their transmuted forms, relate them to similar manifestations elsewhere in the New World, and finally evaluate this
body of material in terms of the hypotheses that open this
work.

CHAPTER II

CLASS DIFFERENCES AND STANDARDS OF LIVING

TOCO LOCAL ECONOMY is an integral, if infinitesimal, part of the world economic order. Its cash-crop agriculture renders the existence of every member of the community responsive to the prices of cocoa and copra set in London and New York. The larger estates are absentee-owned, but whether the manager is owner or employee, the estate must show its profit. The second line of economic defense, the Public Works Department of the colonial government, pays wages determined in the colonial capital. Even the monetary system reflects dual influences, for it is a combination of the pound-shillings-pence formula of England and Canadian-American dollars and cents. Thus prices are quoted and wages paid in sums derived from a shilling count — twelve, twenty-four, forty-eight, and ninety-six cents — after which the dollar takes over, though pound notes are readily accepted, and American and Canadian paper money circulates.

Essentially, the problem of the Toco Negro is subsistence. It is the problem of the rural Negro population everywhere, and to that extent is on broad lines a familiar one — a problem, indeed, of such urgency that within recent years it has had the attention of economic specialists both in the United States and in the West Indies. Yet just because the customary ramifications of the economy into other aspects of the lives of the people are here made the more complex by the presence of a dual tradition, economic analysis is but a single factor in achieving an understanding of the problem, whether this be in the interest of the wider concerns of social science, or for practical ends. That is why in this study the discussion of the economic base of life is a beginning, rather than an end of the analysis; why the attempt will be essentially to comprehend it as it affects the total life of the community; and why, above all, it is to be presented as it appears from the humble place these Negroes have in it.

2

Absentee owners, with their large land holdings throughout the Island, figure in the lives of the Tocoans as impersonal forces like Government or the Church. But in those whose houses line the few village streets, or are scattered along the several "traces" and outlying settlements, Toco knows the categories of well-to-do, comfortable, and poor. The first group comprises those who have the estates — landowners who live in the area and do not rely on managers to operate their holdings. In the "comfortable" group are civil servants, owners of small shops, mechanics and other skilled workers whose employment is not subject to seasonal demand, small landowners, and owners and operators of fishing-boats who, in addition, may act as middlemen in disposing of the catch of others. In many instances these categories overlap; as where a shopkeeper or a landowner has a fishing boat, or even two boats, used by others who deliver to him the customary owner's share of the catch; or where a man, who as civil servant is clerk in a local governmental office, also derives an income from a small plantation which he owns.

The first two classes are greatly outnumbered by those

whose economic position is close to the subsistence level, those classified as poor. They work when and where they can — on the coconut estates, clearing ground on the cocoa estates, repairing roads — with no assurance at any time of earning enough to provide their needs. And since the poor are so much the majority in all of northeastern Trinidad, they give to this society and its economic institutions their characteristic outlines.

Who are those considered well-to-do? The question was discussed with many people, and is best illustrated by individual cases. Consider one man so classified. He is a shopkeeper who has "plenty land" — thirty or forty acres in the cocoa estates area to the west, twenty or thirty to the south of the town where coconuts are grown, besides four or five acres recently left by a brother who died. The coconut estate yields five to six thousand nuts at a time, so that the owner could live on the copra yield alone, without the income from his shop or his other land. As another instance, a Chinese, owner of many acres of cocoa-bearing trees, was often mentioned; likewise, a native of Toco, who has thirty *carrés* of land yielding cocoa and tonka beans, a profitable crop.

In conversations about well-to-do people, it was asserted that there are "more than twenty-five rich people in Toco. Not halfway, they really have." What, however, constitutes "having"? A mutual acquaintance, comfortably situated, was cited: "He mean. He don' let out money. Ask him, he don' give. Don' min' fo' what. He got, yes, but he's a mingy (stingy) man." When such a one is a man of property, no one "cares much," for he fails to live up to the status requirement of a propertied man. He, in turn, will have none of the respect that would otherwise be his in the community. And this, it was observed on many occasions, was actually the attitude toward him. His fellow townsmen gave him the barest of greetings. He shared neither the

warm interchange of an equal, nor the soft-spoken interpolations that were the code for the well-to-do man who had
the town's regard. In contrast, of another "rich" man, perhaps the richest in the community, it was said, "He helps
people too much. He's a clean man. Hard times come and
he was doing for the poor. If not for him, many would go
hungry."

As everywhere in the Euro-American economic system,
the fluctuations of market-prices of world crops can make
for individual economic disaster and this, in turn, is the
commonest cause for change of status. This familiar story
was told by a man who, though not of the poorer group,
was far below the economic position he had once occupied.
"I was a man with forty acres of estate," he said. "I mortgage and they take it. Take it with receiver for taxes, $2,900
due. They promised to give me the balance, but I don't
get it yet." He went on to consider the general situation;
and certain of his comments, as documentation of prevalent attitudes, give insight into the effect this economic
order has on the thinking of those who live under it. "All
people should live loving," he said, "but I'll tell you the
truth, people don' git enough salary. That cause they hate
to the other. Like Esau and Jacob, got to live together. But
in our colonies they aren't giving us enough salary for we to
love them." That to him explained the latent discontent
everywhere, and the outward manifestations of this discontent among the younger generation.

All those who own shops would be included in the group,
neither rich nor poor, who are termed "comfortable." A
count of business places in Toco showed twenty-five such
establishments. They numbered three medium-sized and
three small general merchandise shops, eight "parlors"
where soft drinks are sold, a gasoline filling station, two tailoring shops, one cobbler's shop, one shop where both a
tailor and a cobbler were working, a blacksmithy, and a

house where the owner of the local car for hire could be reached. The butcher also comes in this category, but he usually "kills" only every fortnight on occasion of the Public Works Department paydays, though even then the demand is limited, because so few can afford fresh meat. Often he sells meat brought from Port-of-Spain, for lacking refrigeration facilities he will not slaughter locally and chance having meat left over at the end of the day.

An instance may be given of a person classified as comfortable. This is the mother of a young woman who had died just before this field-work was begun, whose "forty-days" rite of death will be described in later pages. The daughter had been a school teacher, and her mother was to receive her salary for the month she died, a three-months' grant, and also the value of her life insurance policy, an unstated modest amount. This would provide cash for investing in a small business or for buying land. In addition, she was also left the house in which she and her daughter lived, "not a really fine house. One of our kind, but with galvanized" — that is, with a galvanized iron, rather than a thatched roof. With the money she received, or was to receive, and the house assured her, she was regarded as decidedly comfortable.

An essential criterion in classifying a person as well-to-do, comfortable, or poor is whether or not he possesses money — ready cash — though the type of house he lives in figures as well. Even though a man has enough to feed his family and can provide his children with shoes and other essential garments for school, roof his house with "galvanized," and pay his lodge dues, he would still be regarded as of low economic status. "You judge people by the amount of money they have to spend."

Examples of this pattern of judgment were phrased in many forms. A man who perhaps owned enough land for a garden with a sufficient yield to feed his family and himself quite well but could count on no cash income except from occasional surplus his wife might sell in the market to give her some money for a little sugar and an occasional length of material for a needed garment, or shoes — such a man everyone would consider to be very poor. One woman said that though she might have her own house and land that provided her with enough to live on, a neighbor who rented a house, but earned enough in wages to buy food, would be held to be better situated, because the neighbor would have money to spend, and, however limited, some range of choice, whereas the speaker would only have produce for herself and an occasional sale. Certainly anyone who lives in a "trash house" — one that is thatched — is deemed poor. "All about the village there are people with plenty money lent (out), who live that way. But they're thought to be poor just the same." Credit is sometimes extended to persons, even in the lowest strata, if they have a fairly steady cash income such as is derived from work on the road or on the estates. "Many get credit. But some shop don' credit. If you buy an' don' pay on payday, they not credit, even if you dying."

Despite the prestige value ascribed to having money in hand, the land, its ownership, its productivity, and world prices of cash crops figure in all conversations concerning the local economy. One man, intimately acquainted with affairs of the village, estimated that between a quarter and a half of the people have gardens, with the trend showing a decrease in the number of gardens worked and owned as compared with earlier times. Since gardens are rented on cocoa estates from land that had become exhausted, the garden acreage depends on how much has become available, that is, "according to how de cocoa dies off." Such land rents for 1/– a month, "and if it is good land, a bunch of plantains will pay four months' rent." But rare is the estate owner who permits his tenant to build a house on such land.

"De estate claims dey not rent fo' purpose of buildin' house. Dey jus' rent fo' provision gya'den." Also, fewer persons own their gardens now because large tracts of productive land were acquired by the cocoa estates. At the period of this research this land had been offered for garden use because the market for cocoa was very low. Land known to produce good crops was thus being eagerly rented for gardens even by persons who owned other land — perhaps land not so suitable for general marketable crops, planted in coconut trees.

Since almost without exception, houses may not be built on land rented for gardens, the tenant farmers must have houses in the village. Here the rent is 5/– a room, and two-room houses generally cost 10/– a month, though some are to be had for 7/–. In the heart of the village rents are somewhat higher; good houses cost $2.00 a room (8/4 with the shilling at 24¢), whereas poorer ones bring 4/– or 5/–.

In the center of Toco lots could be bought for $30, $35 and $40; those outside the center, fifty by one hundred feet, cost $20. Others, "to de back, but larger" were obtained for $25. It was estimated that half the people of the village owned both the houses in which they lived and the land on which these houses were built, and that another quarter who rented their land owned their houses.

The cost of building a house may be indicated. One which was under construction at the time of this research — of average size, with plastered walls over a woven frame, two rooms, a galvanized iron roof, very substantially built — was to cost about $90. This sum would go largely for labor — "de cya'penter work firs', den de dirt man, den de cya'penter again, some more, and den de mason." A common outlay for the building of a house is about $50; "$20 fo' de cya'penter, $20 fo' de mudman, $10 fo' de mason" (who plasters and paints the outside of the house, and is thus not at all a mason in the ordinary sense). This means a house with coconut-frond thatch, a "straw house," which, as has been suggested, implies low economic status.

3

In the preceding section, the meanings of the designations used to differentiate the socio-economic groups were discussed in terms of standards of the community. They can be further clarified by a series of figures covering various kinds of expenditures, described as typical for poor and comfortable families.

Let us assume our "poor" family consists of father, mother, and three children, the oldest twelve years of age. The work the man and woman do is of the least remunerative kind and they have no garden, so that everything they consume must be purchased. The schedule of meals in Toco is that of rural Trinidad in general — morning tea, at from seven to eight o'clock, or earlier, "breakfast," between eleven and twelve, and supper, at four in the afternoon, or later, if the nature of the man's employment makes the evening meal the principal one. The cost of a characteristic morning meal would be about nine cents — a pound of flour (4¢) , a half-pound of sugar (2¢) , "grease" for frying the flour (2¢) , and a cent's worth of coffee. "Breakfast" may be budgeted at 17¢ — 8¢ for two pounds of rice, 6¢ for a half-pound of salt-fish, 2¢ for cooking oil, and 1¢ for coconut. Fourteen cents buys supper — a pound and a half of flour 6¢, 2¢ worth of salt-fish, 1¢ each for chocolate, coconut, "grease" and cooking butter, and 2¢ for a half-pound of sugar.

To these must be added weekly expenditures of 2¢ for salt, 1¢ for soda, and 48¢ for "coals." This totals $3.31 for the food budget, though half the amount allotted for "coals" would actually go for the cost of ironing clothes, while if the weather were good and wood could be gathered, 24¢

spent for cooking "coals" could be saved entirely. On Sundays meals are somewhat better, and the family might enjoy fresh fish or meat, or have split-pea or tannia soup — tannia being an especially favored kind of yam. Ten cents would thus be added to the weekly sum needed for food for these extras — a half-pound of black-eyed peas for 2¢, a similar sum for onions, garlic, and black pepper, and 6¢ for a half-pound of salt-beef or dried beef.

The lack of nutritional balance in the diet of families of this economic stratum is evident from menus such as these, and particularly when it is realized that the family resources permit little else to be added — only when more money is on hand, or when "ground provisions" can be obtained without paying cash. For this, it was explained, is the scale of "salt-fish families" — those who rarely, if ever, can afford the taste of fresh beef or pork. During harvest time the man might work for a day as a harvest hand, and for this, in addition to any small sum he might earn, he would, when crops were plentiful, exercise his traditional privilege of taking for himself as much as he could carry home. What fruit such families enjoy they must get without paying for it; otherwise fresh fruit is a luxury that cannot be indulged. And in Toco, not a fruit-growing area, they get relatively little — an occasional mango, a few bananas, some guavas, some sugar-cane, oranges.

A standard item in the diet is a "bake," which, though palatable and nutritious, serves to illustrate the high proportion of starch in this diet. It can best be described by giving the recipe for it: "Take a coconut, grate it, and wash it to get the milk out. Add flour, salt, soda, and knead. Then add butter, knead some more, and leave the dough to rise while preparing the rest of the meal. Make one cake, put it in a pot on a low fire; then, when the pot is heated, put coals on top of its tin cover."

More children do not necessarily mean more money

spent, for many families must stretch what they have to cover the cost — they "just fix more gravy with the provision." When such a family has a young child, a neighbor might lend them a goat to milk, or they might buy a "nip" of milk, a half-pint for a penny (2¢) each day. But after a child is two years old, "they don't much worry about milk." Further elements in the living costs of families subsisting on a "salt-fish" scale also throw light on their mode of existence. A weekly charge of 50¢ must be allowed for various items: 8¢ for kerosene, the same amount for a half-bar of soap (both for laundry and personal use) , and 6¢ for milk for the small children; 24¢ in lodge dues for man and woman; 12¢ a month for their church dues, and 4¢ for the weekly church collection ("you're not bound to give, but you want to") . If the family raise fowl, they might on occasion kill a chicken.

Clothing costs must be held to a minimum, as the following estimates indicate. For the man, two pairs of crepe sole shoes at 4/– total $1.92, three pairs of slippers at 50¢ total $1.50; while for the three children, six pairs at 36¢ per pair (which must last, even though they "wear 'em to nothing") cost $2.16. The woman buys dress-goods for $1.00, and pays 50¢ for making a dress. She uses three a year, for a total of $4.50. She spends $1.98 for underclothes — petticoat, chemise and drawers, two sets a year, buying seven yards of material at 12¢ a yard (84¢) , five yards of edging at 2¢, and 5¢ worth of thread for each set. For her daughter she buys four dresses at 15¢ each, four chemises at 12¢, and four pairs of bloomers at 8¢, a total of $1.40. The child could get along with two of each article a year, but even in the poorest families every effort is made to provide her with more, since "you have to dress a little girl better, so her body will be covered."

The father needs two pairs of trousers, which are sold in the local shops at 3/– each, for a total of $1.44. He also must

have dungarees for working, but these are made for him —
two and a half yards of material at 1/– a yard, or 60¢, and
36¢ for the making. For a blouse he pays $1.44, for a thick
khaki shirt 50¢ ("beat it out every Saturday"), the same
amount for an ordinary shirt, and 24¢ for a kerchief. His
young son is provided with a pair of khaki pants or shorts,
the material for which costs 36¢, and a pair of white drill
for the same amount. Two ready-made jackets (blouses)
at 18¢, and two shirts "to wear inside them," at 12¢, complete the outfit. These will last the year, as the lad will
wear them only as occasion demands, "and khaki is strong,
too." When he is not in school, or at other times when his
clothing is not a matter of concern, he wears whatever old,
cast-off things can be found for him.

Other than this, except the savings for the minimum
yearly tax of 5/– if the house they live in is owned by them,
or 4/– if they have built the house on rented land and thus
are responsible for it, there are no resources to allow even
petty expenditures which others somewhat higher in the
economic scale take for granted. If the "galvanized" roof
of the house in which they live has rusted through, there is
no money for a new one — "they use trash." If someone falls
ill and folk remedies do not suffice, the government doctor
can be relied on to care for him, but the official in charge
of the district must certify him as a pauper. "Doctor tend
you. Give you medicine for nothing for four weeks. If you
still ain't better, you have to get a fresh paper. But the doctor don' stop taking care of you." Should a member of the
family die, the lodge will care for burial, and neighbors and
others will provide, as gifts, the food and other articles
needed to hold a modest wake. But this family must accept
these with the knowledge that they cannot reciprocate.

Utensils are of enamel — "they don' break." The iron
coal-pot is saved for use when ironing, and carefully put
away; cooking is done on stones, or in a clay oven. Rec-

reation must not involve any cost. A question concerning the man's haircut brought a laugh. "What money is there for that? He begs a friend to cut his hair." But as for a barber — "Wouldn' study the idea of that." Tobacco is a need deeply felt, and the man makes every effort to get some. "When he has a little change, he may smoke six cents' worth some days." But on others he must go without. And, when "things come up" and a man needs to consult a lookman — a diviner and worker of magic — he pays if he is able, usually spending out of his meager funds as much as a dollar a year for the purpose. But this is a necessity, and if the money is not in hand he either promises to pay later, or turns to parents or brothers or other relatives for help to meet the lookman's charges.

For those with fairly regular work, the margin is not so close between income and subsistence costs. Their way of life, when comparatively considered, is eased. The difference, it will be observed, is more in the matter of choice, though the main meal on Sundays is decidedly less sparse, with greater resources permitting some variety and larger quantity.

Let us look into the standard of living of another family of this economic class. It is the same size as the one already discussed — father, mother, and three children — and the man is a fisherman, or a road-worker, or a coconut-tree climber and "buster" — that is, a family whose head is not a casual laborer, but who enjoys more stabilized employment. Here, as in the previous case, it is assumed that they do not have a garden, but buy all they need. For morning tea, such a family would have ham or cheese (4¢), chocolate, or green tea (2¢), sugar (2¢), and bread to the amount of 4¢ or 6¢; a total of 12¢ or 14¢. "Breakfast" costs 32¢: 4¢ for rice, 6¢ for tannia or yams, 12¢ for fish, and 2¢ each for onion, tomato, cooking butter, oil, and salt-pork. At the evening meal bread would again be served (6¢), with ham

(4¢), and coffee (2¢) with sugar (2¢); thus costing 14¢. Extras would be cake, "moley," "snowball," or rum or wine, or 4¢ worth of ginger might be mixed with sugar of the same cost, and they would have ginger-beer. The Sunday meal besides the basic elements might utilize a pound and a half of pork or beef, at 18¢ to 20¢ a pound, a small piece of fish, okra, tomatoes, onion, and garlic.

The food budget of still another type of family, described as a "well-to-do laboring family" of the same size, may be examined. In the morning, there is coffee with milk and sugar, bread and butter, and bacon or at times salt-fish for the father, at a total cost of 14¢. "Breakfast" would require a half-pound of rice (2¢), fish (6¢), and tannia or plantain, or perhaps both. The woman would buy two tannia for 5¢, keeping one for the next day, for "tannia costs dear" and she could not buy them every day. Plantains are 4¢ or 5¢; she would use one and keep the rest for later. "Grease," onion, butter, and "fig" — bananas — complete the list for this meal, to be had for 19¢. The four o'clock tea includes bread (instead of "bake") with butter, and tea with sugar and milk, and the family might have ham or cheese in addition, the cost being 14¢ or 18¢, depending on the inclusion of this last item.

Menus for such a family's Sunday dinner were gone into in great detail. "They go to market, and buy provisions. Don't mind how much it cost, they buying for Sunday dinner!" This enthusiasm might seem uncalled for in the light of the fact that the cost, in addition to the staples of everyday use would at the most be 75¢, but in terms of prevalent patterns it is quite justified. For the insight it throws on Toco standards of living, indeed, it is to be placed at the side of the comment of the person who gave this menu, to the effect that "In good times, for Sunday dinners people had rum, fowl, and wine that cost 36¢ a quart!"

This family, if they had a chicken in their yard, would

kill it — it could be sold for 36¢, and hence must be considered as having this value in purchasing power — or would buy a pound of beef or a pound or pound and a half of pork. Irish potatoes, a delicacy, would be bought to go with the meat. "Calalu bush" — greens — would be needed to flavor the crab-meat stew, made from crabs the boy had trapped on the beach the day before; then yams, plantain, and tannia, and rice, with mangoes and "fig" for dessert, or extra biscuits (cakes) and bread with "jelly-sugar" (gelatin), and wine or ginger-beer. This is the hard times diet of 1939, a little idealized, for many considered this lavishness beyond their means. In better times, when the thirty-six-cent-a-quart wine was consumed, more elaborate meals could be procured, since in this rural area costs of comestibles raised locally do not appear to rise equally with rising wages, and thus allow a larger real wage than in periods of economic stress.

Such elements in the diet as crab, already mentioned, and fish the boys of the family bring home, or eggs and an occasional chicken consumed instead of being sold, or the "ground provisions" from small gardens or grown by tenant farmers or contract workers on the estates must not be regarded as additions to items that have been described, but as substitutions. The seasonal nature of employment and the small annual wages earned cause such items to be consumed by many families when there is little money for rice, sugar, and "grease," let alone meat or milk, rather than to enrich a diet that consists otherwise of foodstuffs purchased at the store.

Though the portrayal of living standards of the Negroes in the Toco region demonstrates the lowness of the scale and makes understandable how immediate is the problem of meeting fundamental needs, it must, however, be placed in its total setting. The climate is a healthy one, and although the restricted diet leaves much to be desired from the point of view of its nutritional values, the outdoor life, the health-giving properties of sun and sea, do much to correct the grosser deficiencies. Then, too, it may again be pointed out that though the scale is low, the range of variation in it is also low. If the poor are very poor, the "well-to-do" are by no stretch of the imagination rich. People, whatever their place in this society, strive hard to maintain the respect of their fellow-citizens; and a reputation for hard work, and honesty, of keeping a household clean, and having well-mannered children, goes far to compensate for a low economic position.

Except among the young men who have been down in the oil-fields or the capital, reaction to the economic system in which these people live is in terms of a generalized malaise rather than an acute resentment. Opportunities for change in a man's position are few, and in any circumstances are hard to come by if only because of the educational and racial handicaps experienced by the members of a rural community of Negro stock. People do drift away — to Sangre Grande, to San Fernando in the oil fields, to Port-of-Spain, the capital. But at best, with but very few exceptions, they become laborers, with higher living costs to take up any advantages gained in the way of better wages and a place in society that is incomparably less rewarding psychologically than the humble one they had in Toco. For in Toco they shared membership in a homogeneous group having a stable culture. Such an advantage, meager as they may feel it to be, most Toco folk can be said to sense, even though the comment of the younger men constantly echoes their discontent, and such analyses of their own situation as they make emphasize the lack of opportunity that confronts them.

4

In a society such as Toco, there is little encouragement for idling and in most families women as well as men eagerly seek out opportunities to earn money. In this, as in all groups, well-recognized patterns of sex division of labor exist, and it will aid in analyzing the economy under which these people live to indicate the different kinds of work men and women do. These types of labor may best be considered in terms of the categories used by the Toco people themselves in discussing them, after which the techniques employed and the remuneration gained for various kinds of work may be described.

A qualification must be added at this point: though the lines of sex division of labor are in theory well-defined and clearly drawn they are, as in all societies, a statement of accepted practice rather than inviolate rules. When need presses, a man or a woman will do what must be done, without too great thought whether it is proper or improper for a person of his sex to do it. A widow without help will do all the work of her garden, despite conventions that men break the ground and women weed. "No female at all go out fishing — only men," said one woman, emphatically. But she also said, "Sometime de wife help husband with de line," adding the caution, "But fishing is for men." Her statement, "No women go pick coconuts from the tree" is probably correct, but her assertion that no women work at opening coconuts is certainly violated on occasion. Crops are taken to market on the backs of donkeys, and consequently it becomes men's work. "It seem as if it doesn't lie in the woman's job to do — they don't drive cyar, either." However, one Tocoan warned against too strict a construction of the lines along which sex division of labor is drawn while, at the same time, by his tone of voice he showed his personal reaction to violations of the rules, "I seen women fishening!"

In general, when both men and women are employed at a task, the men do the heavier parts of the work, the women the lighter. Thus, on the cocoa estates the men break the brush with their cutlasses, prepare the earth, and dig the holes for the trees which shade the cocoa-trees. The women bring the young plants, weed them, pick and dry the pods, take out the beans from the pod, and with hoe or cutlass cut away the weeds that choke the trees. Both sexes "dance cocoa" — that is, hull the beans, but the men "bag up" the crop, sew the bags, and transport them to market.

On the coconut plantations, men climb the trees and cut down the nuts, and "bus' " them — break them open — so the meat can be extracted for drying, after they have been gathered in heaps by women or young boys. The women take out the meat from the shells and see to the drying, though men may do this also. The men bag the copra, and "sew bag take go to market" as in the case of cocoa. For the preparation of a new planting, the division of labor follows the routine just described. The men "brush," both men and women plant the young trees, and the women weed. Both are employed in "nursing" the growing trees — that is, banking the weeds that have been cut about the trunk of the young palm to fertilize it.

Men are blacksmiths, tailors, cobblers, shopkeepers, clerks in the offices. Women may keep shop, but they are chiefly seamstresses and laundresses. There is little other work that requires skilled craftsmanship. Pottery jars to cool the drinking water are found in every home, but there are no potters in this part of Trinidad, though the women sell the pots, as they do other commodities traded in the local market. Practically all building operations are man's work — carpentry, masonry, mud-work (including "dancing mud" for the walls), cutting grass to "bind" the mud and palm-fronds for "trash," and the thatching itself. Women help by bringing water to moisten the earth when mud is being prepared. Men do all of such lumbering operations as are found.

As has been stated, men are the fishermen, and this is an important occupation in the community. The fishermen may even build their own boats, and do make the nets they cast along the shore for bait, and their lines; they do all the deep-sea fishing, and it is the little boys, rather than the girls, who hunt for crab and lobster among the rocks. Both men and women sell fish, however. Men are the hunters, though hunting is a minor and accessory calling. They see that their dogs are bathed with the proper "medicine" before they take them into the forest, they butcher and sell the meat and, after drying the skins, make chair-seats, knife-sheaths, side-bags, and other articles out of the untanned dried skins. The women as a part of their household duties feed the dogs, and may also bathe them.

Both men and women work on the roads for the Public Works Department, though the proportion of men in the road-gangs that were observed was far above that of the women. The men "plow" — that is, dig up the dirt, spread sand, stamp down the road. Presumably, specialists care for paving, but this is no consideration in Toco, where there are no paved roads. The women "cast the dirt away" after the men have dug the road-bed, bring water to the men, and carry sand. Both men and women clear away the dirt of a landslide that has blocked a road, though in such work only men use wheelbarrows, the women transporting the earth on trays atop their heads. Both roll away the large rocks that the diggers unearth.

When a garden is to be prepared, the men "cut" the land, and also see to it that a "trace" or fire-line, is cut. Both men and women plant, but the women weed the growing crops, the men joining them when it is time to reap the harvest.

The men transport the crops to places of storage or sale, for, as has been pointed out, donkeys or horses are used for this. If the crops are sold "wholesale" to a factor, the bargaining is carried on by the man; if at retail in the market, the women do the selling.

Most of the work about the household is the woman's. She cooks, washes clothes, cleans the house, cares for the children, looks after the pigs or goats and such fowl as the family may have. If the family owns a cow, the man or an older boy cares for it and milks it, unless it is very tame. He also cares for any other large animal they may have — donkey, horse, or mule. Repairs on the house are similarly his responsibility.

In theory it is the man's role to provide for his family; in economic terms he is the producer, while consumption and retail distribution are in the hands of the woman. When a man and woman live together, her earnings supplement his, and are recognized as supplementary. It is only when a woman is the head of a household, living alone with her children, that she becomes the primary provider. To earn extra money women make and sell sugar-cakes, ginger-beer, corn-cakes called *pemi,* and "a thing called moley, a thing floating in a bottle — a root they buy, boil and sugar." They buy "ground-nuts" — peanuts — to parch and sell, and make or buy peppermint and "fix candy and such." They bake cakes called "badian," made of flour, coconut, sugar, butter, and spice, to be sold at a penny a cut on Saturdays, and they also bake buns and tarts for Sundays and festivals.

Work outside the house may be either on a full-time or part-time basis. Some women go to the fields and work three or four days or occasionally a week, to help out, or they "pull" coconuts. "They go 'round and beg for a few days' work." Some do scrubbing for the well-to-do and such city people as may be on holiday, getting for this work from twelve to twenty cents a room, according to size. They may beg for old bottles and sell them, or weed a yard for thirty cents and "breakfast." Laundry-work is a recognized occupation, and is done not only for the well-to-do people who can afford it, but also for bachelors who have no one to care for their clothes. Twenty cents a dozen pieces is a standard price, with twelve cents for a sheet or a man's white suit. Some women do only ironing, with the washing done by others, less skilled. Work on the road is desirable because it is well-paid. "But it's hard to get."

Whether she works to supplement a husband's income or as principal support of her children, a woman's earnings are her own. For in Toco, the economic position of women is high in terms of local standards. If she works a garden, what she receives for the produce she sells is hers; if she works it with her husband, the receipts from what she sells in the market are likewise hers. Only when factors come to the garden to buy the crop, or when the husband sends or takes produce to be sold in Port-of-Spain is the money his. The money a wife gets from trading, or laundering, or working on the road is ordinarily spent on her children and herself, not on the man — a fact the Toco women stress. Yet when questioned they qualify their assertion and add, "It's true according. Some women won't buy anything. They keeps their money. Some men won't give the woman any money at all. Then there's plenty trouble." In most households where a family unit has stability, common sense and need rule the use of available money. But the tradition that a man has no right to the earnings of his wife, and that she spends what she earns on herself and her children, except for such gifts for the man as her affection for him or a woman's strategy dictates, is unequivocal.

Selling in the market is definitely woman's work. "Men don' have time to sit down to sell. That's woman's duty." Only if a purchaser comes to the field to buy his foodstuff

will the man concern himself with selling. The wife sells
what her husband's field produces; and if a man is without
a mate, his mother, or a sister or female cousin will dispose
of what he sends to a local market. A husband knows what
his wife sells, but rarely sees the money she realizes, for, as
has been stated, she spends this on those needs of her family
that are to be acquired only in the shop — soap, kerosene,
sugar, matches, and salt, to name the most important items.
Some hold, indeed, as suggested, that money from sales belongs to the woman who sells, regardless of the quantity of
produce put at her disposal. Sometimes, of course, "when
he's feeling lovely he gi' money to he husband" ("he"
meaning "she") but again — and this is a man's version —
"sometime he rascal an' no gi'."

Formal education in the schools is concerned with more
general subjects than the techniques involved in getting a
living, and training in the crafts is thus obtained informally. Little boys begin work on the coconut estates at
about ten or twelve years of age, picking up the fallen nuts
and piling them. They will braid some coconut branches
into a rope and experiment with climbing the trees. Little
by little they learn to go higher, and when they find they
can repeat their climb several times, they begin "bicycling,"
as going up a tree with a rope is termed. They first climb
the younger trees to "chop" coconuts, and gradually come
to work higher ones. There is no training in these operations, but rather they learn by observation and practice.

If a boy wishes to follow a trade, he is apprenticed to a
craftsman. Carpentry may be cited as an example. If the
father is a carpenter, the boy might learn from him, but
experience has shown this method to have its flaws. "A
father is impatient, wants his boy to learn too quick. Then
the boy get afraid. So the mother ask him if he like his
daddy trade. If he say yes, then she plead and coax the
father to let him apprentice elsewhere. Then when the boy

come back, he get more insight now, and can learn from his father." The boy is not paid during his apprenticeship; he "just helps and learns." After a while he is allowed to do simple jobs, and later goes out to get work for himself. He may try for a government job, but the head carpenter, with apprentices of his own, is not anxious to take on a strange boy, so the lad ends by going back home, getting small jobs, until he earns a reputation as a competent worker, and finally becomes established.

To become a mason the procedure is similar — the lad carries shovels, buckets, and other tools for his master; he mixes sand, lime, and cement, and thus learns the essentials of the trade. "He learn by watching. Don' take years. Boy here, last year helping, now take his own job." Tailors are not too helpful to their apprentices. "He take you, don' teach you too much. Boy pay him a dollar a month, because he useful a little, can make pants already. Otherwise he pay an' go a long time. Don' know how to cut out. Seamstress is the same. Go years — don' know how to cut a dress. Don' show her how." This would seem to indicate that in Toco those making clothing hold to their advantage with the long view, and see to it that competition of those who come to them to learn will not be too severe!

Gardening is learned by watching the other members of the family, helping them in their tasks, and finally assuming a full share of the work. Fishing is learned the same way, but because it requires special knowledge, there is a kind of informal apprenticeship. Most boys in this coastal region know something about fishing, and by the time they are twelve years old catch snapper or mullet, or little pog off the rocks. This is done principally on Saturdays when there is no school. When they reach the age of fourteen, they "go in the boats." A boy asks a fisherman to take him out, and though he is not strong enough to give much help pulling an oar, he "makes himself useful" and is perhaps given a fish to take home or sell. A mother views this vocation with misgivings. "Better be careful," she will say, "the sea got no back door." But the boy continues to help by catching crabs and small fish ·for bait for the fishermen, helping to pull in the boat, and to wash it. In the boat, he uncoils the wires used for lines, and, after a while, "begins to pull. The men say, 'Willin' little feller,' " and the fishermen, who are tired when they come in, are pleased with this help. "After a while any boat is glad to have him." He thus becomes a full-fledged member of the crew, participating when the catch is apportioned and selling his share to the women who go to the shore as the boats come in.

Young girls help their mothers with washing, sewing, cooking, and baking, gradually attaining competence through practice. Nursing is a popular vocation, some of the Toco girls receiving training in the capital on the basis of their school records and of recommendations given them by the minister of their church. Work at home begins at an early age, developing naturally out of the make-believe games they play with each other. At twelve they do some of the washing; by the time they are fifteen years old they are able to wash large sheets, going to the river with their friends, and "proud to have them nice."

There is one Toco code that is held to today by all mothers. Girls are not to be allowed to work on the estates. A mother will herself weed, but however great the need, she will see to it that her daughter will not "go to the field." As was explained, "She will rather have them with some lady or gentleman, who will keep the girl for the work she does" — without paying her a wage — so the daughter may learn "better ways of living." This is called sending them to a "caretaker," and if the child is mistreated, she is taken back. "But some treats them good, like a child in your eyes."

CHAPTER III

WORK, AND THE PROBLEM
OF SECURITY

WORK FOR OTHERS is principally done on the estates, on cocoa or copra plantations, and on the roads. Work for oneself is gardening, fishing, or hunting; occasionally a Tocoan is a craftsman, though this category includes so few persons in northeastern Trinidad that it is of minor concern to us in this discussion. Rarely in Toco does one find a person who works only for himself and never hires out for wages, or a man whose entire support derives from his wages, and who never labors for himself.

There is a form of agricultural enterprise, known as a "contract," wherein a man agrees to cultivate fallow land for its owner in order to produce a cash crop. The essence of the agreement is that the contractor gets new land cleared and planted to produce a crop; all else is incidental. This can be done for coconuts, tonka beans, and cocoa — though when (as at the time this research was carried on) the cocoa market is so low that cultivation of cocoa is unprofitable, such a contract is rarely entered into.

The land is cleared, and then, in addition to the cash crop, a provision garden is planted. All the yield of the provision garden belongs to the worker. After three or four years, when the trees begin to bear, the garden no longer provides as well as it did at first, for the land has been used for several crops, and the shade of the trees keeps the sun-

light from the growing plants. But the trees begin to yield a
crop, and for the duration of the contract this crop belongs
to the worker, so that actually his cash income increases as
the amount of garden provisions he raises decreases. The
contractor is permitted to build a shelter (an *ajoupa*) or
even a "regular house" on the land he takes "on contrac',"
but in this case he must pay the annual house-tax of four
shillings; or the owner will pay it, deducting the advance
from what is owed the worker when the contract expires.

The land-owner derives no income from his land during
the time of the agreement. At the end of that time, however, when he "takes up his contrac' " and pays off the contractor, his hitherto unworked plot will be turned over to
him in full or nearly full production. Rates customary
under this system vary according to the wages prevailing
at the time the contract is entered into. Those that follow
are applicable to the time of his study. On cocoa estates, the
worker at the termination of his contract receives a shilling
for each full bearing tree he has raised to maturity and 6*d*
for each half-tree, with a shilling deducted for each dead
tree. For coconuts, he receives 36¢ for a bearing tree, 18¢
for a half-tree, and 9¢ for a quarter-tree — one which is
healthy, but not yet bearing. In the case of tonka beans, he
is paid 30¢ to 36¢ for a bearing tree, 15¢ to 18¢ for a half-
tree, and 8¢ to 9¢ for a non-bearing tree.

The "contrac' " may on occasion give the one who works
it what are regarded as appreciable resources. Above the
income represented by the produce he grows, he will have
a sum in cash that may open opportunities to him to acquire
land, or otherwise to enhance his economic status. If the
land to be planted and worked is new land, the owner must
pay him $18 a *carré* (that is, two acres) for clearing it. At
the end of the stipulated time, should the owner not care
to take over, or be unable to discharge his obligations toward the contractor, he can claim nothing until the sum

due under the contract is fully met. This is one reason why it is said, "if the land is fertile, you can make much money" by taking a contract.

The tradition of entering into agreements is wide-spread, and takes various forms, though in the total economy of the region these are less important than the aspect just discussed. For example, the owner of a cocoa or coconut field may enter into a "sharing" agreement, under which owner and worker share equally the expenses and returns from the yield of the trees. It is customary in such cases for the worker himself to "cutlash" around the trees — that is, to clear away the undergrowth — or to bear the whole cost of having this done. Other agreements cover the care of livestock. In such cases the equal sharing of the offspring gives the one who tends an animal a vested right "in de mother," and the complete ownership by the original owner of the animal continues only when the man who breeds the livestock receives more than half the young. This type of arrangement customarily concerns cattle, but can be entered into for goats or other smaller animals. Instances were even reported where such an agreement had to do with fowl!

Work is seasonal on the estates, except on the largest holdings, where some hands have year-round employment. Workers receive about 40¢ a day. For this they "supply," that is, plant banana or "cocoa-mother" trees to shade the cocoa, and put in nurslings; they also "brush," cutting away the undergrowth. Men who work cocoa trim trees, pick and break pods, and "dance cocoa" to hull kernels. "Jobs" are also given on cocoa plantations. A "job" is an agreement between an owner and a man to care for a certain plot on which trees are growing, and to pick and prepare the crop. For this the worker receives 5/– a barrel for the harvested cocoa. One Toco small land-owner told of an acre which he had in cocoa, from which he earned enough to supply the needs of his own family and to pay a man to "brush" it. This was at a time when the market was very low; many small cocoa-estate owners simply left the trees to themselves, not working them at all, but gathering what they could or renting the land for gardens.

The principal classes of workers on coconut estates are pickers, who cut down the nuts; gatherers, who put them in piles for the next operation; "busters," who cut them open; and "pullers," who pry the meat out of the nuts so it can be dried for copra. In 1939 pickers received between fifty and sixty cents a thousand nuts, gatherers about twenty cents, "busters" twenty-five cents and "pullers," who are usually women, thirty cents. In years previous to that date, when world markets were high, the rates were 80¢, 1/–, 30¢, and 40¢ respectively. As an illustration of the maximum earning power of the workers on coconut estates, may be cited a young man who told with pride that he had that day picked 2500 nuts, at a wage of 2/6 a thousand, or 6/3 earnings a day at the height of the picking season.

On the larger estates, where men and women are employed the year round as laborers, these steady workers do not perform the duties named above. The men do such work as cutting down the brush; the women weed about the young trees, and dry copra. For this men were paid forty cents a day in 1939, women thirty cents. Women ordinarily dry copra; the only men who are seen drying it are small landholders, doing all the work of their estates themselves. After the copra is bagged by the women who dry it, the bags are sewn by men paid at the same rate as laborers.

On small estates a man takes a "round job." He himself picks, gathers, and "busts," hires women to "pull" the meat, and delivers the undried copra at the rate of $1.40 a thousand nuts. These "jobs" are usually taken by young men, who try to time "jobs" from different estates so they will continuously have work. Usually, however, men who work on this basis also "have a gya'den, then try to catch this job anyway they can get it," and work on the roads as well, or do such other odd jobs as they can find.

One owner of a small coconut estate had about five hundred trees. Only when the market was very good did he employ a picker, otherwise he gathered up the nuts that fell, having them picked every four months. Climbing trees is specialized work, and only a few men are able to earn a living at it, since the demand is too limited to support more. At the period of low prices when this research was done the largest estate in the region employed no pickers. The nuts were gathered from the ground — a process that has a certain advantage, since ripe nuts yield more and better meat, and take much less drying, requiring only a day or two. This estate was averaging about a hundred nuts a day, and those who gathered them were paid fifteen cents a hundred for their work. When the piles were large enough to warrant, workers were called in to perform the operations at regular rates. Though it is not highly remunerative, work on the coconut estates is sought after. As one worker put it, "If you got steady work in de coconut, you earnin' to live on."

2

Public Works Department employment is considered the most desirable work that can be obtained. More than a part-time position is difficult to get, however, for the work done by this agency, principally keeping the roads in repair, is seasonal, or consists of short term projects, such as grading roads or building and repairing bridges. The permanent staff is thus quite small; casual labor is at hand for the hiring when the rough work that makes up the bulk of its needs must be done.

During the period of this field-study a bridge was being rebuilt between Petit Trou, an outlying section of Toco, and Toco village itself. Sixteen laborers and one overseer were employed — nine men and seven women, an unusually large proportion of women. When the bridge was completed, the crew were dismissed, to be available on call when further need for their services might arise.

As in most work of this kind a laborer sets his own pace, and though tasks are heavy and hours strictly checked, there is a flow of conversation to lighten the work, and pay day brings the ready cash that means so much in this community.

Pay day comes fortnightly, an event in the region. Payments are made by the district Warden, who comes from Sangre Grande, stopping at each village which has a Public Works Department center. Table and chairs are arranged for him and the local representative, and as each man or woman's name is called, he comes up, receives the cash due him, counts his money, expresses his thanks, and makes way for the next. Pay days are also the principal marketdays. Smaller markets are held on the days court is in session, for on these days there is no likelihood of as much cash on hand to be spent. Local preachers are about on these important market days, and heads of the humbler cults, both on hand to receive such gifts as the members of their flocks may care to give; sometimes, indeed, they remind failing memories of unfulfilled pledges or unpaid dues. Creditors are also present to obtain what is owing them before the money received by their debtors has been spent.

The importance of the day for the economy of the area is indicated by the fact that this is the largest and most concentrated disbursement of funds. On August 15, 1939, 276 men and women received $1,510.82 for their labor; 32 payments made for materials and miscellaneous services totalled $278.25 more; 26 small estate-owners received $100.38 in quarterly subsidies to encourage copra production (a normal amount) , and there were eight cocoa-subsidy payments totaling $42.81 (a small sum, since the largest amounts under this heading are paid in the preceding months). The amounts of money individually earned varied from 33¢, received by one woman "labourer" for $\frac{13}{16}$ of a day's work at 40¢ per diem, to $18.94, received by a road overseer for twelve full days' work at $1.50, plus four hours at $23\frac{1}{2}$¢ per hour, and a lorry-driver, paid $18.11 for the two weeks at $1.40 a day, plus six hours at $21\frac{7}{8}$¢ per hour.

Tabulation of the wages received by workers, mostly for part-time employment, gave the following distribution of income from this source for the period July 23–August 5, 1939:

Amount	*Men*	*Women*
less than $.50	1	1
$ .51 — 1.00	7	1
1.01 — 1.50	12	4
1.51 — 2.00	13	4
2.01 — 2.50	18	3
2.51 — 3.00	3	5
3.01 — 3.50	14	1
$3.51 — 4.00	15	2
4.01 — 4.50	12	10
4.51 — 5.00	16	1
5.01 — 5.50	7	—
5.51 — 6.00	13	—
6.01 — 6.50	15	—
6.51 — 7.00	17	—
$7.01 — 7.50	30	—
7.51 — 8.00	14	—
8.01 — 8.50	6	—
8.51 — 9.00	8	—
9.01 — 9.50	3	—
9.51 — 10.00	1	—
10.01 — 10.50	3	—

In addition, three lorry-drivers received $12.86, $15.86, and $18.11; two men who hired out with their donkeys were paid $5.93 and $11.81; one road overseer received $16.80 and another $18.94; a "driver" was paid $13.20, and an "officer in charge," $12.00; a carpenter received $17.40, and four masons $11.70, $15.31, $16.62, and $18.00.

Wage rates throw light on the basis on which the socio-economic groupings are sustained, and again stress the low level of economic life in the area. Women workers were paid the lowest amounts. Water-carriers earned 36¢ a day, "labourers" 36¢ and 40¢. Men in the same category of laborers were paid 60¢, 65¢, 70¢, and 75¢ per diem. Minor overseers, called "cantoneers," who do the same kind of work as those they supervise, received 60¢, 70¢, and 75¢ a day, exceeding only the lorry-loaders and night watchmen, whose rate of pay was 70¢. "Head cantoneers" — assistant foremen, as they might be termed — covered the total range of laborers and "cantoneers," but their scale continued upward at 75¢ and 76¢, 80¢, 81¢ and 90¢ a day for various individuals.

The hire of a man and his donkey was $1.20 per diem. "Drivers" as foremen are termed, were paid $1.10 and $1.50, "road officers" received $1.00 and "road overseers" or inspectors, $1.40 and $1.50. One man, named as "officer in charge," was listed as having earned $1.00 a day; another, designated merely as "overseer," $1.50. Carpenters ranged from 86¢ through $1.20 to $1.36; masons, beginning at 92¢, were also entered as earning $1.07, $1.40, $1.50, and $1.52. Lorry drivers received $1.10, $1.25, and $1.40 a day.

For many reasons work for the Public Works Department is considered desirable by Toco people. Payment is in ready cash, made promptly at fixed intervals, and, more important still, is assured. Even more than this, the remuneration, at the period of this research, was at a higher rate than any estates-owner was prepared to pay. A few of' the planters gave experienced and especially able workers wages which ranged up to 80¢ a day. But this figure was the exceptional wage, and a man who received remuneration of this order would have no difficulty in obtaining work with the Public Works as a minor overseer at rates as high or higher. This was a matter of concern to estates owners and managers, a subject which recurred in their conversation. The temporary and limited character of government employment was, from their point of view, the only element that relieved what otherwise would have been for them a critical labor situation.

3

An appreciable number of persons in northeastern Trinidad grow produce for sale and look to their gardens for an important source of income, and in many cases a livelihood. Many among these more modest cultivators own their land, for rented land is used to grow food which supplements wages or returns from fishing or trade.

Knowledge of agriculture is not only widespread, but can almost be said to be universal. This knowledge was, in fact, called upon when the program of subsistence farming was initiated by the Government in the late 1930's. The inhabitants of the area grasped the opportunity of producing the food they needed. Their conversations concerning the governmental program left no doubt that they valued it. The shadow of war that hung over the Island during the time this reasearch was being conducted, recalled unpleasant memories of the near-famine that had marked the first World War, and acted as a further stimulus to the desire of the Tocoans to have land for use and thus have a measure of assurance of providing the essentials of life.

To acquire a garden a man buys or rents land, or, if there is unpreempted land, obtains a government permit to "cut the bush." Land renting is a common practice, and rental, as already indicated, is a shilling a month, unless the land is had from the estate for which the renter works, in which case the charge is one-fourth that amount, or six cents monthly. Virgin land is usually far from transport facilities, but even were this undesirable factor to be overlooked, purchase would still remain a complex affair. For, in the northeastern part of the Island, "estates cover everything way back from the coast." The holdings of one company alone — with offices in Port-of-Spain — extend for miles along the northern shore and reach well inland, and none of this land, of which much lies in valleys highly suited to gardening, is for sale.

Once a gardening plot is arranged for, land is cleared at the end of the dry season, beginning in March and extending through June. Should the farm be in the "high bush," the trees would have been cut down during the previous months, and the severed branches and underbrush left to be burned over. Land previously planted, however, is "cutlashed," that is to say, the season's growth of plant-life is cut. When dry it is burned over to fertilize the land and permit hoeing.

Mutual aid through cooperative work is achieved when one man gives another "a day," and then receives "a day" in return. The Trinidad name for the larger group that comes together at the invitation of a man who is in need of concerted effort to accomplish a task is *gayap,* a créole term. "Men help each other in brushin' field," one participant explained. "No pay, but get food gi' them. That no mean pay, mean we helpin' one another." A *calenda* drum is used to give the beat, and songs are sung to lighten the work. A landowner who is reputed to provide a meager repast is ridiculed in song for his stinginess; these *gayap* songs comment obliquely on the foibles of various villagers who have been gossipped about, and the world at large. There is rum to stimulate exertion — "Mus' buy rum, an' you work mo'. De rum an' de drum put you in heat to do t'rough." In recent times *gayap* groups have not been large, and the tradition was said by at least one Toco resident to be disappearing. "The young men all want to see their money when they work." It may be observed in passing that the *gayap* also takes the form of a house-building "bee," and for "tap-yarin'" — plastering — a house when the builder does not have the means to hire a professional to do this work.

Calendars of planting are variable within certain limits, as the planting cycles, outlined by various persons with whom agricultural techniques were discussed, showed. One of these calendars follows:

March and April — clean ("cutlash") the land.

May and June — plant corn, peas, greens, plantains, tannia, potatoes, carrots, turnips, *edde* and other kinds of yams, "cassada" (cassava) and bananas.

July — "They're growin' now. You haven't much to do."

August and September — weeding.

October — weed; harvest potatoes, "cassada," and greens; and begin to harvest green corn, used for boiling and roasting.

November — harvest ripe corn, potatoes, "cassada."

December — dry corn.

January and February — harvest tannias.

March — harvest other yams, plantains and bananas; and begin the cycle again.

Another version may be given, not only for purposes of comparison, but also because in this calendar the relationship between various crops planted together is indicated. "You begin to clear the land in April, May, June," runs this account. In July corn is planted — a month later than in the preceding calendar — and "this is the first thing you plant." Cassava is put with corn, or shortly afterwards, for "when corn go, cassava take charge." There is a short dry season, called the *canitil*, that lasts from about the middle of July to the middle of August, though another person present who called it *'ti carême* ("little Lent") said this dry period only lasted two weeks, the first half of August. A check on the weather during the period of this field-trip proved both to be wrong — or correct, as the proportion of dry and rainy days during these respective periods might be weighed. What is clear is that there is a "small" dry season at about this time, when "de sun take up." "An' when dat take charge, you have to stop plant," or the crop will be lost.

Other crops — yams, tannia, "fig" (bananas), beans, pumpkins, and cucumbers may be put in before or after early planting time, this version holds, again indicating its general retardation as compared to the other calendar. One kind of bean, not previously mentioned, called in créole *mama zenfant,* is planted with the corn, and also pigeon peas, *pois angole.* Most of the preceding crops were termed by this man "Christmas produce," since they were harvested for Christmas use. Specifically mentioned as falling in this category were corn, ordinary yams, *cush-cush* (a fine yam), pigeon-peas, tomatoes, okra, cucumbers, and sweet potatoes.

In August, "you let it go" and, as in the earlier month named by the other cultivator, little work is done in the field. In September they begin to "clean," that is, to weed; "brushin' " is done in any second field a man might have, and this would be planted during the same month. Weeding continues during October, and the principal harvest is gathered in November and December. During January trees are felled on any new land that is to be brought under cultivation in the ensuing year, and in February and March the crops in the second field are harvested, or any second crop that may have been planted in the old field. It is recognized that the land becomes exhausted after a time, and rotation of crops is, after a fashion, practised. That is, "If corn fails, you plant potato or cassava. And when these fail, you have the land sour. Leave him catch high woods back again, then you fall it."

Still another account of the agricultural cycle, given by a woman, is worth presenting because of the relationship between plants and the account of growing time of the more important crops contained in it. She agrees with the first statement, indicating that corn is planted from May until the end of June. Pumpkins, she said, are planted with the corn, the corn growing faster and permitting the vines of the pumpkin to run between the corn-stalks. "Beans with melon, pumpkins, and cucumbers are planted with corn, and that makes a crop." When the corn is finished, the garden is cleared to make it available for "cassada," tannia, yams, plantains, and "figs." Peppers are planted any time, since they grow even when it is cold. Corn and its associated crops ripen in three months, yams every four months, being replanted by putting a part of the growing shoot into the ground where it takes root. Cassava ripens in six months, tannia nine months to a year, while plantains and bananas require a full year to give a crop.

Produce is sold locally and in Port-of-Spain, but it is held better to sell in the capital, since disposal is easier and surer, and prices are higher. In earlier days crops had to be disposed of locally, or transported by boat around the northern end of the Island to the city. Now, however, with trucks and all-weather roads, the city market is accessible to Toco gardeners at any time. What is sold in the village-market nearest at hand, therefore, amounts to very little in cash terms, as is evident in the sparseness of the market itself, as observed, and in the actual difficulty often experienced of finding enough provisions on sale to meet a visiting family's needs for an ensuing week. In the words of one man who always sent his produce away, "Things always sells in the village for five cents — three or four tannia, four or five plantains, four or five ears of corn, or three in planting season," and the returns are, therefore, meager, for in addition demand is never heavy.

An important aspect of agriculture that has economic significance, since to the people of this area it is as essential in achieving success in farming as the 'requisite technical knowledge, is that which assures to the farmer the supernatural sanctions without which his efforts will be doomed to failure. These precautions are particularly evident where new land is to be worked, but they are also apparent at the season of planting, as will be described later.

Ground to be newly worked is first surveyed for sources of possible difficulties of a supernatural order. Such a one would be a silk-cotton tree. In a case of this sort, the farmer goes to a "lookman," who divines to discover if the tree is "good" or "bad." If good, "then it's a common tree. Fell it right down." But this would only be the case if the tree were a young one. "If it's a big one, is trouble," and "there is things to do" before it may be cut down. The lookman tells what bad things "happen" under the tree — what evil beings do their "work" there. These might be workers of black magic, or a vampire, or a werewolf, or jumbies, spirits of the dead. The cultivator thereupon arranges a feast, and invites his friends to it. "Some buy rum, rice, fowl, egg, cyandle, and white cotton — sometimes red or blue, too." No salt is put in the food to be offered the spirits that live in the tree.

The lookman is the principal figure in the ensuing rite, for it is he who has the professional knowledge of how the spirits are to be placated. He "throws" rum three times, pouring it on the ground. He kills a fowl, sprinkling its blood against the trunk of the tree and placing the head at the base. He breaks three eggs against the bark. "Dey callin' de Satan below dat tree. Dat is Satan wood." Finally the lookman addresses the tree, saying, "I'm goin' to work you now." He drives his axe into the trunk, making the sign of the cross with the first strokes. Only then may the others fall to the task of chopping down the tree without fear of harm. But when it has fallen and been taken away, a bush called *tref,* that bears leaves "with three spurs, like shamrock," is planted "for luck."

Since ant-hills, of themselves, are not believed to harbor spirits to be feared, they are destroyed. But the two-headed snake that is believed to live in each ant-hill — "de mother of de ants" — must be done away with by the use of the proper "medicine," or it will kill the owner of the land if he has not taken the necessary precautions. If there is a stream on the land, the lookman is consulted to find out if a *maît' source* — "master of the stream" — lives in that part of it which crosses the land. "Whatever he give, you take," said one experienced in these matters. "He may gi' you something to guard you, or something to throw in the stream." If he says it is necessary, a feast is offered the *maît' source,* and eggs and rum are thrown in the water. The farmer "begs" the spirit: "Well, I bring that to save me." He also promises to look after the spirit every year, by "feeding" it. "An' that is a promise you cyan' defal' (default) from it. When you do, you fail."

Planting is governed by the phases of the moon. Some plants demand a waxing, some a waning moon, though the reasons for the rules do not seem to be clear to those who follow them. If yams be taken as an example, it is held that tannia is best put in three days after the first quarter, *dasheen,* white and *otutu* yams three days after the full moon, guinea yams three days after the first quarter, red yams "from new moon down, in between moon changes," while Ibo yams are planted "full moon today, tomorrow put them in the hole, and they'll come fine and nice."

Any variety of beans planted with the new moon will be

eaten by worms; these are best put in beginning three days after the first quarter, and "until you get to the full moon." If potatoes are not planted within three days after the quarter-moon, they are covered with banked-over earth and the planting is resumed after the full moon and until the last quarter. If a speedy growth of coconut trees is desired, as when a man has a new contract, they are planted with the new moon. But the "proper time" is after the first quarter, and until the last.

At harvest-time the supernatural protectors of the grower must not be forgotten, and first-fruits go to those beings that have vouchsafed success to the work of the farmer. What is done depends on which are stronger, the teachings of the church or certain extra-Christian beliefs. In the former case the first yield of any plant — grown, not purchased — is taken to church. In the Catholic rite the priest, in Protestant sects the minister, or preacher, blesses it and the one who has brought it. "If two or three or more people bring at the same time, it's a big day." What the minister blesses is "left for the church," and in churchly families nothing, it was said, is "thrown away" as an offering to the family dead at this time. Shouters — the most deviant of the Protestant groups, as will later be apparent — "does have more ceremony. You can see them go behind with different food." But there are those who "throw away" the first fruits for the jumbies — the ancestral spirits. "All de Tobagonians believe in de spirit," said the man who, in telling of the rite, was careful to explain that he was not one of those who follow this custom.

4

"Fishenin'" is important along the northern coast, and many men engage in this occupation to supplement income from other sources. Small craft that accommodate three, or sometimes four men, are used, and fishing is done relatively close to shore, for where tides are heavy and currents notoriously treacherous, a boat rowed too far may find itself on the Venezuelan coast or carried out to sea. Fishing is feasible only about six months in the year, during the rainy season, since the waves are too high in dry weather, and small boats must then remain on the beach. Even during the rains, they may be prevented for days at a time from going out to the banks, as was the case several times during this investigation.

Boats are, in the main, dugouts, with built-up sides, since almost no one can afford a "punchin' " or built-up boat constructed on a rib frame. One fisherman stated that the customary type of dugout cost about $50, but others named the more modest prices of from $27 to $30. To make one of these dugouts a cypress or cedar tree, bought for $4 or $5, is cut down and one side of the log is flattened. The shape of the boat is drawn on this surface; with a small adze the trunk is hollowed out inside this line till the cavity reaches a depth of from eight to ten inches. The outside is then shaped, a keel fitted to the bottom, the sides are built up with boards to a height of a foot or a foot and a half, and the joints are caulked.

In the great majority of cases boats are privately owned. But apparently two men can cooperate in building a boat and can own it together — "Oh, yes, dat's what dey calls comp'ny." In such a case, the two men share the part of the catch that "belongs to the boat." The division of the catch itself, or the proceeds from its sale, is customarily by fourths, one fourth to each of the three men who form the fishing team, and one fourth for the use of the boat. Where one of the men of the fishing team is owner of the boat, he receives one half of the catch, the other two men, therefore, sharing the other half; but where the boat is jointly owned the co-owners share the catch belonging to it.

In fishing operations on a bank instead of by trolling, the "captain"-owner, having the responsibility of determining position and dropping of anchor, as well as of caring for the boat and providing the bait, keeps all the fish he himself brings in. Each of the other two men sets aside a third of his catch for the boat's share, but in this way: If a fisherman gets three fish, a "second-sized one go fo' de boat"; if four or five, "a largest one," if six or seven, two "second-sized" ones; if eight, one or two large. This is "according to whether you have a large or a small catch," since "you have to use your discretion"; for what is regarded as large and what is "second-sized" depends on the kind of fish being caught. Observation confirmed repeated statements that the division of fish by the "captain" rarely raises disputes. He calls his men to watch and check him, and an especially large fish, or one left over after the apportioning, is cut up to make the division an equable one.

Fishing is done almost entirely with lines. The owner of a boat furnishes hooks and lines for "strolling" (trolling), but in fishing off the banks each fisherman furnishes his own. Thus a man gets two-thirds of his catch by this method — "a third is for de owner, a third is for de fisherman and de same is for de line." Lines are of wire, and each of the three or four hooks is attached to the principal trolling-line by smaller wire; one or two fathoms of cord may be used at the end of the line. Care must be taken in handling these lines, especially in playing the larger fish, for if the wire is not properly held the fingers may be badly cut.

Throw-nets, made of a fine mesh fillet with lead weights about the edges, are used to catch bait. When thrown, a net covers a shoal, and the weights pull together, making a bag and imprisoning the school of anchovies, herring, or sprats which the man standing in the water has seen swimming about. After March these small fish are so scarce that if the

Coconut pickers using a "bicycle" to climb trees

Fishermen bargaining for the catch

sea is calm, nets are cast in the small creeks. Fishermen often make their own throw-nets, and some of them are very skillful. The only net-maker in the village gets 80¢ a foot for his nets, or $4.00 for a five-foot net, and takes about a month to make it.

At the period of this study fish were bringing about 12¢ a pound. This must be held as a rough approximation, however, since the retail sales that comprise a considerable proportion of transactions are on the basis of the size of the individual "piece" a woman asks to have cut off a particular fish. Scales are not often used, so that "they value it." The fish are sold first on the beach, where purchasers gather toward noon or early in the afternoon as they see the boats coming in, and bargaining begins as soon as a catch has been apportioned.

A good catch would be ten of the larger variety — kingfish, covally, or barracuda. Fifteen of this type would weigh between four and five hundred pounds, and would net each man about $10.00. But, as observation verified, this would be a rare haul indeed, and in such cases, "even if you get de fish, you don' get de sale of it." What is left after the demands of those waiting on the beach have been satisfied is taken up into the village, or sold to the "jitney," or dried for later sale. The first of these types of disposal is a gamble, and late afternoon often finds a fisherman or his wife, still sitting in a doorway with a fish or two on a leaf in front of him, waiting for a buyer. The "jitney" is the car that comes up from Port-of-Spain to take back fish to be sold there; this entrepreneur pays about 6¢ a pound unless the catch is plentiful, when he gives less. The fishermen, however, in all cases prefer to dispose of large amounts for less money but to a dealer, since hawking takes time, and what remains after the day's selling must be salted for later disposal if it is not to spoil. Fish are dried, "either by de sun or by de smoke." They are then salted and sold for about 10¢ a pound to folk who live too far back in the hills to come for fresh fish.

It is difficult to estimate returns from this supplementary source of income, if only because of its seasonal nature. During the slack period, men hire out to the estates or work on the roads, and even when fishing is good, a man can find time to cultivate his own garden, if he has one. One fisher-man-cultivator estimated that such a person, making from $60 to $80 for the six months' season, calculated as an average return to a fisherman, would clear $30 or $40, since his living cost would be cut down by utilizing the produce he grew. But it is a commentary on the economic situation of these people that few who fish have gardens; which means that they must subsist on what the fishing brings them, plus what they earn at casual work, and consequently achieve at best only minimum support.

A scene at Toco inlet where the fishing-boats put out and come in may be described to document the general statements above. This cove is at the mouth of a creek that runs through the town, shielded by a small peninsula which gives protection against the high waves which come in from the Atlantic Ocean to the east. Across the water Tobago can be seen dimly through the haze. Steep banks, covered with matted underbrush, surround the beach; immediately behind them lie the neatly cleared yards of village houses.

On this occasion three great turtles that had been caught the day before were lying to one side, securely trussed — one especially large "green" one, and two of the axe-bill variety. The former was to be sold for food in Port-of-Spain, and the other two were to be retained for the local market the next Saturday; all the shell would be disposed of to dealers in the capital. Waiting for the boats were a woman and a young girl, customers for fish, and an elderly man, who said he was the owner of a boat and was waiting for his share of the fish. At about 11:15 two boats came in. A third one could be seen rowing westward, and was probably from Sans Souci point, a few miles distant. As the boats approached the shore more people gathered, since word passes rapidly when incoming boats are sighted, and as they came through the light surf, all who stood about helped run them up on the beach.

The larger craft had about twenty-five fish, a good catch, it was generally conceded. These were divided into two parts, one-half for the captain-owner, the remainder to be shared equally by the two men of the crew. One of these estimated his share at thirty pounds, or one hundred twenty for the total catch. The smaller boat brought in ten fish. Four piles were made, each having one good-sized fish plus three halves. Distribution was effected by the "captain," who worked slowly, judging the relative size of whole fish and cutting halves with skilled strokes of his knife. There was no dispute, and each man took up his share to sell. The men said they had got good kingfish on their lines, but the sharks had taken them. The reaction of a bystander to the news was immediate, "Sha'k come already?" he asked. And then, in explanation to the stranger, "Sha'k take kingfish but not mackerel until de sha'k get outrageous. Den he take anyt'ing."

After sales on the beach were completed, the men went up to the village. One of the men who had 30 pounds was disposing of his share steadily: the old boat-owner had sold his halves and had but one whole fish remaining. As a customer came, she told how much she wanted, and this amount was cut off the fish and given her without weighing, and in many cases without dispute.

Later that day the green turtle was taken away. It weighed 400 pounds, and would bring from 3¢ to 4¢ a pound, or about $12.00, when sold "wholesale" in Port-of-Spain; the men who caught it would have to deduct 5/– for "lorry-fee." This variety, incidentally, is deemed to give the best kind of turtle-meat, and brought about 18¢ a pound at retail in the city, indicating a considerable profit for the middle-man. The axe-bill turtles, which weighed about a hundred pounds each, were valuable principally for their shells, though the meat, while coarser than that of the green turtle, was sold at about 8¢ a pound retail in Toco. The shells were bringing 5/– a pound for the two to four pounds each turtle yielded; earlier, in better times, the price was 20/–. It is not difficult to understand how the crew of any boat that brings in a turtle, or better still, a pair of them, is counted fortunate.

Hunting, while it must be listed among the occupations of men, is done largely for recreation in Toco, though near Sangre Grande and farther south, and westward on the Island there are some professional hunters. What the hunter brings in is welcomed as an addition to the customary diet; the money gained from selling the meat of a fortunate kill is prized as supplementary income. Deer, agouti, possum, and iguana are the largest game animals encountered. Dogs are used, and are well trained. Before the hunt they are bathed in water with an infusion of leaves — of lapbush, "cyat-claw" (parasitic vine) , and "St. John," a bush that grows on the banks of streams — and a mixture of tobacco in rum is put up their noses, to sharpen their scent. When a "tatu" (armadillo) is caught, a part beneath the foreleg, "de arm," is cut up and put into a bottle of rum, later to be fed the dogs. This, also, is believed to help them, since "it generates a heat in de dog to catch de animal."

The need to propitiate supernatural powers in the exercise of fishing and hunting pursuits is deemed even more important than for agriculture, which offers less of a direct threat of danger than that which confronts fishermen and hunters. "You must respect de sea," say the fishermen. "Sea have more bad animal than land have." One fisherman explained the matter in this way: "Sea is a woman, an' if you pray to de sea, a little will always come. Say, 'Mother Sea, leave us alone, let us go an' come back. Savior, pilot us. Father, save us.' " There are ways of forcing matters. "Some wicked people get some charm an' get plenty fish for a time. But not for long. Den it stop."

Fishermen understandably help their luck by carrying charms. There is, for example, a bush called *rockshaw* whose leaves they use to rub their hands, lines, and hooks, and to put in their tool-boxes. But this can be too effective: "No be safe, make trouble. Bring sha'k, sha'k damage you. Luck so hot de fish damage you." Sometimes a saint's medallion is attached under a seat to bring luck. This is done at the direction of a lookman, and the saint is that of the fisherman's name-day. Crosses, frequently seen chalked on the rudders of boats or cut into them, are also held to bring luck, while wax candles, taken from the Catholic Church, are inserted into holes bored along the side of the boat as an added protection. Rum is sometimes sprayed on the side of a boat to give it strength, while crosses painted on the side of a new boat are supposed "to keep off anyone who come to make some project." One man had also seen an egg broken against the side of a new boat at its launching, and a whole pint of rum poured out. "But they wouldn't tell me why." Food is given ancestral fishermen in Tobago, but not by the Toco fishers.

In the woods the hunter must beware of the *papa bois,* a short, hairy, human-like creature with a "funny" head — "a little like an animal." The *papa bois* is guardian of the animals, and if one is wounded, the *papa bois* cures him. He also takes vengeance on hunters who do wrong, "like kill and only take a piece." One Toco man said some years ago he went into the "high woods" in the southern part of the Island, near the oil fields, with his brother and a hunter who lived there. The first night, while he and his brother busied themselves making an *ajoupa* to sleep in, the hunter killed a deer for supper, but "only took a piece." The next day they killed four *kwenk* (wild hogs), but the day after they saw the *papa bois*. "He stand, an' grumble, grumble, grumble. Pull down de *ajoupa*." The hunter was saved only by his "trick" — the charm he carried — and never went into this forest again. For the *papa bois,* who tolerates but "don' like no hunter" can make one who has offended him lose his way and wander aimlessly until he dies.

5

The problems of saving for future needs and of providing some security for old age are major concerns of the Toco folk. Of still greater importance is the need to be certain of having a "proper" burial; this is seen to at the cost of great sacrifices. The problem of saving is met by a group arrangement so widespread that in the past five years it has won recognized status in Trinidad law. Provision for old age, the most difficult problem of all, was in some measure being solved by a pension scheme instituted by Government at about the time of this investigation. Proper burial is made certain through membership in a lodge.

The savings arrangement is called "susu." An invitation to belong is phrased, "Join our meeting?" to which the response is, "How much to pay?" It takes the form of a co-operative pooling of earnings by those in the group, so that each member may benefit by obtaining in turn, and at one time, all the money paid in by the entire group on a given date. Members each contribute the same amount. The total of the weekly contribution — for this is the period most favored in Trinidad — is called a "hand." It is paid to the "captain," and given to the one whose turn it is to receive the money. In Toco such sums are modest, though in wealthier centers they may be fairly large. The point of importance is to have a membership able to make the stipulated contributions when these are due. A *susu* group, for example, made up of Public Works Department employees would not take in a man or woman whose employment was casual. An astute move for such a *susu* is to make the "driver" its captain, since, when personnel are to be laid off, he will see to it that members of the group are not among them.

Both men and women may belong to these groups, which may, however, also be restricted to persons of one sex. Nor is a member limited to joining but one *susu*, for if his earnings permit, he may belong to several. The most important member is the captain, or treasurer, who must be a person of responsibility. This does not always occur, and it was abuse of the *susu* mechanism by unscrupulous but plausible organizers that led to the recognition of the institution in law and the consequent protection of members against such exploitation. This danger is fully recognized in Toco, where it is held that a treasurer who draws the first "hand" is a person to be watched.

The organization is thus of the simplest. A number of people agree to pay in a certain amount of money each to the common fund at stated intervals. Then, in turn, each receives the total amount for a single period. This makes it possible for a person to purchase some article — a bicycle, for example — which he desires, but for which he has not been able to amass the necessary sum. Some of these groups, perhaps most of them, are ephemeral, lasting only for a "round" or two. But there are others that endure for a long time. And though, as such, they have no grounding in any kinship structure and do not involve any associations such as lodge-membership brings, their usefulness is recognized by all, and they have a firm place in Trinidad culture.

This is not the place for a discussion of lodges, except to indicate their function as organizations which provide for their members the kind of burial that validates their status and the status of surviving members of the family. Men and women strive to remain in good standing with their lodges, as arrears mean that the benefit of a fitting funeral will be denied them in the event of sudden death. The lodge concept, it may be remarked in passing, has been extended to meet another economic contingency. This was revealed when one Toco resident pointed out the meeting-place of the "Union Lodge," a new type of organization for Toco in which the members paid 12¢ a week dues as in the others, "but they give something new. They see member don' lose the job." Several incidents where this had occurred were cited. This is obviously a diffusion from the industrialized south, which shortly before the period of this research had faced serious labor difficulties.

Extreme poverty and neglected old age are the fears that haunt elderly people. Both are not uncommon, since it is with advancing years that the absence of support from a broad relationship grouping is felt. Children do what they can to aid aged parents, and collateral relatives and neighbors help those in dire poverty, yet there are enough persons in both categories to bring these fears into the thoughts of the villagers, and to bring the subject into many conversations.

The poor allowance for the county in which Toco is situated was in 1939, 36¢ (1/6) a week. At Sangre Grande, it was only 24¢ (1/–), because the appropriation, when distributed among the certified cases, was insufficient to pay a higher allowance, even though in reality the cost of living was higher there than in Toco. Sixty-eight persons received this amount, 17 in Toco, 20 between l'Anse Noire and Sans Souci, 15 in Cumana, and 16 in Grand Riviere and Matelot. Understandably, these persons could not live on the small sum given them. One old woman on the list, who had no family and no children, would beg food from passersby, or ask for something she might sell. "People here give a few plantains, a little fish. But not as much as they used to. Toco people are poorer now." Others who receive the allowance are women with small children otherwise unprovided for — "Women make plenty children, all small yet, an' de husban' dead" — or those who because of illness cannot support themselves.

There is a government poor-house for the aged, but the idea of living in it is distasteful, for it is held that most of those who go there die. "Don' live there long. Man here is 110 years old. Say he won't go to Government house. He live alone in a shack made of sticks. Everybody give him something. Still we don' know how he live."

The prospects of the aged were somewhat alleviated by the action of Government, which shortly before 1939, extended a system of old-age pensions to the county. The maximum sum paid at that time was $3 per month to help make up the desired minimum income of $6. This operated in such a way that a person whose income was $3 or less received the maximum amount, while if his income was between $3 and $6 he received the difference between that sum and the desired minimum.

The following data, taken from old-age pension cards in the Warden's Office, Toco, indicate the disbursements then contemplated under this system. They may be considered in the light of the fact that the total population of St. David County, as given in the 1931 census, was between five and six thousand persons, and that the numbers indicated below represented about 80% of those 65 years and more eligible for old-age pension. In Toco, 62 persons were to receive $3, and one each of the following sums: $2.70, $2.50, $2.20, $2.00. At l'Anse Noire, 16 persons were to receive the maximum, one was to get $1.58, and one 80¢. All 26 eligible in Sans Souci were listed as recipients of $3, while in Grand Riviere, 38 were to get the maximum, payments to the remainder ranging from $1.00 to $2.50, and in Matelot 18 were to have $3.00, one $2.95, one $1.50 and one $1.00. To the total of 180 thus to be benefited were to be added 45 more persons who had made application for relief but whose cases had not as yet been passed by the board.

CHAPTER IV

THE STRUCTURE OF TOCO
SOCIETY

THE LEGALLY and religiously sanctioned union between a man and woman is marriage. It is the form espoused by the whites who are the governing and propertied group, and is therefore a prestige-giving institution. More than this, on occasions when letters from the local minister or priest or preacher are needed for a better job, or an opportunity for a son or daughter to get a secondary education, or some other preferment, marriage properly solemnized and recorded brings definite rewards, and this economic aspect of conformity is phrased by the villagers in all discussions of mating.

Another form, equally institutionalized, and recognized in law if not by the churches, is called "keeping" or "living." In terms of sanction, of duration, and of the relationship between the principals this form is comparable in many ways to marriage, though there are distinctions to be drawn. These distinctions not only concern its prestige role as contrasted with marriage, but also have to do with whether the keepers — as both parties to this form of union are called — enter into the relationship with family consent, or as a form of trial marriage without parental approval, or as an expedient of mating when either or both parties are separated from a legally married spouse without divorce. Not uncommonly, a man and woman who are well into middle age, and who have been living together for years effect legal marriage for the position it gives the family.

Deviant forms of mating that are socially frowned upon or at best the object of gossip, are "living around," and prostitution. Here, too, distinctions must be made. A man may have a wife or keeper and be living around as well, in which case he makes presents to the woman he visits for intermittent favors from her. Another form of living around is had in the instance of a woman, not young, who has no special keeper, who is in fact economically independent, and distributes favors among several men, often younger than herself, but not on a commercial basis. There are also some young women in the village who are available at a price, or often in "comradeship," appearing, however, on Public Works Department pay days to capitalize on both friendship and generosity. There may be an instance of a man and a woman, each head of a household, who are "friends" and are said to be living around, for their relationship is neither regularized by a common residence, nor by his support of the woman, nor by any presumption of permanence.

There is, however, one form of relationship which the community excoriates. This does not concern the professional prostitute. The abhorred type of mating is the promiscuous one, when pregnancy occurs and a child is born with no identifiable father. No greater shame can befall a family, no failing is so unanimously condemned, or so mars the reputation of a girl. Such occurrences are not common, but they are more frequent among the adolescent girls than among older ones, for these know how to prevent the birth of an unwanted child.

One point needs to be made clear at the outset of this discussion. As regards children born to any of these forms of mating, not excluding even the promiscuous type, there is no social disability imposed by the community because of legitimacy or illegitimacy. The only differences between them arise out of such advantages as they may enjoy because of a more favored economic position of the parents, or of personal endowment.

2

Marriage, as described by the villagers, is costly. Many women who hold it important to be called "Madam," the title which designates a married woman, work and save for many years to come by the sum required for a church wedding. "A woman needs a ring, and a 'guard' to keep the wedding ring on the finger. Don' bound to, but they does get it," runs the account. These will cost "from a pound sterling to ten shillings, or perhaps even $2.00." Then, these days, "they wants a motor car for the church, and a white silk dress, and a veil, and flowers." They give a lunch "with cakes and wine." Six months before the wedding, they "print the cards." The woman buys "shoes one week, stockings the next, a dress," accumulating what she needs little by little, sometimes over a period of a year or several years, a procedure not always safe in terms of her fiancé's continuing interest in her. However, "Most people don' have the money for it. They got to start keepin'."

If poor people insist on a church marriage, then "they go to the family and ask who can to help." The bride buys an inexpensive dress, they walk to church, and the couple "just go home" — that is, there are no festivities after the ceremony. This type of church marriage, while lacking the greater prestige of the formal wedding, is nevertheless respected by the community, for it has the family "behind it."

But the action of a young man and woman in everyday clothes going to the priest or minister to be married, and then going home to a furnished room in the village, would be looked upon quizzically, and even mockingly as a form of pretentiousness. Here an important factor enters into the attitude toward marriage as the Tocoan envisages it. Not only is it necessary to meet the cost of the religious and social ritual, as prescribed by usage — the church fees, and the outfitting, and the refreshments — but marriage presupposes the attainment of certain economic standards in terms of maintaining a household. The man should have a house to which to bring his wife; in Tobago, it is pointed out, the families of both bride and groom help to build a house for the new couple, and "establish" the household by providing them with a cow, and fowl, and other appurtenances. But "here in Toco they don' take marriage so serious," and a man could marry without having his own house.

Whether owned or rented, the house must be furnished. A girl's mother buys at least the linens for the sleeping-room — "She'll mortgage her land to buy linens" — and she will also provide a chest of drawers, a washstand, and a wash-basin, if she can afford this. The man must provide the bedstead and mattress. "It's the custom." Above all, the man who marries legally will have what in terms of the local economy is a means of livelihood; in other words, he must be able to support his household, however modestly. Thus it is to be seen that marriage is not only a prestige phenomenon in terms of social or religious values, but equally, if not more importantly, has to do with economic stability and position.

Let us now examine in greater detail the forms of customary behavior that bear upon marriage. Here must be considered not only those practices that are ideally indicated, though in the reality of the situation of today are not too often followed, but also the variants that are deemed permissive.

When the conventions are observed, courtship begins in more or less casual contact between a young man and woman. It is continued through more frequent meetings, and leads to formal addresses to the girl's parents. These are in the form of a letter, in which the young man asks permission to wed their daughter. Copies of such a letter and the response written in reply to it are given here, unchanged except for the names of the principals:

> "Paria Main Road
> "Toco

"Dear

Mr. and Mrs. James it is with the greatest respect I take upon myself to adress you this letter on behalf of your loving daughter Jane; I hope you will not be offended by my doing so. It is clearly known that a time will come that you have to receive such notice; and now is the time . . It is fully twelve months now since I was watching your daughter; and she was also watching my movements; now the time has come for both of us to reveale our secret . . Mr. and Mrs. James we are deeply in love with each other; and by her request I write this letter, trusting it will not be in vain. I cannot say much more at present when I shall have learn your intention I will have a plenty to say. I am awaiting your reply at an early date.

> "Yours Obbdt;
> "J. H. William"

The reply is as follows:

> "Toco Proper

"Dear

Mr. William we have received you letter quite safe; I was much surprised when I opened it to see your title . . I had no thought of you whatsoever but I must

say that we all is quite glad to know that Jane has made
a good choice . . . I was always looking at you as a
gentleman; as far as I can see; I trust this letter you
have written that I might live to see the good result of
it; Madam and the sisters also the brothers is quite
proud to know that their sister has made a good choice.
I hereby give you full permission to visit my place;
and when we shall have seen each other we will have
some face to face chat; I close with love and respect to
you my son . .

> "Your loving Father and Mother
> "J. T. James"

Each of these letters had affixed to it a two-penny revenue
and postage stamp, to indicate its contractual nature, for
after an interchange of this kind, failure to carry through
the obligation that has been assumed can be taken to the
courts by either party, and damages collected. An alteration of the agreement by the young woman or her family
will be followed by a demand for the return of any gifts
the young man may have made, the value of which is re-
coverable in law; while the young woman can sue in an
action comparable to a breach of promise suit.

Obviously, not all requests of this kind find as hospitable
a reception as the one cited here, in which event the young
people might well, and in perhaps a majority of cases actually would present their parents with a *fait accompli* by
moving into the category of keepers. In such an instance,
the parents of the girl have no recourse but to accept the
fact. They will, therefore, either permit the experiment in
living together to continue until it is shown whether the
pair can achieve an adjustment, later arranging for a marriage; or disown the daughter and allow her to go her own
way. This latter procedure would, however, follow only
when there was active dislike between the young man and

the girl's father, and the union was consummated after prolonged dispute between the girl and her family. A step of this kind would not be taken on grounds of objection to the keeper relationship as such, but because of personal failings of the young man. Certainly if taken for the former reason, the sympathy of the community would be with the young people, and the parents of the girl would be the object of criticism, at the least, and open ridicule if popular feeling about their action was aroused.

In actual practice marriage among Toco people most often follows upon a period of varying length, during which the couple live together as keepers with or without parental consent. But this is not true in theory, and detailed statements of the steps toward marriage given a questioner will omit this aspect, since such an episode is held to be outside correct procedure. In theory, a marriage is not arranged until the families of the young couple are satisfied regarding their maturity, competence, and position. In outline, the young man writes his letter asking permission to court the girl. He then comes to her home to see her, and from time to time offers his services to her parents, giving two or three days' work in planting season, doing odd jobs about the house, and aiding them in other ways. This is not obligatory, "but the mother and the family are pleased, and if he likes the girl, he will do it." The girl, in visiting his parents' house, similarly takes occasion to demonstrate to her prospective mother-in-law that she can wash clothes and iron them. Each contributes gifts of food if a relative of the other dies — though this, likewise, is not exacted. The families of each are investigated by the other, and it might even be recalled that the grandfather of a grandmother "had a bad, bad reputation."

Yet, as has been stated, matters actually proceed in this theoretically regular manner only in a few cases. Because men in Toco have in recent years been drained off in appreciable proportion for work elsewhere, and since men have so much greater mobility than women, especially once children are born, procedures and precautions of the kind just described do not often precede a mating, or they are carried on only in fragmentary detail.

"A man live in a room," the women explained. "One day a daughter doesn't come home for the night. Next day she come for her clothes." The experiment has begun, and her parents watch to see how successful it will be. If the couple remain together, the girl's mother, as she visits her daughter, brings gifts that aid them to equip their household. At the same time, each family may quietly be investigated by the parents of the couple — that is, provided they do not come from the same village, where everyone knows everyone else. And arrangements may likewise go forward for a church wedding, unless they are content to live as keepers.

Today in Toco the custom of consulting the ancestors as to the advisability of a match, and obtaining ancestral sanctions for it, is not as prevalent as in earlier days. This part of the rites incident to marriage consists of reel dances, and *sakara,* an African designation for the offerings given the ancestors to obtain their consent to the match. In present-day usage, the dances are not often held. "Don' have reel dance again. Have weddin' dance. I don' know if they throws away food. They must do it, but you don' hear. If you marry today and have old parents, then you do it. You used to go whether you were invited or not. But now they dance at home." The more general view, however, is that a lookman is consulted, and if he sees no obstacles, the reel dance is dispensed with; otherwise it must be given.

These reels, or *sakara,* when held, take place the night before the wedding. Each family gives one, though the two dances are combined if the families are fellow villagers. Those invited bring gifts to help the host. "Long time ago they had a drum — a kettle drum — tambourine and fife.

Now does have clarinet, bass, and play jazz. Sing any song. Then ripe [mature] people, like meself, they dance." While the drum plays, and the younger people remain inside the house, singing songs, the offerings are prepared. "They kill fowl. Some does kill goat, and kill pig, big so, too!" White rice, peas, yam, and other vegetables are cooked with the offering, and they also have bread and cake and rum and ginger beer, to round out the refreshments.

A portion of each of these foods, especially white rice and the blood of the offering, is cooked separately, without salt. Corn is parched, ground, and mixed with sugar. This is called *sansam,* and is a special food for the spirits. The head of "any of de meat dey kill" is also prepared separately, without salt. At midnight an elderly man takes all this food, the *sakara,* and "cry outside, he talking in language like Yarriba. Everybody don' understand what he saying. Say, 'All a me people from Guinea, all you come. Come, this are we own food.' " Then he throws the corn and the rice on the ground, and a libation of rum. "When he start to eat, dey does eat, too. 'Me, the headman,' he begin, 'all of we pickney want you to help us in de livin'. Tomorrow dey go tie 'em. All we pickney from Guinea, all we Congo come join. Join in we marry, so we are all marry decide.' "

The susceptibilities of the dead must be respected, and the officiant specifies that none has been forgotten. Named or nameless, they are all welcome. "Can't say me no tell all you. Me no lef' out one of you." He takes the drinks, and calls out, "Who a drink rum, drink. Who a drink beverage [non-alcoholic drink], drink," and cries "Music, music!" at which all the older women begin to dance. He has a little bell which he rings three times, and then whistles. The others present turn their backs; no one looks at him as he watches the door. "They say, now he talking to Guinea." He goes off a little to a nearby bush of a special kind, presumably a sacred bush where family offerings are customarily given; his head is covered by a black cloth, with a wide red cross in front. Except for a "small cloth, like de Indians wear," he wears no clothing; but when he returns from behind the bush, he dresses in what he had on before.

The food that has been specially cooked for the ancestors is separated into portions, and placed on banana leaves to be put down at a spot that has been meticulously cleaned for the occasion. Two men and two women, the oldest in the family, and the one who has summoned the ancestors and performed the rite just described, do this. "One give the calling." This man calls the name of each ancestor three times; then all five officiants call together, and finally all "throw away" a proper offering. As the man calls, he puts down a portion, to which the others add. They recall as many names as they can; then, when finished, they circle the house, saying, "We girl going off tomorrow. Come help we. Come, give you blessing." Then, when they reach the place where the food is, the one in charge says, "All we no remember, you come and eat. Look, we put you own here." They put down a larger portion of food, and to make sure the wrath of none of the dead is incurred, he repeats, "All we no call, look! We put all your food now." When this is finished, the officiants have their own dance, with their own tambourine, in a "tent" — a temporary thatched structure — marching from where the food has been placed to the "tent" and back three times before beginning their dancing.

Another account of the ritual of obtaining the friendly intercession of the ancestors to the end of a successful marriage was as follows: "Man who throws away the *sakara* does all the talking. There are four of them with him, two males, two females, that make five. The four have candles. He takes white chalk, a big piece. He doing every work. Start from tree, go so [counterclockwise] and make marks. Stoop down and talk as he make them. Make it [sacred symbols] where the four stand, at their feet. Only do it around there where food is. When he done, all go right around the house [where the family lives]. He mark the four with cross on forehead. He have his red [piece of red cloth]. Everybody sit still and watching them. No singing. After he goes round three times, goes to bush again. Undresses. You hear, 'Guinea, Guinea, Kromanti, Hibo, Hibo, Hibo!' Stop. Silence for a good little time, and then he call, 'Music, music!' Everybody marches. Then they go yard hut [to the open shelter that has been erected]. 'Music now, me boy,' they says. . . . He [the chief officiant] say, 'Who we no remember, I leave for you all down there.' So if he forgot somebody, and they come, they would still get food."

Later the bridegroom is brought, and leaves that have been gathered are rubbed on his head, forehead, and the soles of his feet to test him, and to make certain that no spirit hostile to the match will bring disaster to the union. In the instance being cited here, this was not done to the girl: "She is all right. She is family. But they want to prove de boy." When they touch the man's feet with the leaves, the officiants call out, "Ah, no pass," or "Ah, good man," or "Yes, goin' to be a good marriage." If the ancestors are not favorably inclined, the match can be stopped at this point. "Do it when rubbing de man. Say, 'No good, no good. Me been a Guinea, me been a Africa. Me been a *tampo*. (Don' know where that is.) No good.'" Individual forebears may also speak. "Tom Henry say, 'No good.' Pete Joseph say, 'No good.' What about Aunty Rosie? 'Aunty Rosie say don' want at all.' Say, 'Bad man. Boy goin' to die if he marry.'"

An incident of this kind is rare, for in a family well enough versed in ritual to carry out so elaborate a rite, precautions against such a happening would have been taken at an earlier stage. As actually happened in Toco some years ago, where the ancestors forbade a marriage, the two families involved would be, and actually were, enemies for life.

"Dey ain't marry. Family give back what his. Girl keep what she have." The man who had been rejected would leave the village and would seek a wife elsewhere. But belief holds that a verdict of this kind, cruel though it may be, is for the best, since through it evil otherwise in store for the couple is avoided. In most instances, however, the *sakara* rite and the rubbing confirm the match, and the festivities continue until the morning.

Another practice, less common today than earlier, is for the old people — grandparents, uncles, cousins — to join with the parents of the girl as a kind of family council to investigate the desirability of the match. But the old grandmothers are today no longer called upon to be present on the wedding night to certify the bride's virginity. "There used to be plenty songs about that. Sometimes the girl was sent back. Always the families quarrelled about it," was the comment about the bride who was not a virgin. Today in marriages arranged by well-to-do families, virginity if not exacted is still a marketable asset in terms of what the groom or the groom's family consents to provide in the way of luxury gifts, and later in the amicable relations between families.

A married woman is called "Mistress" or "Madam." This designation is jealously exacted of all, whether or not the original match endures or, after separation, a woman enters into a keepers relationship. Even a young woman's own mother calls her daughter "Madam" and her son-in-law "Mr. John." For the wife likewise exacts respect for her husband, and calling him by his first name, even by intimates, is disapproved. She, in her turn, will not answer to her girlhood name. If she is taunted "Don' you answer good mornin'?" — for, as in all Negro societies, the canons of politeness are of importance, and must be observed — she will answer, "I don' know you speak. My name Madam James now." That this is an open invitation to quarrel is apparent, and such a response would bring forth further retort that might carry the dispute before the court. But the principle that the prestige of legal marriage must be upheld by use of proper titles is agreed to by all. "De husban' self does call she *Madam*. An' she call him *Mister*. After all, she want hers. Well, she have to give him his."

Patterns of exogamy are changing, as are those which govern other aspects of the life of the Toco community. "You can't marry a cousin on your father's or mother's side, but they are beginning to do it. But the older people don't like it at all," is a general observation. "When young people see a cousin they marry her." Theory has it that to marry a second cousin is undesirable because "blood is more deep, and the family is getting stronger." But the young people say "Second cousin no family," while all agree that the marriage of third and fourth cousins, and those more remotely related, is permissible. Generation and kinship prohibitions forbid a person to marry an uncle or aunt, a union that is held to be reprehensible indeed.

A kind of restricted sororate and levirate is sanctioned, though matings of this kind are not the rule. That is, a man may marry the sister of his dead wife provided no offspring had been born of the earlier mating. "If there are children, say, she is uncovering her dead sister's nakedness." The same feeling applies to a widow who goes to live with her dead mate's brother; this is sanctioned only if "he lef' no seed." Otherwise, were such a union to be established, a child would have to call his father's new wife, "stepmother as well as aunt. An' we don' want that." Furthermore, "If he say, 'I want to take care of my brother's children,' we say 'We'll take care of them.' " This last was the comment of a woman in whose family such a situation had actually arisen, and who was describing the reactions of herself and others to this proposal.

3

An unmarried wife — "keeper" — wears no ring; and in more than one Toco household, gossip says, the woman exerts constant pressure on her man so that he will take her to the church and obtain for her this outward mark of defined position. If a man has a keeper, however, this does not mean any "affairs" he may have will be the less resented by her than if she were legally married to him, nor has he any less responsibility for maintaining the economic activities of the household, or toward the children; nor, as has been stated, are the offspring of such a mating penalized by any stigma of illegitimacy.

A member of the local clergy, speaking of one woman who had been living as keeper with several men after an initial prolonged relationship, said, "She's a good mother. She is supporting five grand-children." He remarked that there is much experimenting in forming unions and that, though alliances generally last only a short while, some endure for the better part of the lifetime of the participants. Marriage, he pointed out, is no guarantee of stability, since a married couple separate just as readily as if they had been living as keepers. Once separated, moreover, such a couple do not trouble to gain their freedom through the courts, but each moves into a new keeper mating.

In examining the keepers type of mating, we are thus, in reality, viewing a pattern that fits harmoniously into the texture of Toco life, for as is demonstrated by the fact brought out in discussing marriage, a trial period of living together as keepers often precedes actual marriage. In addition to the reasons already given, this trial period may result because the families of the parties to a match are not yet able to undertake the expense of a formal wedding; or because the young man has not yet demonstrated his ability to provide, however simply, for a wife and children; or be-

cause the man, on his part, wishes to be convinced, possibly
because of some family history concerning the girl's relatives, that she will not be barren, or shiftless. A few examples of such keepers relationships may be given to clarify
these points.

John is a likable young man, but of a family not particularly noted for thrift or prudence. He is a hard worker,
earns a living of sorts at casual labor, and does not refuse
any type of work. But he will not hesitate to walk many
miles to a dance in a distant village, and will spend gen-
erously. The mother of his keeper will not permit her
daughter to live with him and their child in a room in the
village, as she feels that he has not yet demonstrated enough
responsibility to "have she trust she daughter to him." He
must visit his child and his keeper in the grandmother's
house, and what money he gives toward their support is
turned over to his keeper's mother.

Sue is the youngest daughter of a family once numerous,
but now consisting of but herself and three other children,
a brother and sister keeping, and another brother, who is
away in the oil fields just "living around," as his mother
hopes, for she disapproves of his forming a permanent attachment with a girl she does not know. Sue has had advantages. She can read and write well, she has done domestic work in the capital in an important family, she has
brought back clothes from the capital and wears them with
an air. But she is a timid girl, and is dominated by her old
and shrewd mother. Before Sue had left for the capital she
had been keeping with a man from another village. Their
child was stillborn, and they separated. Now he is seeking
to renew the keeping relationship, and because Sue's mother
does not have the funds necessary for a "proper wedding,"
and this suitor is well established, with good prospects of
being able to support a family, Sue is preparing to go to
him. Before this was decided, the mother had called upon

both lay and professional advice, the latter including both a lookman and a Baptist preacher of the Shouters sect.

Peter is a shopkeeper in his thirties. As Toco standards go, he is well-to-do, and he associates with estate owners and law enforcement officers. He had been keeping for several years with a woman, but had separated from her, and is now keeping with a young girl, whom he is planning to marry. Both families approve of the new relationship and the forthcoming marriage.

Amy and Andrew are keeping in a room in the village. Amy's parents had objected to Andrew's courtship, but they were presented with a *fait accompli*. There is now a year-old grandson, and Amy's mother is bending all effort to reconcile Andrew and Amy's father so that there may be a marriage soon.

The foregoing examples of keepers matings include types of unions which, as the Tocoans say, "have the family behind them." In this category are the matings which are not looked upon as preliminary to marriage, but as permanent unions, which do not eventuate in marriage because of lack of means, or disinclination to attach too much importance to the marital state. As may be anticipated, such unions are to be found preponderantly in the socioeconomic class called "the poor." Nevertheless, no identification can be made between the institution of keeping, as such, and socioeconomic status. This is because of the addition to the group of keepers of those from all classes of this society who, having been married legally, later separated, and without obtaining a divorce contracted other unions. Many of these once-married keepers enter into this latter relationship with the consent of their parents, while many others are sufficiently mature when these separations occur, so that their right to go their own way is granted by all, and their new arrangement may also be spoken of as unions that "have the family behind them."

The last category of keepers comprises unions in which a young man is joined by a young woman in defiance of the parents of both. Their behavior is considered so reprehensible that the older people will not be reconciled to the union. This occurs only in the rarest of instances, for whatever dislike parents may have of a young man or a young woman, if a union of stability is established, with the man earning enough to support the family, and the woman observing some code of fidelity and thrift, the families will not long remain estranged.

It has been seen that a prerequisite to marriage, as ideally conceived, is a man's ability to establish and maintain a household. In the establishment of the household he is aided by both his own family and that of his wife. Moreover, not only the living members of the family, but the family ancestors are called upon to promote the well-being of the new household. Whether this appeal to the ancestors takes the more elaborate ritual form of giving a reel and "proving" the groom, or of giving a dance and providing offerings for the dead, or of secretly consulting a lookman and taking whatever precautionary measures he suggests, the effect is to aid both actually and psychologically in the success of the union.

In the keeper relationship, the man has an equal obligation to provide for his household. This specifically includes a place to house the woman who is his keeper, and money or provisions to feed her and their children. If he cannot afford to clothe her, she is expected to supplement his earnings and to provide this herself, and where there are children, she will try to earn enough to clothe them before she sees to her own needs. Food and shelter are, however, the minimum requirement. A man who cannot provide subsistence, however meager, will be "living around"; he will not be keeping.

Rare would be a mother, moreover, who would not visit

a lookman and "do something for the dead" when her daughter took a keeper, whether with the family's initial consent or not. However, to give a reel or other dance for a keeper mating would also be rare, except where a young girl, a virgin, was given as keeper to a well-to-do man who had left his wife, and had not got a divorce. From the point of view of the girl's family this would be considered as important an event as a marriage, which would be prevented only because of the formalities imposed by "government."

The extent to which keeping is a normal expression of family life is apparent from an analysis of the marital status of a considerable proportion of the families in Toco and its immediate vicinity. These may be classified as follows:

Married	37	33%
Married, but with premarital offspring	24	21%
Keeping, but one or both mates previously married	20	18%
Keeping	31	28%
	112	100%

If the first two categories are combined to indicate the married couples and the last two to indicate the keepers, the figures are:

Married	61	54%
Keeping	51	46%
	112	100%

It may be indicated, moreover, that of the married couples listed as having premarital children, these in many instances had them by keepers to whom they are now married, or by other keepers, or that a man or woman is married to one who had a child by an earlier mate. Those listed as keeping but with one or both mates previously married, represent cases where marriages have been broken, and a new union has been formed by a member of it without the formality of divorce.

Just how long such a keeper relationship may last cannot be estimated, but the listing included numerous instances where such entries as "keeping a long time," "living with her man a long time," "keeping for ten years," "keeping good long time," "married — wife leave him; keeping now a good time," show the durable nature of many matings of this type. The man or woman who has moved from one keeper mating to another, however, is thought of as no different from the one who leaves a married spouse to become part of a keepers union. But the prestige in which marriage is held, especially by women — as commented on in earlier pages — and the stability and nature of the keeper mating are both strikingly documented by the case of a man who, after having lived as keeper with a woman long enough to have a daughter now keeping, was planning to use his savings for simultaneous church marriages for his daughter, and for himself and her mother!

Our list of families, their types of mating, and the children in each household already cited, also yields data that help us understand the place of the father in the Toco family. To be considered are those unions where, after matings had been broken, children remained with their fathers rather than their mothers, being cared for by their fathers' new keepers. The entries, though not numerous, are sufficient to indicate that there is no strict rule in the matter. In seven cases of the 112 noted, children by a previous mating were living in a father's present household, while in fourteen households the woman had with her the children she had borne in a previous mating.*

* Notations such as the following indicate the nature of the facts: "One child by another woman"; "two girls before marriage living with him"; "separated, he kept two boys, woman took two girls"; "two from wife, three

Attitudes toward the keepers relationship are further illustrated by the case of a man, previously married twice, who discovered his "keep woman" with a policeman. The matter came up for discussion in connection with this officer's death in a "jitney" accident, the result, in popular opinion, of the magic set against him. The offended mate had preferred action against the officer before his superior. But he lacked witnesses, and the woman declared that, "It was a policeman but not this one" — answering the Inspector's further question as to the identity of the man with the typical Trinidadian's response, "That my private business" — and no case could be made.

The man then went to a worker of magic, to set charms against the officer. But before the charm could "do its work," the woman gave birth to a child. "She come back, say the child is his own. He say, 'No.' She say, 'Whether yours or no, I livin' with you when the child was make, an' you got to acknowledge.' He acknowledge it. An' they make back." But later she took this child, and two others, and returned to her policeman, leaving one child for him. Then, "Somebody tell him she back with this man. He had a workman [worker of magic] come up behind him. Say, as long as this man live will always make trouble." It was after this that the car overturned, killing the officer. But the affair was not over, for the policeman's family had gone to a diviner, who had declared that magic had been the cause of death. "Well, they ain't goin' to leave him so. They go behind him now. But people say, 'Who have more mouth water, go soak more farine!' " And since the man whom the woman had left was well-to-do, and could afford to engage the best "talent," there was little doubt in Toco as to who would be the winner in this contest.

---

with keeper"; "has or had with him three premarital offspring"; "he had one before marriage, she had two, now seven children in the household"; "one (child living with him) not had with wife."

The Shouters, who, as will be seen, are a closely-knit group which functions socially as well as religiously, have much the same point of view toward marriage and keepers as the rest of the community. "Living," as they call it, is quite sharply differentiated from promiscuous relationships, for however brief such an attachment may be, there is at least an assumed permanence, and presumed exclusive right to the other party that lends to an arrangement of this type its sanctions. Indeed, the Shouters will not have an unattached young man or woman in their group, since they are certain there will be "running around" and subsequent difficulties. Such a person must acquire a keeper, therefore, before being permitted to join the group.

4

To enter into a mating where parents are presented with a *fait accompli* is simple, but otherwise, even where young people are permitted by parents of the girl to live together for a time as keepers, until they can test their ability to set up a household, the man must demonstrate that he can care for the woman. One point must again be stressed, both for the sake of clarity and to assure proper perspective. In the minds of the Toco folk, both marriage and keepers are relationships entered into in good faith, between persons attracted to one another, who have the intent of establishing a permanent union and bearing and rearing children. That the two types of matings have differing degrees of prestige attached to them is a by-product of an historical experience that has introduced the concepts of legal and illegal matings, and has given to the former type all the support that those in a preferred position could accord it. Yet keepers unions are never casual ones, and the difference between a woman who lives in such a relationship, and the woman who confers sexual favors promiscuously and for pay, is incomparably greater than between the common-law wife and the legally married one.

One need but listen to village gossip about the girl who "leads a life of least resistance" to sense how acutely the difference between marriage and keepers on the one hand, and sexual promiscuity on the other, is felt. In one family, where the daughters are all reputed prostitutes, communal distaste has woven tales of an ugly alliance between one daughter and her father, by whom she is said to have had a child, and about the mother, who it is whispered gave another daughter to her lover to conceal the fact of their illicit relationship.

Talk of another young woman of "questionable character" tells how she is the "friend" of two men, and how she knows to use position to her own advantage. "She is thrifty, yes?" they say, "Her house is nice, nice, nice. She is building a gallery [verandah] now. She has a big standing-up machine for sewing, bicycle, many things." It is told how this young woman takes trips when she pleases for a day or two — "Don' min' how much it cost." On the favorable side, gossip relates that she "is nice to her mother," adding maliciously, "Her mother say, if she marry, won' have all the things she is used to."

As in any small community, any deviation from customary usage is threshed over minutely by the members of the group. One such instance is that of a union between a woman who married a man much — "but much" — younger than herself. And though this couple have lived together "nicely" for several years, "they talks still."

Another situation where deviant behavior makes for talk is that of the parents of the young woman, the celebration of whose "forty days" rite of death is recorded in later pages. Her father, some years before, had left her mother, and was still living with the woman with whom he had formed a union. Before her death, the deceased had begged her

Working on the road

Paying off workers, Grand Rivière

father to return to her mother, and he had consented. At the time of the rite, he was sleeping "at home," but had not entirely deserted his keeper for his wife. "He cyan' stop all at once." He had had no children by this other woman, but all his clothing was at her house, so "he have to pick up clothes one, one, till he get away." Otherwise, she would keep them. It was anticipated he would remain friendly with his keeper. Once he sleeps at his earlier spouse's house "and he wife cook and wash for him, well, he home."

The quality of gossip of this sort is, however, tempered and sympathetic rather than malicious, and indicates the manner in which socially sanctioned forms of the family are distinguished from unsanctioned relationships. With either mates or married folk, the daily round is a reflection of capacity for adjustment. "Sometimes you hear them bitin' an' fightin' an' grumblin' an' tumblin'. Neighbors have to separate them," said one woman, speaking of married people, as she summed up her views of the institutions of marriage and keepers. "Others pass, hear them laugh, sing, play gramopho'. Always conversation. An' they keepin'."

CHAPTER V

THE FUNCTIONING FAMILY

THE DEFINITION OF the Toco family, in any functioning sense, must give a prominent place to the individual household. Kinship, of course, is important, yet the fact that a child can be sent from a parent to grandparent or aunt when his mother or father takes a new mate, and thereupon becomes a full-fledged member of this grouping, shows that it is merely one of a number of factors. Similarly, economic considerations enter, as is shown by the case of a woman who, having supported her daughter's child during its first six years, indignantly rejected the suggestion that she might at some later date care to return her grandchild to its mother on the ground that, "Mary never spend so much as a penny on Jane. Jane is mine. I bring she up, feed she, clothe she."

Whether the relationship is that of marriage or keepers, children are regarded as the normal end of mating. The desire for offspring and the affection and care shown children is a characteristic aspect of Toco family life. Many households number among the family group children born of a previous union, though where such children are not wanted by the new mate, they are sent to live with a relative. "Some men don' mind if say child not theirs," was one comment, reinforced by many specific examples where "they treat it good, good, good."

When a father dies or goes away, it is customary for the mother to keep her children with her, being aided in this by her own family and at times by the family of her children's father, until she enters into a new arrangement. When a mother dies, the father keeps the children if he can. Otherwise he sends them to his family or that of their dead mother, paying for their support until he can take a new mate, or continues to support them at the home of the relation with whom the children are living even though he has set up a new household. Stepmothers vary in their treatment of such young: "Sometimes we see things and we say 'Dead have no power' "; that is to say, the children are mistreated by the stepmother. A situation of this kind depends largely on the personality of the father, or his ability to earn enough to support his family. But a stepfather who mistreats his wife's offspring is rarely countenanced by a mother. If she cares very much for the man, "she wouldn't growl" but would send the children away. The more common practice, however, is for her to leave him, taking the children with her.

Because of these different kinds of arrangements it follows that the number of children in a given household does not necessarily represent the fecundity of the man and woman who have formed it. To attempt a numerical analysis of family size was a matter of some interest. Though any first-hand census of the village was precluded, an inquiry, as systematic as could be under the circumstances, of third persons concerning their neighbors and friends, made possible an approximation of the membership of households. Firsthand contact with a not inconsiderable number of families suggests that the data given here may be taken as reasonably valid. The reservation must be entered, however, that the average figures represent a slight understatement of the actual mean number of children per household, as will be explained later.

Number of children living in a given household	Number of households
0	28
1	13
2	21
3	11
4	10
5	6
6	8
7	4
8	2
9	2
10	1

In the 106 households represented in this table, the average number of children is 2.6; for those 78 households where there were children — that is, omitting the 28 cases listed as having none — the average is 3.4. That these twenty-eight households without children constitute the largest single category, and that of the households having children, the most frequent number is of those that have two, shows how heavily weighted the distribution is toward its lower end.

Explanatory comments on the individual household that were made when the information was gathered, corroborated by cases of families with whom firsthand contact was had, document the complexities of the situation. Almost every mating analysed, and almost every household visited, was found to have produced offspring who died subsequent to birth, while the tale of stillbirths was appreciable. That the birthrate is higher than the table would indicate is made plain by the fact that so many households had mature offspring in the city or in other parts of the Island, or by a different mating had children who were living elsewhere — with an earlier spouse or keeper, or with grandparents.

Yet in some measure this would be counterbalanced by gains per household where grandchildren were living, or where adoptions had been made, or in the few instances where children from more remote village homes had been sent to Toco friends, to benefit from such advantages as this small community afforded.

If preconceptions of what constitutes family stability lead to the impression that this society is one in a state of demoralization, the conclusion must be revised. There is nothing of family disorganization in the facts cited, any more than there is anything pathological in the dual system of mating. Here the range of permitted behavior in organizing, as in instituting the family, is simply wider than in other societies. For, in the final analysis, the family in Toco quite successfully performs the task allotted to it — the propagation and rearing of the young.

Another factor must here be considered. Given a community of households where custom lends preference to the rearing and training of children by the older, more experienced adults, the growing child is little concerned that he is brought up in a family where grandparents or an uncle and aunt control him, if he is given care, affection, and a sense of security. Allowance must understandably be made for the effect of differing individual personalities, yet within most Toco families, however constituted, the child comes surely to a knowledge of his culture, and achieves adjustment in it. Moreover, just as there is no stigma of illegitimacy to plague the offspring of a keepers union, so there is, as a rule, no difficulty where children of married and keepers mothers live together. They are, in effect, members of a single family; and where this is the tone set by the adults of the household, the solidarity of the group in face of the outside world is not affected by the circumstance of birth of the individual members.

We may gain some insight into the family life we are

studying if we pause to analyse the household of the woman who was mentioned in the opening lines of this chapter, indicating its composition and the attitudes its members have toward each other. This woman, Viola Thomas, has at the present time four children, two of whom are living with her. The oldest, a girl, Iris, was born of a keeper relationship. The second, Mary, was born to Viola after her marriage to Anthony Thomas. Mary is now a young woman in her middle twenties and is the only child Anthony acknowledges as his. She resembles him, and, according to Toco reasoning, is "lucky," because, "when a daughter resemble she father, he cannot claim she not his, and will look after she." About the third girl, Sally, there had seemed to be much suspicion as to her paternity, and there was quarrelling between Anthony and Viola; but about the son, Alan, a minor still, there was no doubt at all. and Anthony left her, eventually to take a keeper.

Viola's later experiences in mating are of no concern to us here, but a recounting of a few incidents in the lives of the children will be profitable. The oldest daughter, Iris, has a son, born to her in a keeper relationship that, by all accounts, was an unhappy experience that embittered her. Viola's view is that Iris has nothing more to do with men. Iris's son is living with Viola, his grandmother, whom he calls "mama," and is being cared for with solicitude, but Iris is made to pay for his care, and to pay for it as well as repeated letters detailing actual and sometimes imaginary ailments of the boy can bring results.

Mary, born in wedlock, had her first experience of motherhood still in her early teens, when she gave birth to a son, after one of those little esteemed attachments, with no keeper relationship to eventuate. Anthony, Mary's father, whom it will be recalled she resembles, assumed responsibility for the care of his daughter's son, and has supported him from birth. The boy is now living temporarily with Viola, while Anthony is away on a trip; but his upkeep continues to be met by Anthony. This same daughter bore Jane, to whom we have referred at the beginning of this chapter, but by another man. Anthony was incensed at Viola for her laxity in guarding the girl, and refused to contribute to the second grandchild's support, and since once again Mary's mate either could not or would not assume responsibility, Viola took Jane, and has seen to all her wants. Jane is growing up into a comely child, and calls her grandmother "mama," and her own mother by name, Mary. Jane has more than solicitude from her grandmother; she has her warm affection. "Jane is mine. She is more mine than Mary herself. Nobody help me with she." Mary has recently borne still another son by a keeper with whom she is now living. This infant is with Mary and its father, and is thus not part of Viola's household. Though there were more than intimations that all is not well between Mary and her keeper, there was little likelihood that this child would join the other grandchildren, for already there had been an offer from the parents of Mary's keeper to take the child, and bring it up for their son.

Mary's younger sister, Sally, fully adult, seems not to have had the urge — or perhaps the opportunity — to adventure sexually. She is hardworking, and is an excellent nursemaid to the children living in her mother's house, who are in reality under her care more than under Viola's. The young brother, Alan, is at school, a likable, easy going, surprisingly immature lad for his age, at fourteen spending much time with boys younger than himself, telling stories, and sharing sophistications. Friends of the family deplore that there is no man in the household to equip Alan for the the life of an adult, for his father died shortly after he was born, and could not assume even that limited direction which conscience or affection might have indicated in the kind of relationship that existed between Alan's parents.

Local opinion explains the relationship as one that might have eventuated in a regular keeper mating had the man lived, but at the time it took place he was married and living with his wife and family.

The important point to recognize in the organization of this household, which may be taken as a type met with frequently in the community, is that, whether with grandmother, with grandfather, or with mother, each child was being adequately provided for, was being trained in the ways of living, being given schooling, and will eventually take its full place in society. In short, this example, like the more general orientations that were presented, indicates that although in Toco society kinship holds its full importance, the ties of kinship and of residence do not necessarily coincide.

2

The possibility of mishaps attendant upon the birth of children are realistically present in the minds of Toco women. This does not make of pregnancy, however, an anxious or burdensome experience, since the desire for children is buttressed by social pressures of tradition and the Church. Abortives are not often employed, though a young girl who finds herself pregnant, particularly where this will "make people talk," may, with her mother's aid, halt her pregnancy. Such a step is taken only under great stress, and is carried out secretly, since a husband or keeper will seriously object if he discovers later that this had occurred. There is, moreover, fear of the dead, who are believed to disapprove of abortion, and to punish it.

This brings up a more immediate reason for not taking measures of this kind, for there is the fear that an abortion causes a woman to become barren. It is not at all uncommon for a man to leave a barren woman and seek another who can give him children. So strong is the dread women have of being barren, indeed, that this attitude serves as a device to promote stability in mating. For it is said that a woman who takes a man from another incurs the danger of becoming the victim of what is called "jumby belly," where an apparent pregnancy proves to be but a growth in the womb. "Belly coming up all the way. She tell husband she going to have baby, an' believe so, too. Nine months, ten months, no baby. Then belly go flat. They calls it tumor, but we believe it's jumby belly."

The common and incorrect assumption of the ease of childbirth where women live lives presumed to be in some way more "natural" than those of urban societies, and particularly in those groups who inhabit the tropics, is not shared by the Toco women, who take all precautions, both medical and supernatural, against mishap.

The diet is watched. Pineapple, *pirah,* and unripe mangoes are in no case to be eaten. "Green mangoes make you chuck up baby. Salts, too, plenty of it, clean it clean, throw it away. And limes, all this sour acids and rum and salts cut it up bodily." For these are abortives. Women of means go to the doctor for monthly examination; the poor go to the clinic. Some, who themselves "know what to do," do not visit the doctor at all, while others not only go to the doctor or clinic, but also give attention to such measures as boiling milkbush roots to make a tea which is given the expectant mother to drink on five or nine successive days. "It cools down the body," they say of this medicine.

When a woman experiences a first pregnancy, or where she has had miscarriages, or her children have been stillborn, or have died shortly after birth, a diviner — the look-man — is consulted. The object of this consultation is, above all, to determine whether the child will be good or bad; or, more especially, to be sure it is not a "maul," which is no baby at all. "Can't change 'maul' to good baby, so they give her medicine. Give to throw it up." But if the lookman determines it is a "good baby," he prescribes "things to drink and medicines to bathe." Where there have been previous unsuccessful pregnancies, he comes to his patient's house to bathe her himself. "But he do so at night, so people doesn't talk." Ordinarily, he is consulted only once, however, and leaves his prescriptions. "Then they goes to the clinic, too. Because they wants both sides."

As at marriage, when the first child is conceived, the family dead must be notified and their aid and that of other supernatural beings sought. This is also done where several miscarriages have been experienced by a woman. A fowl is killed, and white rice cooked — a little kept unsalted. A piece of the fowl, boiled together with the unsalted rice is "thrown away" outside the house on the ground, and with it is "thrown away" water and rum. The known dead of the woman's family are called by name, together with those others whose names have been forgotten, and all are begged "to help the poor pickney (child)." The dead of the husband's family are called in like manner — the known dead by name, and then, as a group, those whose names are no longer remembered. In addition the aid of the saints is asked. "It doesn't matter if they're a Roman family or not. Saints, and the Virgin, and St. Joseph belong to everybody." Finally, the spirits of twins are invoked. "Ask twins, too. Twins are very important."

Three months after conception, the woman takes two teaspoonfuls of castor oil, beaten up in milk or water, to keep the bowels open. Her urine is watched, and "if they sees dregs in it," doses of salts, a teaspoonful mixed in hot water, are given until this condition is cleared. In the eighth month, the dosage of castor oil taken early in the pregnancy is repeated, followed by milder doses as necessary, perhaps even once a week until within seven days of the expected time of delivery. Should there be repeated attacks of vomiting, the gizzard of a fowl is boiled with salt and butter to make a broth. It is put uncleaned in the water, and a little of the broth, which is strained, is believed to be enough to check the vomiting. The use of this remedy, which is applied to all cases of vomiting, whether of children, pregnant women, or the sick, is so widespead that the gizzards of all fowls killed are put aside and kept in the kitchen for just such a contingency.

The techniques of delivery vary, for the clinic nurse has the woman lie down, while midwives prefer that she squat on a large wooden tray, placed on the ground and covered with cloths. When a midwife officiates, the expectant mother is walked up and down the room until the "real pain" comes. Then the midwife rubs the vaginal passage and abdomen with "sweet, good oil," while the husband, who with the older women of the family is present, holds his wife's shoulders to keep her in position.

When the infant arrives, the umbilical cord is cut with scissors about four fingers' lengths away from the body, and the infant is bathed in tepid water to which a little rum has been added. The scissors, of the ordinary type, are put beneath the place the baby's head is to lie, and left there for nine days, when mother and child first emerge from the house. The umbilicus may fall the third, fifth, or seventh day, though it is sometimes still in place when the rite of the ninth day is performed. It is given to one of the infant's parents, or an older relative, who digs a hole for it, and plants a fruit tree over it — usually coconut, banana, or plantain. This is not kept secret, and when he is old enough, the child is told which tree it is. The after-birth is placed in a round calabash, put on a bed of buck-buck or "fig" (banana) leaves with salt and rum or bay rum, and is buried. Over it a fire is lighted, and kept burning for nine days; if this fire goes out, it is rekindled. No one must take coals from the fire: "This is done to prevent the mother from having after-pain."

After the placenta has been removed, the midwife first pounds wild coffee, called *malame,* and boils it, giving it to the newly delivered woman to drink. "As much as she want, a big glass full. That is to bring out all the bruised blood." The treatment continues as follows: "Then I take plum-bush, put it in a dishpan, boil it in water. I let the water half cool, then I lift up the woman and sit her over it. The steam come up. I beat she belly [demonstrating vigorous massaging], beat, beat all over. Then all the mortification drop right down. Don' take long, about five minutes. Then I give she a glass of malame water. I feed she on this water three days. Then she clean, clean."

If the birth is a difficult one, someone has "tied the baby in her belly." The same is believed if the pregnancy is prolonged a month or two. "Somebody is doing things to keep it from being born" — that is, magic is being used. In either case, the lookman is consulted. The best remedy, according to one midwife, is cobwebs taken from the ceiling, boiled, and given the woman to drink. "Then baby born. Must born, even if a lion tie him. Before the drink is finished, is born."

A caul present at birth is given to the mother, who wraps it about a bottle where it remains until dry. It is then tied in a parcel, and put away in a trunk until needed. From time to time, a little of it is parched and ground, and fed to the infant in his "pap" or gruel. For the child born with a caul will "see de spirit," and everyone says, "This will be a lucky child. This will be a sensible child." A child with the cord about its neck (which sometimes results in the infant's being born dead) is believed to be the result of the mother's stooping.

A child with six fingers is desirable. "Say it's lucky. Say

it's a giant breed, a strong family. Get presents plenty. The parents say 'Through the luck of this child I will live.' The parents are glad." But the extra digit is cut off when the child is big enough to have this done. On the other hand, children born feet-foremost are held in great mistrust. They say the Devil has come to kill the mother; that it is a dangerous infant. "If the child live, the mother have a different eye for it." And later, if the circumstance of its birth is known, parents will be reluctant to allow a child of theirs to marry such a one. Magic set by an enemy is held responsible when a birth of this kind occurs. For the good of the child, a breech presentation is kept a close secret.

Twins constitute a special category. They are welcome in the household and the community at large, for they bring luck. The rite of emergence from the house after nine days is in their case more elaborate than for ordinary infants. "There is more to eat and drink. Everybody come and bring nice cup of sago. Who have cow bring nice bottle of milk so the mother have plenty milk to nurse them. Everybody brings presents. Say, 'What lovely babies. I must give it luck an' luck for me, too.' " When the twins are brought out, they are carried to the nearby houses. "Everybody give (each twin) pieces of silver. It's luck for the baby and luck for you. Give two pieces, really, an' the same. They are jealous people, you know, twins."

As they grow older, they are dressed alike, if of the same sex. Should one of them die, they "make a kind of covenant" with the dead in the presence of the surviving twin. They speak to the dead, and say, "You're goin' to meet your Savior. Go in peace. Go. Don' look back for Nancy. Go, leave Nancy give me to help me." As this is said, the dead child's eyes are closed, either by the mother or some older relative, usually a grandmother. If the twin is grown when it dies, it is the grandmother who cries out to the dead, "Leave me this one. I grown old," and thereafter, when the living twin eats, it "throws away" some of its food for the dead one. But if it is not old enough to do this itself, the mother, or whoever feeds it, performs the rite. When new clothing is bought for a surviving twin, the matter is explained to the dead one. "Take this, and make your brother (sister) road clear. We still remember you. But don't come for him."

The most unfortunate and most dreaded contingency is when one child after another is stillborn, or dies shortly after birth. This is believed to be due to the action of a werewolf, or a vampire, and thus the result of evil magic. "They suck him dead. Doctor can help it, if navel bleeds too much, or catch it some way when they see the blood go. Otherwise, if they don' catch it in time, the baby die." This explanation came from a woman, three of whose children died in this way. She knew, she said, a rich, "fat woman," who sucked their blood. On the recommendation of the lookman she gave this woman her next child — that is, the woman was asked "to stand up for it" as godmother. "Never take no more from me." As is customary when an infant lives after previous children have died, this child was given a "funny name" — Sel. The mother pretended she did not care for it, and would say, "Stay or go, I don' care." She never dressed this daughter too well, but the child thrived, was never ill, and did not mind the apparent neglect. "That girl love me the best of all the children."

3

These abnormalities are talked of more than the frequency of their occurrence does in fact justify. In actual experience, children are born without too great difficulty, and the normal procedures associated with the care of mother and infant take their customary course. This does not mean that infant mortality is not high, for it is rare to talk to a woman who has not lost more than one child, and many tell of several children whom, early in life or later, they have buried.

The diet of the mother for the days immediately following the birth of her child is watched. She is at first given tea with milk, then chicken broth with rice, also chocolate, tea, and cornstarch — "that's cooling." After three days she may have boiled plantain cooked with sweet oil. Salt-fish and cooked cereals are also fed to her, and a special kind of plantain called buck-buck, which has had the seedy center removed. After nine days almost any meat may be eaten except pork, which she does not take until she resumes her normal diet forty days after parturition.

The length of time a new mother rests before taking up her daily pursuits varies. If the child is her first, she will convalesce longer than after subsequent births, though her economic position will have much to do in determining how long she is to remain free of the more taxing work about the house. In a poor family, even with a first child, the mother may do the washing after three days, assuming her full household duties after nine days; but this is unusual, since even among the poor there will always be a friend to help with the heavier tasks. The majority of women resume their full normal round a month after the birth of a first child; and as has been stated, in all instances the time is less with subsequent births.

As for the infant itself, from the time it is bathed until its mother can nurse it, it is given boiled water to which a little sugar or honey is added. The child is put to the breast every half hour, whether or not the flow of milk has begun. "Even if it get nothing, it draws," and the breast is pressed and massaged to encourage the flow. After the milk appears, the infant is fed whenever he cries — five times a day but, if he demands it, every hour or half-hour. When the mother's milk is not sufficient, it is supplemented with equal parts of condensed milk and water, or scalded goat's milk, with sugar added. After two months, nursing at the breast is alternated with bottle feedings of a mixture of sago, arrowroot, and corn-starch gruel. But if the mother can nurse her child adequately, this gruel, the first addition to its diet, is given after the infant is nine months old. The nursing period may end at that time or may continue until the child is a year or eighteen months old, depending on the child's health, the flow of milk, and the tradition in individual families. The other foods given are Irish potatoes with "good butter," or tannia yam and melted pork soup, or white rice, "cooked soft, soft."

When the baby and its mother emerge from the house nine days after birth, a ceremony is held to present the new member of the family to relatives and to the family dead. The infant is dressed as finely as the resources of the parents allow. Both mother and child are bathed at the entrance. "You put the baby to lie down, then go throw water — an old person, not a young one. Say, "God bress us to give us a little gran. Come in and see it now, but don' take it away from us.'" This is addressed to the dead: "They call by name, 'Jane, Mary, Henry, all we dead family, come an' see.'" The dead of the father's family are also called. Fowl and white rice are cooked without salt, and they "carry a dishful give the family dead." They say, "The mother and father family coming from Africa, all of you there, come and merry with us." The feast is as bountiful as the means of the parents permit, aided at times by both families with gifts of provisions. All the members who do not live too far away attend. Presents are given the child, "plenty presents," and it is a happy occasion.

As soon after the "nine-days feast" as feasible — that is, "if the parents can afford it and the child is strong" — and in any event before the infant is three months old, it is baptized. The child is named after a godparent, and if a "grandmother or aunt" now dead is thought to have helped with the delivery, her name is also given it. One baptismal name is held secret. The infant is then taken home, where all who come "give some little thing for present."

The role of the godparent is usually important in the child's life. The godfather and godmother ideally have the rights of parents to correct their godchild, who looks to them for help when in difficulty. Yet on occasion, particularly where some prominent member of the community has been asked, as a gesture, to act in this capacity, the contact between him and his godchild may be very slight. "Some godparents, christenin' over, don' know you till marryin', an' if they are not kind, you don' bother about them. Don' tell them even if you marry."

When it is judged time to wean the infant, the bitter tasting, milky juice of the aloe is spread on the mother's breasts. If a child persists in taking the breast despite this, it sleeps for a few nights away from the mother. Another method of weaning is to give the child a "toddy" of condensed milk, sweetened with four or five drops of rum to the cupful, when it cries for the breast at night, and is unduly restless. This supplements the use of bitter aloes. Should the infant fall ill before the flow stops, the mother may resume giving it the breast for a time, even though it has been weaned. But this is done only rarely, being considered a critical expedient.

When the flow of milk persists, a hot piece of iron or a heated brick is placed on the floor and the milk pressed out on it. This is believed to dry up the flow. Or a cork and nine grains of corn can be tied with a cord that reaches about the woman's neck and allows these to fall on both breasts. Then a leaf "of a thing they call cabbage," is greased with sweet oil or lard, and fastened on the breast. "But some people milk come so heavy that wouldn't do," in which case the method of the heated brick is resorted to, with certain efficacy in three or four days.

Babies sleep beside their mothers on a deer or sheep skin that is put over the mattress for protection. Should it be necessary to leave an infant alone in the room, while the mother is doing the washing or working in the garden, an open Bible is left with it to protect it from harm.

A girl-child's ears are pierced for earrings when she is about three months old. Should the family have small gold earrings, or be in a position to buy them, they are inserted when the holes are made. Otherwise, pieces of thread, attached to the needle which pierces the lobes, are left until earrings can be acquired.

Since the parents are eager for the child to begin to talk at the proper time, they are extremely careful not to cut the infant's hair too early, for they believe this "will turn him mumu" — dumb. One mother, for example, plaited her son's hair in four braids until he was quite able to talk. If a child fails to talk when most others of his age do, some "naked" water is pounded in a mortar, and a formula such as the following is recited: "We pound this water in the name of the Father, the Son. Help me to make the little child talk. All my dead, all the souls, the saints that is, O help me to give the child speech. The Mother, the Father, the Son and the Holy Ghost." The water is then poured into a small calabash, and the child is given this water to drink. Then he should begin to talk. If they are in season, he is fed uncooked green peas from the pods. "Then he talk like a parrot." Food for the dead is later "thrown away," in gratitude for their aid.

Girls are "put to sit" — propped up — at about the age of three months and boys, a month later. "When they sit good an' try to stand, help them." As they crawl, they are encouraged to walk. Considerable variation is recognized; whereas some children walk at twelve months or earlier, others do not walk until they are eighteen months or even two years old. Whoever notices a first tooth must "pay" either a fowl, or a pig or goat; or, if poor, a shilling, six-pence, or even six cents — "something silver." Lateness in teething causes no concern — "They always come" — nor is there any anxiety whether upper or lower teeth first appear. Even though the mother is the first to notice the teeth, as she generally is, she waits for someone else to dis-cover them so the child may have its gift. When the first deciduous tooth comes out, the mother throws it on the roof of her house, and says,

> "Rat, rat, rat
> Take this tooth
> And give my little boy (or girl)
> The next one."

Teeth are cleaned with soda and a piece of cloth. In earlier times people chewed orange sticks to keep the teeth clean, but now this is not done so much as formerly.

Little attempt is made to teach sphincter control in the earliest period of children's lives, but "when they have sense, tell them to go on the pot." Later, if they wet the bed, an attempt is made to ascertain the cause, for it is believed that some children do this "because de midwife went home an' de navel drop off an' fell on de floor." To cure bed-wet-ting caused in this manner the child is given the heart of the sour-sap fruit to eat, while the bladder of a cow or any other animal killed by the head of the family is put to dry. When it is thoroughly dried, it is filled with water, which the child drinks through the tube. "That cures it. But it's bad to let the navel drop on groun'. Make the child go weak inside always."

When children's bed-wetting is not caused by a dropped navel cord, parents "flog them, flog them plenty, too." Neighborhood children cover their faces in mockery and sing,

"Little girl (or boy)
Pee a bed
Pee a bed
Fie, for shame!"

Only after the children have left the culprit hiding in a corner, does the mother or grandmother come and caress the child, urging it not to offend again. One elderly woman told how her father had looked at the sleeping-mats each morning to see if any of his children had wet them. If so, the children were flogged the first few times, but if the offence was continued, he would put flour on the offender's face, "make it white, white." Fowl's feathers were put in the child's hair, a frog — *c'apeau* — was placed in a pan fastened with a cord to the child's back, and the culprit was sent to walk on the highway where there were "plenty people." Other children, with sticks, would follow, singing a variant of the song just given:

"Little girl, little girl
What you name?
Little girl, pee a bed
Cry for shame!"

This elderly woman can still recollect how she used to lie awake nights, in terror that this would happen to her. When she awakened to find her mat wet, she would put in her place a younger brother or sister, and take the dry place herself.

The baby is continuously introduced to new foods. After the first soft diet that follows weaning, well-to-do or comfortable families give it fowl or fish, or a little beef if this is available, soon after the second birthday. If the child is not too well, it is fed a little fish-broth. White rice cooked soft, with coconut oil or butter, is standard in the diet at this period and later; children of this age are also fed mangoes, fig (bananas), mashed tannia yam, or tannia soup. Plantain and oranges enter after the third year, though children are given some strained orange juice from infancy. "Clinic didn't teach us that. We know it by ourselves."

Cassava is eaten when a child "come big and walking." The root is sliced, put in the sun until dry, pounded in a mortar, the resulting flour sifted, and "pap" made of it. "It's nice, yes? I like it myself," said the woman who explained the process. "Better than things in the store." If the parents can possibly afford it, milk is given to young children. "But after they walks, if you haven't got milk, you don't worry. Cut up cane [sugar cane], an' they suck it. That does help them. They goes on fine."

A bush called *fell* is used to clean the eyes. "It's a thin bush, don' grow wild." A piece is broken off and put in clean water; later it is exposed overnight to the dew, with two sticks across it, "so that those dead will not use it first — that no good." In the morning the infant's eyes are bathed, to wash out the film, until it is a year old. The same treatment is given, however, "if the eyes come bothered" any time later. Children's ears may cause trouble. For earache, "you syringe with hot water and something out of the doctor-shop."

For other childhood ailments there are well recognized popular remedies. An infant who has "gripes" — constipation — is given a tea of pumpkin bush and bud lime, lightly brewed, to stop the crying and restlessness, and relieve the condition. For measles, either *crapeau* pumpkin ("with spreckles") or garden pumpkin is boiled and strained. The water is given the patient to drink, and the meat, prepared without fat of any kind, to eat. "If you feed them on this pumpkin and barley water, it wouldn't stay on very long." Should the disease have been contracted outside the house, the child may go out, but if he contracted his measles while indoors, "then it kill him" if he were to go out before re-

covery. A cure for whooping-cough is wide red braid tied
about the neck. Once a day the patient is given boiled coffee
which has salted butter in it. As for colds, drinks made
of Christmas-bush, greta-wood, or "yella-black" sage are
brewed. "That red cloth suck the cough; you put red flannel on the belly (chest), too. But if it's bad, you take him
to the doctor. Children die from whooping-cough." Similarly, should typhoid fever appear, "Go for de doctor right
away."

4

Formal education is given by the schools, which are under
church direction and are operated with government grants-
in-aid. Since none of the Toco schools reach the level of
secondary education, it is necessary for the few children
from this area who wish to study at this level to go to one of
the Island's larger communities. The earlier grades are well
taught. Such a high standard of performance is demanded
and achieved that the proportion of those in the district
who can read, write, and figure is quite high.

Children begin school at the age of five, and continue
until adolescence, when they become full-fledged workers.
Some who dislike school run away. Here the economic
element enters, since they are generally children who have
no shoes or adequate clothing to wear, or, as importantly,
whose parents cannot afford to give them lunches to take
along. The other children share food with them, but since
these poorer ones are often mocked, it is not strange to find
that they become what is termed "locobeach." Only one or
two of these were to be found in Toco during the time of
this study, and the hope was expressed that these, like others
of the type before them, might "come to take ambition for
themselves" and induce someone to teach them what they
had missed in school.

The child's training for participation in the life lived about him is gained primarily in the household, and begins at a very early age. When a child is only two years old, it is taught to put things away. A few months later, a little girl is given a small broom so she may sweep a few strokes; still later, twigs are made into a yard-broom, and she is expected to help keep the yard clean. "They start to do it and are pleased." At five, when they are ready for school, girls "can do a little anything." When young children come home at half-past three or four o'clock, they are given some "domestic work" — the girls helping to prepare the meal or aiding with housework, the boys "changing" the goat to a new grazing place and gathering "hogmeat" vine to feed the pigs.

Boys do not "go to the gya'den" until they are six years old or more. "Beginning with six, the boy pick up the food you dig. That self time he bring home something from gya'den, as much as he could eat. Some are glad to do it, proud to carry plenty. Some don' be glad" — especially those who have been kept home from school to help with the garden. By the time he is ten years old, a boy can help with the planting, and knows how to weed. On Saturdays, the boys go "to pick wood." This is competitive, and since boys of all ages work together, a younger lad tries to bring in as large a "bundle" of sticks as he can manage. They work steadily, and a lazy boy is teased by the others.

Little girls seldom go to the garden. If it is not too far and the weather is good, "father take she on a donkey," but the girl does no work. "Not everybody does carry children in de gya'den." By the time a girl is ten, however, she has learned to help with the weeding. Her household duties consist of dusting, or mopping — "a little, but she must do something." If the spring or brook is nearby, she helps carry water in a little pan. By ten years of age, also, she has learned to scrub and wash simple pieces of laundry, such as towels. If the mother knows how to sew, she begins to teach her daughter. "But not every mother could sew, so she wouldn't be able to teach."

Girls are also taught to cook when quite young. At five, even, they are shown "little things." By the time a girl is twelve years old, or even ten, she can prepare the family meal, "but some don' learn 'till they're fourteen or fifteen, and some are not industrious at all, no matter how you teach them." Such girls are obviously problems to their families, for inability to carry on the tasks of a household means that an adjustment will be difficult for them to achieve in later life. Such girls are warned by being told tales like that of the girl who dressed nicely, married, had "a gold wedding ring and guard, and a ring from her mother," but who could not carry on the household tasks. When her husband sent her back to her mother, they made up a song about her:

> "You han' full of gol'
> Cyan' wash a bowl
> Pack she back
> To she mother."

The tale goes that "everybody beg the man to take she back. Mother go there an' keep house for a long time, stay with her till she learn. She 'bliged. Before she only care for dress, dance."

When they are young, boys as well as girls help about the house. "Have some boys can cook better than a girl, and like to do it, too, while small," said one person, discussing the activities of young folk. "Some boy can do everything like a girl. But when they grows up, don' want to know anything about it at all."

It must not be assumed, however, that school and home duties tell the entire tale of the child's life. Understandably, there are few, if any, organized activities for children, but the boys play marbles, make grava wood tops and spin them, play cricket, make kites and fly them, trap mongoose, crabs, and other small animals, and fish from the rocks. The girls dress dolls and play at keeping house. Though there are no "church leagues," occasionally there is a school entertainment. One such evening, to be described later, was witnessed. If it were representative of this type of performance, as it seemed to be, it can be understood why it generates no special enthusiasm among the children. But these same children, among themselves, tell Anansi stories with dramatic skill, and great alertness in listening and telling.

Before the onset of menstruation, when a girl's "breasts begin to come," she is given a potion made of boiled bed-grass root or sera seed bush. She is also given a little oil, and "a little salts to keep the blood moving." After her first menstrual period, the drink is given again, "so the flow should always come good." No taboos are associated with menstruation except as regards church matters, and as concerns sympathetic and black magic. A girl who is a member of the Anglican church does not commune while menstruating, and though she may go to service if her period is near its end, she will take no part in it. The Shouters will not baptise a menstruating woman, and will not permit her to "go to the mournin' ground" while in this condition.

As for the magical aspects, the cloths a woman uses are not washed until the end of the period, since it is believed that to do so sooner would bring on the flow at more frequent intervals, and cause it to continue longer. Care is taken not to leave the cloths about, for they are potent in concocting evil magic. To insure against this, the first cloth used by a girl during her first period is burned, and the ashes are poured into water and given the girl to drink. This, it is believed, will forever prevent her being harmed by anyone who might utilize her menstrual fluid to make magic with which to control, or otherwise overpower her. "But not everybody know to do so."

Education in matters of sex is given informally. Girls are constantly warned by mother and grandmother against sexual adventures, particularly at the time of their initial menstruation. Mothers often examine their daughters, possibly with the idea of inducing abortion should the girl be pregnant. Small girls and boys who are discovered "playing together" are flogged. For while virginity is prized more perhaps in theory than insisted upon in practice, if a man courts a girl with the understanding that she is a virgin and discovers she is not, she will be returned to her mother. At puberty, also, boys are "talked to" by their fathers, who warn against sexual excesses, and of the penalties for rape.

Of other manifestations of sexual activity, masturbation and homosexuality are known. Regarding the first, it was said, "Don' like it, but don' know they do it." Both boys and girls are said to indulge, and they are flogged if detected. Homosexuality is considered a disgrace. The homosexual is an object of ridicule and abuse. An older man discovered to be exerting an influence over a young boy would be prosecuted by the boy's family. Among women, it is termed "making *zanmi* [friends]," and there is much, talk and "plenty song" about such persons. In one case elsewhere in the Island, known to a Toco woman, the active member in the arrangement, "mind that woman, make she plenty present of shoes an' dresses. Give parties for she" — to which only "females" were invited. But no such cases existed in Toco or its surrounding areas.

Another form of disapproved behavior is dealt with by calling on the dead: "If you got unbelieving children, especially girls go bad, don' work, don' cook, don' wash. Dance would be at Matelot, go, don' mind what cost. Wouldn' obey, wouldn't hear. Go with men, come back late at night, hear dem make disturbance, singing. When mother warn she, she give no head. Laugh. So de mother mix sugar water an' call it beverage — some takes rum an' water — an' throw it as she wake in de mornin'. Throw it down de steps, as she open de door, outside now, say 'Mother, Gran'-mother, Auntie May, Uncle Peter Joseph — an' all de others — come to dis pickney. I prefer you to take it. She wan' to go bad. She won' hear to me. She wan' to bring disgrace on we family."

The account goes on to tell how at first the girl laughs at all this. But "de night surely you go hear dis people come. They cookin' food an' rice an' de same beverage leaving on de table. She goin' to hear de knives an' plates raklin' [rattling]. Put out good plates. Mus' be all white. An' white rice, but no salt. Mix de beverage, get goblet an' put in de center. Hear dem drinkin'. De nex' mornin' woman say, Buddy Harry was here tonight. He say 'Help you mother' " — here the teller imitated a gruff, nasal voice.

"Nex' mornin'," the narrative continues, "de girl get up. Then girl get fever. Do it to son, too," came the explanation, almost as an afterthought, "but most often to girl." Then, returning to the principal theme, "Daughter now sick, begin to cry, to beg. Say she sorry, say goin' to behave." That night the mother sets the table as before, and prepares the same food. "They come again, say, 'Warn you. We warn you' " — in the nasal speech of the dead. "Tell mother, now, bush to pick [leaves] for bathe her. But if dey come to take her, de girl really bad. She sick, sick now. Mother have to get reel" — the dance to placate the dead.

Thus the wayward child is punished, first by correction administered by its relatives, then by action of the dead. The matter can be pursued no further, nor is it often necessary to do so, for belief permits little question that in such extreme cases as that described here only a new way of life, or death, could result.

5

In the manner described in the preceding sections, the child is brought to maturity and trained to become a member of his group. Something of the relations that exist between the members of these households, and their rights and obligations toward each other must still be indicated. Particularly important to assess is the role of father and mother in family situations where matings are constituted, broken, and reconstituted in a manner sanctioned by the community.

In defining the place of the mother in the household, the Tocoan himself gives the unequivocal answer, "Always your mother first. No matter what the trouble, your mother there the first to help." Or, more picturesquely stated, "You mother always behind you. Don' you hear the song say, 'Pack she back to she mother'? An' the mother always there to help. Don' mind what it mean, she there to do every little work for you."

But it is made clear that a mother's aid is also to be counted on in achieving normal aims as well. "Mothers don' only help in trouble. They the one to take ambition for the children. See daughter study nursing. See son learn trade, or fin' some profession. Father, if he have estate, want he son to work the land, but mother want she son to have education."

Another illustration was given, to show how the mothers strive to save small sums for their children. "When provisions is scarce, a family will sell as much as it can, for prices are high. The father he fret, 'My house come first. I de plant. I wan' to eat.' But no matter what he say, she carry it away sell it. She try take the best before he come to the gyarden. See a nice plantain put it aside, take home one no so nice, say we wouldn' get sale for them all the time." All this she saves for the children, "so when they growing, they have things."

When a man and woman separate, the children born of their union are either divided between them, or, far more generally, the woman takes the children to live with her or her own family. Whether the children's father contributes to their support depends largely upon his economic position, and in no small measure on the relationship of the parents after separation. If the father owns land, or if he is still a resident of Toco with some assured means of support, he will contribute to the care of his children. But aside from such contribution, or such provisions as may be required of him under law, custom dictates certain minimum obligations that must be validated if a man is to maintain a position of respect in the community. An example of this is the requirement that a man must provide a funeral for a dead child, even if he is separated from its mother, and doubts that the child is his.

One comment on the role of the father was, "Most fathers love their children. They work hard, work to feed them and give them things. Teach their sons to work the land, teach them to be men. If there is trouble with the law, they will mortgage the land to help. Brothers do that, too, and the whole family. But fathers not so patient as mothers. Little troubles you hide from the father." Another version was, "If father have, he give, but if hard times come, a man lose courage, then he can't think of children. Mother, she go beg to feed them, but he sit with he jaw in he hand."

All opinion holds that whether father or mother plays the dominant role in a household depends principally on the socioeconomic position of the family. In the family — whether based on marriage or keeping — belonging to the "well-to-do" or "comfortable" groups, a man is the head of his household and its court of last instance, except as this can be modified by the ingenuity of the mother or by the prestige of the mother's family. In the category of the "poor," once more whether married or keepers, the role of the father in the household depends upon whether he earns at least enough for subsistence. Though individual differences introduce differing emphases, rare is the man who allows his voice to be the one more subdued in such a household. The mother as a contributing wage-earner resorts to less indirection to gain her points in the family's conduct when she is not entirely dependent on her mate.

Another group of households consists of those in which the woman has either been abandoned, or has left her keeper, or she and her children have been left behind in Toco while he is away working in the oil-fields. If the woman is mature and has an assured means of livelihood, she heads her own household; such a one is Viola Thomas, whose family has been described. If the woman is young, she makes her home with her parents, or her mother's family.

Thus far, the expressed feeling tone of the Toco villager toward his father and mother, and the role of the man in the household, as determined by his socioeconomic status, have been considered. Tradition establishes a role of equality for mother and father in such practices as addressing to both parents the formal letter asking for a daughter in marriage, or, when the dead are to be appealed to for aid, invoking and propitiating the ancestors in the families of both mother and father. In other words, whatever the actual roles played by parents in given situations, both parents have a place in the life of their children, recognized by the Tocoan, and regularized in Toco custom and behavior.

The problem of inheritance within a household in which the father is already dead and the mother dies intestate may be met in the following manner. "The family comes now, mother's brothers and sisters. They talk. Boys ask for more.

Uncles say, 'A man need more, he got to work to keep wife, children.' Aunts say, 'What, take Mary's things give another woman?' They now pulling for the daughters. They argue, but don' come to a big thing. They would divide. Girls they think take care of mother's things better."

This relates to personal property such as furniture, clothing, utensils, and perhaps some more or less expensive trinket — a ring, earrings. "Land they divide equal, and money, too." But the qualification was entered that often land allotted to a daughter is for life only. "They have a paper make out for that. Give her one, keep one. If she die, then if the man she married to or keeping with is a good man, give him nex' sister, if there are no children from the first." What if there are children? "Then the keeper say to the mother, 'Come, take her things.' He wouldn' crave what hers. The children go backward and forward from grandmother to father. If he near, and lived nice with the daughter, she would even cook for him and wash his clothes. People say, 'Mary, why you so good to that young man? He ain't no family to you.' She say, 'A good livin' better than a bad marry.' "

Children, it is said, get on well with all their grandparents, but there is recognition that the maternal grandmother figures most importantly in their lives. In trouble, one turns to a mother's family for aid. "Say they're more lovin'. Don' know why." If the father's side is in better circumstances, "Then you go to them first, still hangin' on to the mother's side." But while living at home, "Child may be more friend with father than with mother. Some boys love the father more, follow him everywhere. Girls follow the mother."

CHAPTER VI

THE RITES OF DEATH

ALTHOUGH TOCO KNOWS no institutionalized cult of the dead in clearly defined form, any adequate understanding of Toco culture requires that the rites of death and the attitudes toward the dead be given their full weight. For as an intrinsic part of the life of the people, these not only furnish dramatic incidents for conversational relish and material for gossip, or bring villagers together at wakes to enjoy the recreation that is an overlay to the more serious aspects of these rites, but act as a stabilizing, moral force. They give to the older men and women of the family who officiate a respect in behavior and a prestige in council which makes for cohesiveness and adjustment of the group.

The necessity of having a proper funeral has already been discussed; and the funeral in conjunction with the other rituals of death may be thought of as affording a kind of transition — logical and validly ethnological — between problems of the natural world and a discussion of the realm of belief. Since the funeral, the ceremony which separates a human being from the world in which he has lived his life and launches him on a more mystical experience, bulks so large in Toco, our analysis of this aspect of the culture may begin with a description of it.

UPPER LEFT: The "father" of a Shouters group. UPPER RIGHT: "Yarriba" woman singing. CENTER LEFT: Woman (Negro type) on way to market. CENTER RIGHT: Negro man on donkey. LOWER LEFT: Drumming for the "Yarriba" songs. LOWER RIGHT: Negro woman with headtie.

TOCOANS

2

We may consider the case of a man, the head of a family, beyond middle age, who has been ill for some time. The nature of his ailment, and the course of his life, allow no suspicion that his death is being caused by evil magic. His condition has been steadily deteriorating until one morning it is apparent that death must soon come.

Members of the family, or friends nearby, are sent to telephone or telegraph relatives who are elsewhere in the Island, while a lad is dispatched on a bicycle to summon relations who live within reach. Once death comes, wailing begins, and the neighbors, hearing the cries, come running. "They sees the family carry on, and they is sorry, and bawl, too. There's plenty loud bawling." Hysteria is discouraged, and when those outside the family see someone giving way to grief, they "take a kerchief and lash you." They also "tie you belly," that is, take a towel and tie it about the waist, thus giving physical support to those whose weeping is likely to overcome them. This is done to men and women alike; though "a man when he catch himself would loose he, but a woman stay on all de while, till next mornin'."

All who come bring gifts to help with the wake that night and the funeral of the next day — money, rum, plantains, tannia yams, rice, candles, biscuits (that is, cakes), and sugar. A friend of the family is dispatched to buy rum, nails, tacks, flannel cloth, candles, and turpentine, while others go to get rice, salt-fish, and cooking oil. Friends and neighbors prepare food for the wake, and care for the family of the dead, relieving the mourners of any tasks in connection with the death rites.

The coffin is made in the yard, or under a nearby shed. The carpenter who makes "de box," is not paid for his work, but is reimbursed for the cost of the planks he uses.

"But there is plenty rum there. They drinking all the time, wetting the wood." If the dead was poor, the shavings that "plane off" the boards are piled where the head of the corpse is to lie to give the effect of a pillow, and over these old white cloths are laid, "to make it comfortable." But in the case of the man we are considering, the wood is stained and varnished, the coffin is lined with "plenty flannel," and trimmed with " 'boss work" — carvings — and "nice hardware."

Tobacco, rum, and "jumby balsam" — to give a sweet odor — are placed in the water with which the corpse is washed. This water is kept until the coffin is taken from the house to the cemetery, where it is thrown after the dead. The white cloth used to dry the body and the nail-parings and hair of the dead are made up into a parcel and put into the coffin. The specialist who bathes and shaves the corpse is given the razor and the soap in remembrance of the dead man.

The body may be dressed in either a white shirt and black trousers, in which case the shirt is sewed to the trousers, or a pajama suit is made of new flannel. No pockets are provided, but if the trousers had them, no one troubles to sew them up. New white socks are put on the feet, but no shoes. No belt is used. The arms of the dead are folded, and a "real pocket handkerchief," scented with jasmine, is laid against them. Ears and nostrils are stopped with cotton. If the mouth is open, "the jaw is bound with a cotton cloth"; a copper coin is placed on each eye, otherwise, "they say he's looking back for somebody."

If the dead man belonged to a lodge, his membership card and his regalia are placed at his side. Some lodges, especially the Masonic order, close the coffin in a secret ceremony. Ordinarily, however, when the coffin is ready, the body is placed in it, and all come to look at the dead. If the dead man liked flowers, friends make a wreath of jasmine to put about the corpse, or take "len'-liana" to form floral offerings which, with cardboard crosses decorated with flowers, are carried in the funeral procession and deposited on the grave. While the man lies in the coffin, the principal mourners sit beside it and receive condolences.

That night there is a wake, for the dead is never left alone. The wake, an essential part of the rituals for the dead, is an important event in the life of the community. All who attend make their contributions, for everyone present must be served coffee, bread and biscuits, and rum, while candles are needed to read the hymn-books, to play cards and other games such as forfeits, to dance the *bongo* dances, and for the groups who tell Anansi stories. Some member of the family selects a man "so he come for chairman," to assure order and proper direction of the night's activities. "He say, 'The topic for this meeting is for Mr. James Thomas, deceased. We want perfec' order. No rudeness. Anybody can't behave themselves we put them out. All you 'gree, say "Yes."' Then go on for the night."

First a series of hymns is sung and then "people go on to play (games)." Refreshments of coffee and bread are served at about ten o'clock. Singing, *bongo* dancing, and card and other games are resumed outside the house until midnight, when coffee and biscuits are again served, and rum. "Now it's a big intermission." Before anything is drunk, however, some member of the family makes a circuit of the outside of the house, sprinkling rum on the ground. A libation is also poured in front of the coffin, or before the bed on which the corpse lies if the coffin is not yet ready. Before the chairman, who is first to drink, tastes the rum, he likewise pours some for the dead. Smoking is not permitted inside the house where the body lies, for "this will make de dead purge," or weep.

The hours until dawn are whiled away with stories and riddles, hymns, games, *bongo* dances, and wine or chocolate may be served early in the morning. If the dead is well-known, the gathering is large, and most of those who attend remain the entire night. There is hesitation to be the first to leave a wake. "Nobody likes to go first. But the rude boys that play (dance) in the yard, don' mind who go first. Plenty of them go together."

The grave is dug early the next day, by a party always made up of an uneven number of men, sometimes as many as twenty-one, sometimes eleven, or as few as five. The better known and liked the dead, the larger the group, and the family have rum and food — rice, tannia, and soup — sent for each member. The digging is done with hoes, pick-axes, digging forks and shovels, and the grave is about six feet deep, its length and width being determined by the dimensions of the coffin. An extra space is dug to indicate where the head is to go, in accordance with the precept, "head to the rising, feet to the setting." The men exercise caution in digging, so they will not hurt themselves. "Many men don' worry with that, but some would be afraid, yes?"

If a person dies very early in the morning or during the preceding night, burial is the afternoon of the day of death; or the following day in a case such as we are considering here. Four o'clock is the favored hour, but they will delay as long as possible to permit the arrival of relatives living at a distance. If they wait too long, the funeral will not be over before sunset and the swift tropical darkness will over-take them. It is mandatory that burial take place no later than the third day, for at that time the body "rises," and this may take place only in the grave.

Even if the dead had quarrelled with his children, they come to his funeral. Weeping, they beg forgiveness, and it is said the dead hears them, giving recognition by opening his eyes. A child who is ill or who has suffered misfortune will call on the spirit of the dead for help, holding the great toe of the corpse. But all this must be done before the body has been bathed. Sometimes, when father and son have had violent quarrels, the dead is unrelenting. He will not grant forgiveness, and if the son attempts to carry the coffin, "then the box heavy on the son's side. The dead puts all his weight there, and the son must let someone else carry his father's coffin. He goes off and cries. He's ashamed too much." A child of ten or even more, is sometimes passed three times over the coffin, especially when a man has said, "When I die, take the child pass him over my coffin three times and bathe him in my water." This is a preventative against evil magic: "Nobody can do anything to the child then." But these practices are today less frequently encountered.*

The funeral procession moves on foot, and in the instance of the man whose death-rituals are being described, the cortege is of appreciable size by reason of his lodge memberships. As preparation is made to take the coffin from the house, the family renew their wailing. When the body of the dead was put in the coffin, the room was swept and the dust put in the corner. Now, in accordance with the saying, "Don' watch the box, or the spirit will harm you," those present move away, and as the coffin goes through the door, the water in which the corpse was washed and the dust that had been swept up are thrown after it. "You sweep quick, quick, as the funeral is moving, and throw that (dust), too. If that lef', he lef' " — an occurrence none would care to contemplate, since the spirit of the dead, reluctant to leave his home would, by remaining in the vicinity, become a restless and, therefore, a dangerous ghost.

Church participation in the funeral depends on the affiliation of the dead. We assume, however, that in this case the dead was a member of one of the more conventional

* A Barbadian, resident in Toco, stated that in Barbados a child is passed three times over the coffin of its parent. If one has a pain "you beg the dead before he is washed, and it is cured."

church groups, and that his lodge is in charge. The marshal would have summoned the membership to attend the burial, absence from which is subject to a fine of a shilling, strictly exacted unless an acceptable excuse is presented in writing. At the funeral, the president and other officers carry the society's banner at the head of the procession. "De ribbon come down nice on each side." Then comes the coffin, carried by members, "de head tippin' to de banner." Full regalia are worn. "You can tell an officer by the initial embroidered on his sash." If the coffin has no handles, two cloths are slipped beneath it, an end of each held by the bearers. Chairs are brought along on which to rest the coffin when those who carry it tire, for the distance traversed may be long. Since the coffin is never carried on the shoulder, bearers are frequently changed.

After the church ceremony, they proceed to the cemetery, where the rites vary with the church affiliation and the "order" or lodge to which the dead man had belonged. Ordinarily, no offerings are put in the grave — "they open the grave with rum, but after that, don' put in nothin' again." Those not related to the dead stand quietly by — "only de fam'ly bawls." If the dead had been an Anglican, or a member of one of the other conventional Protestant sects, the minister throws earth on the lowered coffin as he pronounces the formula, "Dust to dust, ashes to ashes . . ." However, should the dead have belonged to a Shouters group, each member throws in a twisted handkerchief as the coffin disappears from view. As the grave-diggers work to fill in the excavation, people leave quietly, two by two, and only the family and close friends remain to watch until the mound has been tamped down by the flat of the diggers' hoes.

At the house, the bed on which the dead man lay during his last illness is washed in a running stream by friends, unless the disease had been communicable, in which case the "public health" burns bed and bedding. They use water containing limes, "jumby balsam," and black sage, and the bed and other articles are thoroughly washed and put in the sun to dry. No ceremony attends this work — "don' hear them say words when they clean the house." Everything inside must be made ready for those who will come that night, and the eight nights following, to sit with the mourners in a series of "small wakes." Another rite called the *cropover* — a term interpreted as meaning "we are finished," somewhat like the wake — is held on the ninth night after burial. This is the principal ceremony between the funeral and the "forty days," which will be considered in some detail in later pages.

3

The rites of death vary with the sex of the dead, with age and socioeconomic status and, as has been suggested, with religious affiliation and membership in lodge or order. The procedures in various kinds of burials can be sketched to indicate, in their divergences from the rites just described, something of the range of accepted funerary custom.

The "shroud dress" of a woman is made of mauve colored cloth, while that for a young girl is white; both are trimmed with "plenty white flowers." The hair is combed and plaited, and over it a cap of mauve material is placed or, in the case of a young girl who sang in a church choir, a white "choir cap." The coffin is lined with flannel, as for a man, and shavings are used for a pillow if the family is poor, but a woman's coffin is never carved. The persons who wash the body are in this case women, and as in preparation of the body of a man, the family watch the work to make sure that body fluids are not secreted, later to be employed

for magic. The women who do the washing take for themselves the garments last worn by the dead, the soap they
use, and the comb.

All body openings are "plugged," especially the vagina.
"They say, let her be closed," and this principle applies to
all females more than a year old. A mixture of balsam, tobacco, charcoal and "soft candle" is used for this purpose,
a cloth being placed over the vagina after the manner of
menstrual cloths. Ears and nose are closed as for a male,
and the chin bound should the mouth have opened, while
pennies are also placed on open eyes to be sure they will be
closed in death; as has been said, the dead must not "look
back."

A woman's earrings, rings, bracelets would have been removed during her illness; if death is sudden, jewelry is
taken away before the body is washed. These trinkets are
given to a woman's husband, or her mother, if she has no
mate, and can be disposed of as the recipient sees fit. In the
coffin goes the same kind of "good" white handkerchief,
scented with jasmine, that is placed in the coffin of a man,
and, if the dead woman was active in the church, her hymn-
book and confirmation certificate are buried with her. Membership cards of the lodges with which she was affiliated,
her regalia and any other "cards" are put there; lodges and
religious organizations function at her funeral as they would
for a male member.

If it is suspected that death was caused by evil magic, the
dead, whether woman or man, is instructed to return in
nine days to tell who was responsible for the death. In order
to assure proper punishment for the culprit, the corpse is
provided with two whips, one in each hand. One is cut
from the calabash tree, the other is of the type called a
mayama whip. To the corpse, they say, "Nine days after
this time, show we the example of the person who did this."
Some also take a whip and "lash the grave, ask the dead to

rise and get he enemy." When such measures are taken the results are awesome. "Nine night, hear running around the house. If the person who is guilty is outside, the dead licks, licks him, then he howl, running, running. Licks him till he can't find his house. You can hear him stumble. The next day he sick, sick till he himself is dead. The doctor can't find out the complaint." Measures such as this are obviously taken secretly, so that whips would be placed in the coffin just before it was closed and only in the presence of one or two of the closest relatives, while the rite of "lashing the grave" would be done after the funeral, when no one was about to gossip.

Wakes are held for women as for men. Their size is determined by the age and social position of the dead rather than by sex. More gifts of food and drink are brought when the survivor is a widow or a mother than when a man is bereaved, "A man doesn't get much, because he can look out for himself." Gifts of this kind brought for the wake of a wife are not given the widower, but rather to the "female" relatives of the dead. "They wouldn't look for the man himself. He doesn't take care of such things."

As when a man dies, visitors come to extend condolences the day following death, until time for the funeral. A woman's burial rites parallel those already described, except that orders participate less frequently at women's funerals, since membership in these organizations is usually restricted to men. On the other hand, church rites would be more important at the funerals of women, for women are more active in church affairs in Toco than are men. The small wakes, the *cropovers,* and the "forty days" are all held as for men.

The death of a very young child is marked by little, if any ceremony. The father buys a soap-box and the carpenter "knocks it up" into a coffin. It is covered with cotton cloth, and the body, clothed in an infant's garment, placed

in it. Then "one man take it under his arm so, go bury it."
But for a child of five or six years of age, there is a regular
funeral. "They make a lovely coffin," and, if the family of
the dead boy or girl can afford it, put it in a car with children too young to walk, while grown-ups and older children follow on foot. A wake is held for a dead child, and the
"nine day night"; but the "forty days" is for adults. "They
don' worry about that for children."

Rituals do not vary with the circumstance of death.
There is no stigma attached to the death of a woman in
childbirth. "People are just sorry." In such a case one could
be sure that the corpse would be instructed to avenge the
death, and whips would be placed in its hands. Those for
whom contagious diseases prove mortal usually die in the
wards of the Colonial hospital in Port-of-Spain. If an illness
of this type is hidden and the patient dies at home, dis-
covery of the cause of death brings officials to "burn everything." For a man who dies in prison, the family hold a
"forty days" wake if the news reaches them in time. "Everybody come and bring things. Say, 'Look at what a death he
get.' " Death by drowning is not infrequent. "Who is strong
and have more constitution will be save. Other don't." A
priest is brought to "pray on the water," while search for
the body is made along the shore, and fishermen — since
death by drowning rarely comes to other than fishermen —
seek it in the vicinity of the accident. In such cases the only
rite is the "forty days." It is "bigger than if he had died on
land," for all the fishermen attend, bringing generous gifts.

Obviously the economic position of the deceased largely
determines the character of his funeral. Not only can those
of means provide more abundantly of food and drink for
the wakes, but the presence of orders and lodges is contin-
gent on the ability not to fall in arrears on dues and assess-
ments. On the other hand, where family relationships have
been made unstable by the absence of family-owned land,

old people too often find themselves "on the gover'ment," and die in the poorhouse with none of the rites described here. An instance of such a death, though not involving institutionalization, occurred during the course of this study. This case afforded an example of how very low economic position could even bring about a complete disregard of the conventions of care of the dead described in the preceding pages. It also showed how this disregard could introduce a flood of uneasy gossip, as if the entire community felt a sense of guilt for having allowed this to happen.

News of the death came with a visitor, who explained that there would be no ceremonies because the dead man was poor, and had no relatives in Toco at the moment. He had been a plumber, and was well thought of; his wife had gone to a leper colony and his adopted daughter was visiting an uncle in another part of the Island. A passing lorry-driver discovered his plight, took him from the floor, put him on his bed, and "cleaned up the mess"; an old man stayed with him the night of his death and "tied his jaw." Except for this, the body was given no care at all.

During the morning, hammering on "de box" could be heard from the nearby Public Works Department headquarters, for in the case of the destitute, that agency pays men to "dig a hole and knock a box together." Later that afternoon a young man came to record songs. He carried a hammer, and told how he and three others, having finished making "de box" took it to the dead man's cabin, placed the body in it, nailed it down and, in the heat of the day, took it to the cemetery where it was "put away in the hole" without any rites at all. "Of course the priest would not come for a man as poor as this one." The Star of Bethlehem lodge, which would have assumed responsibility for his burial, was absolved by the fact that his dues had long since been in arrears.

The following day, talk heard everywhere criticized what

had been done. "I've never seen it happen before," said one minor official, "and I've lived all over Trinidad in my lifetime, and have seen many poor people die. It isn't as if he was a beggar. He was hard-working, and people liked him. But to be carried off to the graveyard in a rough box by four laborers in work clothes. . . . They didn't even have anyone to carry chairs to set the box on when they rested, but put it right on the ground! No varnish on the box. Why, you wouldn't bury a pet dog like that! It's just like getting rid of the carcass of a pig — a hole in the ground, in he goes, and stamp down the earth. I hope nothing like that ever happens to me. Wake? No, of course not. No one bothered. You'd have thought some preacher would have come say a prayer." Another regretted the dead man had not been a Shouter. For even if a person is unable to pay his church dues, this group comes and gives him a fine burial. "It's nice at the grave. They whisper the hymn from one to another, so they all starts at once without saying anything. They wouldn't have let him go like this." Still other comments expressed resentment that the body had been carried to the grave shortly after noon, instead of in the cool of the day.

Later it became apparent that the spirit of the dead was properly outraged at the lack of respect shown his corpse. For on the ninth day after death — and local talk did not miss pointing out the significance of this — at noon, a time, with midnight, when the dead manifest themselves, children coming from school, stopping to pick fruit from the mango trees at the dead man's cabin, saw him, angrily glowering, in the branches. Shrieking with fright, they ran to "the jun'tion" — the crossroads — where the angry jumby could not harm them, throwing away the fruit they had picked and their school books as well. From then on, the trees and the vicinity of the shack were avoided carefully by all who had occasion to pass that way. For, in addition, report had it that the man who had found the dead stated that the unfortunate creature had cursed liberally before his death, while the tenant of the other half of the cabin had been hearing sounds through the partition, and was making immediate preparations to move elsewhere.

4

Outstanding among the rituals of death are the wakes. The first of these, as has been seen, is on the night of death, when friends come to watch the body, to sing hyms, to play games, and dance. As at all wakes, this occasion honors the dead, adds to the prestige of the surviving members of his family, and affords to the participants a break in the monotony of the daily round. The second in this series is the *cropover*, the end of a week's vigils following death, the "nine days night." Finally, the most important, is the "forty days night," which ends the cycle. A death which had taken place shortly before the beginning of field-work in Toco, that of the school teacher of whom mention has been made in an earlier chapter, occasioned a ceremony of the last type. And since all wakes, by report, follow a similar pattern, a description of this "forty days" may serve to introduce a discussion of this phase of the cult of the dead.

By half-past eight of a brilliant starlit night, on the paths just south of the town, were to be found many on their way to the ceremony held at the home of the mother of the dead. Inside the principal room of the house, about nine by fifteen feet, some eighteen or twenty people were sitting at a table, with about ten others standing by. Outside, sheltered from the dew by the "galvanized" metal roof of an open structure sat another group, while others, mainly young people, stood or sat quietly by, talking and playing cards. Those in the house and in the shelter were hymn-singing groups, the ranking one being inside the house.

On the table, covered with a white cloth, was a lamp with a shade on which were traceries of flowers and on which "God Bless our Home," was etched in broad letters. According to custom there were two "chairmen," but they did not get on very well. The elder of the two lined out a hymn, without interruption, prefacing the hearty singing with an injunction to "go to fundamentals," but when this song was ended, and the second chairman called a number and began the tune, the first objected, pointing out that it was written with a breve that was not being observed. This occasioned a hot dispute, after which the group settled down to steady singing, until nine o'clock, when an intermission was called and hot ginger beer was served.

The elder of the two chairmen left with the injunction that there be no singing until his return, but his associate, nevertheless, permitted one of the women to start a song, whereupon the first chairman rushed back, angered that his instructions for an "intermission" had not been followed. The two men again fell to quarreling, and were quieted only by the intercession of the host, though not until the outraged "authority on music," as he termed himself, had expressed himself freely, calling his co-chairman a "musical numbskull-hardskull" as his mildest epithet.

This quarreling between co-chairmen is a matter of usage, and the attitude toward it almost ritualistic. "They always has a little scramble," was one explanatory comment, while another person said, "It's as two lawyers. When the case win, they make friends." At times, disputes are said to wax so warm that the two come to blows. Then the men present make a circle and cry "Heave!" to encourage them, though if there seems to be danger that they will harm each other, they are separated. "Otherwise, they make a fun of it."

In the shelter, the singing in competition with those inside the house quite outdid that group, for not only were more persons here, but harmony marked the relations between the co-chairmen, and no untoward incidents interfered with the hymns. Nearby a game of "high-low" was in progress, and another somewhat farther away, while behind the kitchen a *bongo* dance was in full swing. Here, in the main, were younger people, formed into a ring about the dancers, only two of whom performed at any one time. The dancers were principally men, though several times young women, or an older, more experienced matron would enter the ring to dance intricate steps forward, then backwards, to the complex rhythms. On occasion, it is said, these rhythms are beaten on a small wooden bench. None was available this night, however, so two men held a short pole, each using his free hand to wield a small stick with which the rhythm was sounded. Sometimes a third man would use two sticks to hit the same pole and thus add to the complexity of the beats, while at other times those who held the pole did not beat at all, but two others, each wielding two sticks, would play the four rhythmic strands that seemed the most desirable accompaniment.

The songs, of leader-and-chorus type, were lively, to fit the dance, and were principally topical. Some young men from the nearby town of Matura, half-brothers of the dead girl by the same mother, were present, and there was little doubt, from performance and from acclaim, that this night they were in the words of one of the songs, the "kings of *bongo*." They, themselves, fully realizing their virtuosity, were critical of those who beat the rhythms. The best of the visiting dancers repeatedly objected to the poor timing of the beats, while his partner, on one occasion, exclaimed, "Too many Seven-days boys here!" the reference being to the Seventh Day Adventist followers, who are scorned as the equivalent of "mama's boys" by those who take life at a more exuberant pace.

Coffee and bread were served shortly before midnight,

after which the hymn singing, the card playing, and the dancing were resumed, though enthusiasm began to diminish. Those in the open-roofed enclosure ended their hymns, much to the loudly-expressed disappointment of their chairman, as this meant that the singers in the house had finally prevailed. The *bongo* waxed and waned, some card players left their games and others began new ones. Rum, brought as a gift, had been distributed, but except for a few who had supplemented what was provided from personal flasks, no one seemed to have had enough to bring forth uncontrolled enthusiasms. But the enjoyment of the Sankey and Moody hymns, rendered strictly as written, with no rhythmic modifications, and with the countless verses faithfully given, was patent. As a matter of fact, the hymn singing, done largely by the women, outlasted both *bongo* and card games, and it is worth noting that those who were somewhat "rum-happy" distributed themselves impartially between the singers and the dancers.

By one o'clock, people were leaving; the ceremony had passed its peak. Except for the "heartfelts" which ended the rite, and for which only those close to the bereaved family remain, the festivities were ended. Before this, there had been little to indicate that this ceremony had been in honor of the dead — "to make the spirit of the girl rest, an' not walk about" — except one remark made by the "chairman" of the hymn-singing team in the house, when, as he called the group to order, he named the purpose of the gathering.

For the "heartfelts," each man present is called upon in turn to make a speech appropriate to the occasion, and each woman to "call the number of a Sankey." Prestige accrues to the man who commands the apt phrase and the gift of parable; shy young men leave or hide until the danger of being called on has passed. On this occasion, a lad of no more than twelve "made a toast," and was loudly praised by the assemblage. who volubly compared him to an older boy who ran away because he was afraid to talk. During the giving of "heartfelts" the mother and father were present to hear the praises of their dead daughter.

Any who wish to honor the dead may give the "nine days" rite and the "forty days." At times, several of these are given simultaneously, as when a husband, a child, and a grandchild of an elderly woman, living in the same village, each gives a "forty days" the same night. The one described was given by the father of the dead girl. The mother, it was said, would later give a special service in the church, for the father was in process of moving his belongings from his keeper's house to hers, where he planned again to take up his residence in compliance with his daughter's last wish, and consequently mother and father constituted one household.

The ceremony described represents the "public" portion of it, at which friends and neighbors participate; that simultaneously other rites are also performed emerges from discussion of the ritual with the villagers. "When it commence to midnight," said one, "some old relations, men or women, take glasses of water and beginning with one spot pour it as they go round the outside of the house. Say, 'We pourin' this for you to make the path clear. We know you with us tonight. We doin' this for you.' They go right around. When they come back to where they started, they add rum to the water and go round again. Come back, they wash their faces in the rum and water and say, 'Cousin Doris, I hope you here with us tonight.' They speaking to the dead. Then they call all the others [the family dead], pouring clear rum, going again, throwing rice cooked without salt. Say, 'Come and feast with us, and work with us, and bless us.' " This is at the "forty days." On the night of the death, a similar ritual is held, this time the rum and water are poured in front of the coffin, or of the bed if the body has not been placed in the coffin, and rice is thrown. They say,

"Oh, you are gone! Don' let us see you walking about. Go, and rest in peace. And help we. Guide we."

Reference to the past life of the dead is made more usually over the body at the wake, though this may be done at later rites as well. As one account had it: "Chairman is there round the table, gives lectures: 'Look, this man was a very peaceful man. Don' like no noise, no disturbance, no dispute. We want everything to go on nice.' Or, 'Look here, all you behave. You know this man when he living, he don' make fun. Nobody can come in his place, nobody can touch anything. He was a devil. As he is dead now, he may be bad the same way. So all you behave you'self. He dead, but he still here. Let him see in his las' going out how we behavin' good for him.'" Here co-chairmen begin to disagree vehemently. "They couldn' keep quiet about a man like this. One give out a hymn. Other one growl. Always a disturbance. So how man live, so he die."

Proper measures must be taken for a dead person of this kind. "Chairman say, 'Bring a little rum here.' Bring it, he take it. 'Well, Joe, you needn' vex with me for speakin' the truth, man. We all men. You gone in front. I behind. I not comin' with you, man. Go that side. You do enough already.' He pour rum in his hand, wash his face with it, and throw some in four directions. He's in front of a window or the door, so he's speakin' to the dead man now. 'I drink, man. Have a drink.' When he sit down at the table he sit with his hand over his eyes. They say his eyes tie up. The jumby comin' on him, so he call for rum. People laugh, but what he do in the house, don' mind." But because the spirit is near, they go outside to dance. "That's the time the *bongo* come sweet."

At the "forty days," *sakara* — offerings for all the ancestors — are given, as well as for the recent dead. The one officiating rings a little bell three times, then whistles. The four older members of the family who assist him and all others, turn their backs, though curiosity may make some bold enough to look. "We peeps, yes?" The officiant places a black cloth over his head, on which is sewn a red cross. "Look like the bishop." When he whistles, he goes behind a bush, and removes his clothing, wearing only a small cloth, "like the Indians wear." Here he whistles again, and they say, "Now he talking to Guinea."

5

The conventions governing the conduct of relatives of the dead give insight into the manner in which the soul is thought of as continuing its association with the living. A widow is expected to stay away from her garden for about four weeks after the death of her husband, and during this interval his friends work it for her; a man would wait a week before resuming work. A surviving spouse, man or woman, in most cases waits a "decent" interval before taking a new mate, though "some women go to the grave and bawl, but next week have another man." It does not seem that faithfulness is exacted by the dead; as it was phrased, "They doesn't be afraid here at all about taking a new man or woman soon. I don' know why."

The wearing of mourning, though not compulsory, is customary. "Some believe that if he doesn't wear mourning, too much things will happen, while others don't." In general, however, a woman wears black and white on ordinary occasions, and black for church, while a man wears a black suit for a wife or parent for from a year to eighteen months after the death. Children wear mourning for six months, though if the black clothing is of good quality and lasts, it is worn as long as it is presentable. A sister may be mourned "equally with the mother," but some mourn a sister for three months only, and then "don' worry with she no more." A poor person will sew a black ribbon on a white dress, or a black band about the sleeve, or on the lapel of a coat. "They wouldn' go in deep black if they didn't have the money."

On occasion, however, mourning is put on for a relative long after his death. Sometimes a sick person on consulting a lookman finds that a grandmother, or even a greatgrandmother, has sent illness as a punishment because "nobody wore proper mourning for she." Even a poor person, "if the dead is vex with you," wears black for the prescribed period, five or ten years or even longer after death. For if this is not done, "the dead people grumble." They trouble their descendants first in dreams; if this warning is ignored, illness or other mishaps will beset them. Belief holds that when the injunction of the diviner to wear black has been complied with, the illness disappears. Prevalent attitudes toward this question are perhaps best summarized in the following comment: "It's a sort of love. People say daughter is mourning, say she loved she mother. But if she don' wear mourning the dead notice it, too."

The need to be watchful wherever the spirits of the dead are concerned pervades Toco thought. One who had quarreled with a man about to die "would come to de sickness" to ask pardon; if this were not granted, he would stay away from the funeral and, at all events, however close a relative, he would refrain from joining the grave-digging party. Separated mates, unless they were on good terms, similarly would not participate in any of the rites for the dead, but would instead provide themselves with a guard for protection against the ill will of the ghost. This might be something to drink, or a magic charm, furnished by a lookman, to be worn about the waist. Such a person would also make some contribution toward the funeral, a shilling or two. If a carpenter, to cite another instance, cut himself while working on the coffin, he would take some of the shavings, rub them on his skin near the cut, take some rum, rub this on the cut and say, "Look here, I makin' you box. I got cut.

Take care you no go an' do me bad." Only then would a
bandage be put on the cut and work be resumed.

The dead may become yard-spirits, hovering near the
house of descendants, who "feed" them. There are those
who say every "yard" has its own spirit, "some person belonging to you, whether he died there or not." If the presence of such a spirit has manifested itself, offerings of food
are given to it and, symbolically, to all the family dead
whenever food is eaten — a practice, incidentally, which,
once begun, must be continued. If the custom of giving
food to such a spirit, once it has revealed itself, has not been
started, however, it is not essential to begin, though this
merely means that those who live in the yard do not benefit
from the continuous vigilance of such a being in their behalf. But, "If they vex, they really do put on the lash," and
as a result, there are those who prefer to forego this protection. One such person explained: "I know some people
who are always saying, 'Got to hurry go put me mother
food on.' 'But you mother dead?' She say, "What, you
wan' me mother capsize me upside down, make me die.
too?' "

An account of "feeding" the dead — which shows how
intimate is the relationship between a person and his dead
forebears, and how human these beings are conceived to be
— may be given here. "What I does, now, every good day,
Christmas, Easter, New Year, I always throw. I go down the
steps, say, 'Look, I don' make it a promise. Also, you mus'
take whatever I give you.' I don' make it a promise for no
special place, either. Give beef, a little cooked apart without salt, rice, ginger beer, rum, cake. When I go down the
steps I call everybody I can remember to come. I say, 'My
ol' daddy like to smoke. I go len' you a pipe and tobacco.'
Leave it, stop there the whole night and the morning, then
say, 'Well, you finish with the pipe. Well, I take it.' In the
night, I leave the table set, food on the table, drinks, the

pipe in one corner of the table. Put that pretty cotton on the table, too. When you get up, you smell tobacco strong. Say, 'He enjoyin' it fine.' "

Another example of how the dead are treated much as the living is to be seen in the case of a woman who, having dreamed of her mother, and having had this dream interpreted, had been told that it signified the desire of the dead woman to be "fed." She had done nothing about it as yet, however, waiting until she returned to her home in Port-of-Spain, and found the means for the necessary offerings to comply with her dead mother's wishes.

All Saints' Day, though formally more important to Catholics and Anglicans than to members of other sects, is an occasion when the dead are widely feted. Their graves are weeded, and covered with flowers, "nice, nice," and candles are placed about them. At home, during the afternoon, a table is festively set with dishes, glasses, knives, forks, and spoons, and decorated at the outer edges with strands of "cotton" from the silk-cotton tree, "pulled out nice, so you can see through it when it's held up, so they can get themselves a kerchief if they wants to wipe their faces."

At about sundown, the family go to the graveyard, leaving the house unlocked. "Nobody goin' into your house that night!" The candles on the graves are lighted, and the dead are addressed. "Ask them for anything." On returning to the house, a lighted candle is placed before the door, and a bouquet of flowers. "Rap on the door three times," and as the first one enters, he says, "Good night, good night. Who is here? I come, I come." Then the family seat themselves about the table, and say; "We, weself go now drink a little rum in the bottle on the table," and say again, "This dinner is for you, so we sit to help you enjoy it."

As the family sit chatting, they become drowsy and, as in a dream, hear voices say, "We come. We eat. We drink. We thank you all. We merry. We glad. You hear de stick break, that we" — that is, in passing a bush on the way from a grave, when a twig breaks, a person turns and hears a laugh, and he knows, "that my dead telling they friends, 'That my family.' "

When those about the table awake, they take a little rum, pour it on their hands, wet their faces with it, and eat the food before them, even though, since it was prepared for the dead, it is unsalted. As they eat, they say "Aunt — or uncle, or grandfather, or mother or father — we eating this food. We hope you always here to prevent us from harm." Then the family hear a "growl." "They glad." When the candles are burned out, the family go to bed, but in the morning the wax is put in a small box and saved as a remedy to cure a cold, or a rheumatic hand or foot, or other ailment.

The spirits of the dead, as jealous guardians of what is theirs, can exact fearsome punishment, as is illustrated by the tale of a Toco woman's experience with a jumby. This will be seen as of the pattern already related of the adventure of the school children with the spirit of the old man whose recent burial had been so casual. Many years ago, when this woman was quite young, and was carrying her second child, she was on her way to join the women who were washing clothes at a little brook. On the road she passed under a mango tree, and since her pregnancy made her hungry, she plucked three mangoes and ate them. When she arrived at her destination she became ill, and fell into a stupor. She was brought home, where she remained unconscious for several days. This was followed by a prolonged spell of vomiting, after which she fell into a normal sleep. In that sleep she dreamed she again walked on the path that led under the mango tree, and as she neared it, she saw a very black man sitting in its lower branches. He cried out, "Why did you steal those mangoes from me? They are my mangoes, not yours!" She begged his pardon, pleading that she had not realized she had been doing wrong, whereupon he asked for blood and rum.

She awakened her husband who was sleeping, and telling him her dream, urged him to give this spirit what he asked. But her husband mumbled that this was nonsense, and went to sleep again, going off to his garden early that morning. Still very weak, she made her way to a neighbor, to whom she gave some money to buy a chicken and rum. Tying them and a knife in a cloth about her waist, she crawled on hands and knees to the mango tree. Though almost fainting from the effort, she was able to throw the rum on the ground, and to kill the chicken and sprinkle its blood under the branches. "I beg and beg and beg as I cry out to the man not to hurt me any more, and to forgive me, and let me get well." She does not remember how she got home, but she began to mend steadily. "I don' know who the man was. I never see him before, and I never see him since. But he own the tree. I gone under it many time since and see other people take mangoes. I wouldn' touch the fruit for anything you could give me."

6

The reel and bele dances are the outstanding rites for the dead. The first is essentially a curing ceremony, while the latter, wherein the dead are feted to assure their continuing benevolent surveillance over their descendants, has a more generalized character. No clear expression was to be had as to the occasions that called for one rite as against the other. "Is according to what the dead say," or "This is what family is used to give before." The dead may name their desires in a dream which is said to recur three times either to the same member of the family or to three different members, or else a lookman who is consulted about difficulties that beset the family, speaks the will of the dead.

The reason for this lack of clarity, it was explained, was the secrecy that surrounded these dances in more recent times. No rites were more difficult to witness, and frankness in discussion of them was come by very slowly, for both reel and bele were vigorously opposed by Anglican and Catholic priests, who not only preached against holding them, but marked down as undesirable citizens any who gave them. This was a matter of importance, since testimonials as to the reliability, character, and standing in the community of a man or woman had to be obtained from priest and vicar whom they thus, if only on economic grounds, could not afford to offend.

This attitude of those who wielded power, as it bore on a small community having the psychological tensions that accompany the social and economic setting described, and the divergent religious stresses that are to be discussed, was a constant invitation to gossip, and more than this, to tale-bearing as a means of reprisal for real or imaginary insult or harm. It was small wonder that those few who directed reels and bele dances belonged to no church, and those church members who were obliged to give these rites, gave small ones in strictest privacy, telling but the closest friends and relatives. Even then it was considered of no little risk, as "someone always tell when they give it."

The songs at these rites differ. The reels are danced to "reel-songs" of Scottish and Irish derivation and to quadrilles, in the French manner; the bele music — or *juba* as "we calls the same dance in some of the other islands" — is of a less European type, and accompanied by single-headed drums which, though made of staves, are of the kind known as hollow-log drums. Such dancing as was demonstrated for the reel indicated little modified execution of the conventional reel, the dancer performing his figure in a circle until replaced by others, or with men and women facing each other to dance the figures of the quadrille. The bele dance, non-European in style, is nevertheless grouped with the reel, as the dance beloved of the ancestors. These two are to be differentiated from what is called "ball" — the two-step, waltz, and other forms of modern secular dances — and the highly individualized steps of the *bongo*.

The reel, whose principal purpose, as stated, is to effect a cure, is given on the order of a lookman when other measures have failed to aid a client whose illness has not yielded to treatment. Food is prepared in quantity, though without salt, while a goat, fowl and rice are offered as sacrifices to the dead. The name of each of the family dead is called three times, that each may come and help bring about the cure. A description of such a cure, under the direction of a lookman named Jones in a settlement not far from Toco, may be described in the words of an eye-witness.

"A young man, goin' to be married, come sick. He couldn't work, so they called Jones to work on him. [At the reel] the musicians were playin', and dancin' goin' on. Man came in that no one see before, wore nothin' but a pants short. His head was grey. He was a black, thin man. Everybody stopped dancin', folded arms and stood by. They couldn't move. The man ask the musicians to play, and they play nearly every reel they know. Play till they hit one that catch him. He sittin' so, on the floor of the room between the fiddler an' the tambourine player. Now he stand up, wheel roun' two times, third time he go outside, now come back with bush in he han'. He go to the bed where the sick man lie. Man Jones rubbin' the sick man, rubbin', rubbin'. He no better. This man go to the bed. Jones go off in a corner. Stranger wash his face and head, rub, rub, rub with bush. . . . Now he bathe sick man, ask for three fowl eggs. Go outside and throw egg at the sick man in the bed. Egg hit the man on he head, break. Do it again, hit right on the head, hit the third time. Ask for fowl, wring its neck.

The blood flow as fowl flap he wing, spatter everybody with blood, till he lie still. Soil me new dress. I was vex.

"Now the man call family to come. Was two families. They inherited property an' didn' want this young man to get he share. So they sen' a spirit come on this man. That spirit one jumby. This man now make them all stan' up in a row near the bed where the sick man lie. Take a strap, lash, lash everybody in the family, lash till they bawl. They boun' to bawl when the spirit lash. Now he command the sick man to stand up an' go dance. This man now disappear. Nobody see him again. Say it's some man in the family long dead, come to cure. The reel was hot that night, an' before I leave, that sick man well. He able to go to work. Short time, he marry."

According to another account, a person learns in a dream that he must give one of these ceremonies. Shortly before the period of this research, a woman on the Cumana road had such a dream, in which her mother appeared and instructed her to give three bele dances. She had already given two of them, and was preparing the third, which was to take place the following December. The dead also indicate whether they wish a reel or the simpler form called a "sing." A diviner, as mentioned, can transmit to a person the desire of the dead to have a reel held, if the dead do not themselves care to "come" in a dream. A small reel will be held when a woman, several of whose children have died, again conceives. "Then the spirit catch someone" — that is, possession ensues — "and they tell what's making the children die, an' what to do. Some spirit see clear." Such a ceremony as described in an earlier chapter of "proving" a prospective bridegroom, is also in the reel category, as are all rites of calling the ancestors on the occasion of a betrothal or marriage.

What is said at a reel is understood by all. "They don'

talk *unknown* at reels, much. It's accordin'. Most of the time, they talk plain English. You call the dead by name, stand and call them, say 'Come help we tonight!' They hear an' they bound to come. When they call the spirit, they whistle. It's spirit language. You yourself hear them whistle every night. . . . No, ma'am, it's not frog. Frog make rough noise. It's spirit. They talking to each other that way." Of the bele dance, it is said, "The ancestors like it. All the time they used to dance bele." A dance of this kind, which was described early during this period of study as a purely social dance, had its true nature revealed when a woman, in speaking of it, asserted that it will "fall down" early, and go badly if it is not preceded by an appeal to the ancestors.

A bele dance has its "captain" who must know how to "speak de language, an' how to get de dead to come." He may be a lookman, but need not be a professional, though in any event, for his own protection he must "have tricks or so" while coming into close association with the dead. A goat and fowls are sacrificed — all must be "certified" as "proper healthy" — and rum and rice are given. The animals are killed by the "captain" and an assistant, who are helped by the young men present. All those in attendance, especially the drummers and singers, try to get some of the blood for themselves, to which they add a little salt before they drink it. The meat is cooked, and the dance continues until daybreak.

We now come to a phenomenon associated in the minds of the Toco people not only with the ancestral cult but also more specifically with the bele ritual, and which has to do with the ownership by some families of a shrine consisting of a cross and a large earthenware jar, half-buried, and filled with a healing fluid. A funnel projects from the mouth of this jar, and behind it is a cross about two feet high, while special kinds of bushes are planted around it.

"It's Toco, Toco I'm speaking of now," said the person who told of this, emphasizing both the importance of this complex and its divergence from ordinary aspects of Toco life.

What is contained in the jar cannot be said, but it was intimated that the blood of the sacrifices at the bele dance forms at least one component. In a family that owns one of these, when relatives who live elsewhere on the Island return to Toco, they at once go to this jar, removing it and throwing "a little water" in the hole. "They talk language" there, it was said. But in the case of illness, others, not necessarily of the family, come for some of this liquid as a remedy.

7

The conception of the world of the dead held by the Toco Negro is essentially the Christian one. Yet this conception enters only lightly into the system of belief and practice that has been under discussion in the preceding pages. Certainly it seems to be less important to those who hold to it than are the concepts of death which underlie the functioning of the dead as active spirits that reward or punish, that cure the sick or bring illness, that protect or menace, as determined by their inherent character and the manner in which the living accord them their due.

The term jumby is applied to all spirits of the dead, without apparent reference to quality. "If we now good people, we good jumby," said one person. "Bad people make bad jumby. But we all jumby. We livin'. But what's livin'? Jumby with breath. Me, you, everyone, all is jumby." Yet when the question of the relationship between the jumby and two other concepts often met with — soul and shadow — is raised, the matter becomes clouded again. "The soul? They can't hurt the soul," it was said, referring to the "capture" of a ghost by one versed in evil magic, to be used to further his ends. "The soul pass to God. It's the spirit part of you they catch." Or, "When you die, your soul go to Paradise." There is no agreement as to the nature or role of the shadow. Consensus of opinion holds that the shadow is "of the body," in which the spirit lives, having no important function. "It's the spirit that's trapped. It's either a good or bad workman" — that is, it is the spirit that performs good or evil. Nonetheless, as against this must be recorded the remark, "Spirit's there when you're alive, but it's always workin' as a shadow."

This matter of the shadow seemed to be of importance where illness that follows evil magic was involved, as became evident when the point concerning what happens to soul and spirit while a person sleeps was raised. "If you is a blessed soul and you lie down, they is both with you. But if I'm bad, they go rogueing about, sometimes together, sometimes not. Go round trouble people." According to one belief, it is the spirit that, as the shadow, is taken, and in such an event, the person whose spirit is gone falls ill. "You become stupefied. Even a person who don' know you see you and say, 'Oh, oh! That person shadow gone. Somebody has taken it.' " A case of this sort then resolves itself into a type already discussed, wherein a reel dance is given to effect a cure. The dead are called, and when they arrive, the patient is bathed, told to rise, and recovers from the illness that followed on the theft of the spirit. But no one is clear as to how the spirit is returned, or by whom, except through the inference which attributes all this to the family dead who come when called.

There are those, indeed, who hold that it is not the dead themselves, but "the soul, waiting around for the judgment day" that does the "work" of the dead for or against the living. Such persons, with complete inconsistency, say that the dead, of themselves, have no power. The case of young children was given. "You see nex' woman come, flog them, starve them. Children stay underneath the house, afraid to come in when their father is away," while the spirit of the dead mother, at least on its own initiative, does nothing. Yet at the same time it was insisted that if help is asked of the dead, it is given. "If you go to the cemetery and call them and throw sweet water [sugar and water] and bawl out their name [of the person who is mistreating the children, for example], in nine days' time they come for said person. If it's jumby or devil, I doesn't know. But they come when they hear their name."

Definitions and distinctions of supernatural forces are never a theme on which the ethnographer looks for uniformity of view. Yet it is currently not possible to record any systematic statement of belief comprehending the nature of the entities that make up the world of the dead that is convincing to the Tocoan himself, nor any clear differentiation of such concepts as soul, ghost, jumby, spirit, and shadow. Beliefs concerning the dead must be abstracted from statements in which they are reflected in expressed opinion, or as they lie implicit in descriptions of rituals, rather than taken down as explicit formulation from those who, as leaders of a recognized and established cult, have as their principal concern the reconciliation of conflicting beliefs into a workable, unified series of concepts. Such individuals did live in Toco until a short time before the period of study reported on here, but it is not the custom to replace at once a person of spiritual power, and none was to be found at that time living in Toco who might with professional detail resolve conflicting statements.

Yet despite the absence of an organized cult, and the conventional outward acceptance of the practices of the dominant groups in the population of Trinidad, the importance of the dead as beings who enter actively into the ordering of life is emphatically affirmed. For whatever other powers may rule the Universe, and however needful it may be for an individual to be alert to the demands of the natural world, it is essentially to one's own ancestors that one turns for aid when in difficulty. And, by the same token, it is to them that one must dedicate ritually decreed observances. For otherwise they might not only fail their descendants when called upon, but turn on them in recrimination..

CHAPTER VII

THE ROLE OF RELIGION

THE CHURCHES WHICH INCORPORATE the more conventional manifestations of the religious life of Toco are the Anglican (Church of England), the Roman Catholic, the Seventh Day Adventist, the Moravian, and the Baptist. Baptists, however, are of two kinds, those who worship in restrained form, popularly called the "carnal" Baptists, and those who "shout," or the "spiritual" Baptists. These latter are so named because the "spirit" is said to enter their bodies and fill them with joy, causing them to shake, to dance, and otherwise to express their worship in the complex of rites associated with the term to "shout." In the ensuing discussion, the "carnal" Baptists will be designated as Baptists, while the "spiritual" Baptists, who also refer to themselves as Baptists, but who are known in the community at large, as well as in the language of the ordinances that prohibit this worship, as "Shouters," will be called by this special name.

An important church in Toco is St. George's, the Anglican center. Its minister, addressed as Father by the local people, is the representative, under the Bishop of Trinidad, of the Church of England. Its buildings are nearest the center of the village, and it has a good school that is attended by children of communicants and non-communicants.

On the road that skirts the northern coast going westward away from town are a group of buildings that make up the Roman Catholic center. They consist of a church, a half-open schoolhouse, and a parish house. These buildings are atop a hill, overlooking the sea, with more space about them than St. George's, and an effect of graciousness that none of the Protestant churches afford. This quality is particularly lacking in the Moravian center, a mile or two farther along the same road. The Seventh Day Adventists and the Baptists have more modest churches, small structures, much like the dwellings of the less well-to-do residents, though at the period of this research the Baptists were erecting a somewhat larger building.

In regard to the relative numbers affiliated with these denominations, the Anglicans and Catholics are said to have the most communicants, then the Baptists — including both the "carnal" and the "spiritual" groups — and the Adventists, followed by the Moravians. Among families whose economic and marital status has already been reported upon, church affiliation was as follows:

Denomination	Number	Percentage
Anglican	56	45%
Catholic	30	24%
Baptist	19	16%
Adventist	10	8%
Moravian	2	2%
Affiliation not known	6	5%

To what extent this is representative cannot be said, but it is reasonable to assume that the proportion of Baptists and Moravians is lower than among the entire population of the village, since many of the families enumerated live on the outskirts of Toco, some distance from the Moravian center, and also somewhat removed from the local Baptist church. Since, except for the Anglicans and Catholics, contiguity is a factor, this should be taken into account in evaluating the estimated figures and percentages.

One woman discussed church membership in these terms: "The Catholic stick to their backbone, but the Anglican go here, go there. The Baptis' new, and make many converts." She went on to philosophize about the proselytizing activities of these groups — since, as elsewhere over the world, the competition for souls is always present; and though sometimes overlooked by those engaged in the struggle, this point is not lost sight of by the objects of their attention. "Is there one God?" she asked. "Who you lookin' for, runnin' aroun' with a match-box?" Her reaction extended to practical matters, also, for when she was asked how so small a community could support the number of churches found there, she replied, "They all starves."

The churches are financed by dues, by gifts, by the receipts from "socials" and "concerts," "auctions" and "bazaars." Dues, as was stated when family budgets were described, are low, and so, at least for most people, are the contributions to the weekly church collection taken up at services. The sums given there were twelve cents a month dues, and offerings of about four cents each week, per family, for the socioeconomic group classified as poor. The comfortable and well-to-do families would be expected to make proportionately larger contributions. Small as the dues are, every effort is made to see that they are kept up, for membership in the congregation is forfeited if there is extended delinquency. Preaching about the importance of meeting this obligation is common. A minster of the Anglican church who preceded the incumbent functioning during the period of this study went so far as to post the names of those in arrears, though apparently this heroic step had the unlooked for effect of causing some of those whose names were posted to "stop from de church." Other ministers do not go this far, but it was said that "they does talk plenty" about the delinquents.

The practices of the Catholic mission differ in this regard from those of the Protestant groups, for Catholics do not pay dues. Yet the priests are vigilant that their communicants fulfill their obligations, and stay within the Church, and tales are recounted of the sharp reproaches of the priest to one who has left the Church, or to a member who fails to send his children to its school, or is remiss in making his proper contribution. Pressures are also exerted that children do not fail in attendance at Sunday school.

Two examples of other kinds of money-raising activities that were witnessed may be briefly described. The first, at St. George's Church, was a "concert and dance" given with the object of helping finance the acquisition of a piano for the church school. An audience of perhaps fifty persons paid admission of twelve cents, and each person who attended was expected, in addition, to bring a parcel containing something that could be auctioned in the course of the evening. A local jazz-band, whose performance was of the quality that might be expected, was present to provide music for the dancing, and incidental selections to fill intervals between events.

The "program" consisted of embarrassed children reciting "pieces." The vicar was the announcer, but gave way to an official of the congregation when it was time to auction the parcels, which were bid on without the bidder's being permitted to know what he was getting. The resulting inappropriateness of the purchases brought forth much laughter. The audience dwindled in number as the auctioning continued — this was not ended until midnight — after which the young people danced. It was intimated that the style of dancing did less than justice to the skill of the village youngbloods, but that the extreme restraint was due to the church setting, and particularly to the presence of the vicar. The dance ended at about two o'clock in the morning. How much was collected toward the purchase of a piano was not made known, though fifteen dollars would be a liberal estimate.

The "harvest festival" at the Catholic Mission, held on the morning of Sunday, August 6th, was preceded by a procession about the Mission grounds, and a mass. After this, in theory at least, the priest blessed the offerings of first fruits, produce and animals that had been brought there for the purpose, though the only produce or animals to be seen on the ground were some coconuts, some sugar-cane, and a pig. The ceremony was a quiet one, obviously with less movement than that described in the *passé* song of the reel cycle sung in the village, and indicative of how even such rites of the Church are grist for the song-maker's commentary:

> "The twenty-fourth of November,
> It have a harves' an' a festival at Maria;
> Everybody carry something,
> But Oma carry pussy.

> "Oma-o, Oma-o,
> Oma pussy go 'way.
> The pussy run, the pussy jump
> The pussy run through 'Sia back door!

> "The parson vex, the sexton vex,
> Say, Oma pussy go 'way;
> The harves' would a make more money,
> But Oma pussy go 'way."

The bazaar was, again, much like similar events everywhere in Euro-American communities. It was held in the half-open schoolhouse, and here the fifty to sixty persons in attendance paid six cents for a roulette number, a shilling for a chance on a pillow, bought odds and ends donated by members of the women's organization, and consumed ice cream and other refreshments. The purpose was to raise money for general church funds, and since the affair lasted the entire day, it is to be presumed that the sum realized was considerably larger than that collected at the Anglican social; though here, too, the amount was not made public.

2

The Shouters must be given a place of prominence in any consideration of the religious life of Trinidad. This is true even though they are not too numerous, though they are proscribed by law, and though their places of worship are humble in character. For it is from beliefs and practices such as are found among the Shouters, and in the acceptance of divination and magic as techniques for controlling the immediate problems of living, that the Tocoan attains a sense of being part of a Universe that can provide him a place of dignity and security in this world as well as the next.

In addition to the conventional churches, the Shouters, and the complex of practices that concern divination and magic, two other factors function in Toco religion that have no institutionalized representation there at all. For despite their absence from the local scene, the Salvation Army and the Shango Cult are themes that weave through discussions of the religious experience of the Tocoans.

Knowledge of the Salvation Army comes to Toco through the shelters for those without homes and without means that are maintained by this organization in Port-of-Spain. The help thus given the men who go to the capital in search of work is remembered with appreciation, and "de Army" is often mentioned with approval when examples of how Christian theory can be put into practice are cited. "If you are in trouble and hungry," one man put it, "you go to the Captain and he help you, but if you'd go to the priest and ask for something to eat, he'd sen' you away."

It is not only for its social services, however, that "de Army" is esteemed. As in other parts of the world, the appeal of its revivalistic emotionalism is felt, but even more than this, and the material aid they render, is the fact that "dey pounds de tambourine" and though "they don' exactly shout, their songs are nice." To this is added, "Government is not against them," so that it is safe to attend their services as spectators. The Army, then, is present in Toco as an example, as a memory. As far as could be ascertained, few from Toco have joined it, or experienced conversion through its preaching, even while in the city. But in the minds of the people it stands as an example of what they feel applied Christianity should be, and though it will not be necessary to mention it again in treating of Toco religion, it cannot be omitted from any discussion of the total range of Toco religious thought.

The influence of the Shango Cult is more deep-seated, for it is in the background of Toco thinking, as a kind of last resort when other modes of appeal to the supernatural fail; while its physical manifestations are from time to time found in the district, if not in the village itself, in the persons of members of this cult who are called from Port-of-Spain to "do a piece of work." This form of worship, like the Salvation Army, centers about the capital. Its shrines are found on the hills about the city, in the towns that lie close to the eastward, and in the valleys of the extreme northwestern part of the Island. Its African gods, identified by the Shango cult-group with the saints of the Catholic Church, have become beings who need not be envisaged as emanating from a remote ancestral past, but as of the everyday world about them, only bearing new names in a new land.

The interest which the Toco Negroes show in this form

of worship makes pertinent the question why none of them follow it in their home community. The answer to this is primarily to be sought in demographic and economic terms — that is, in rural settlements, there are not enough people and not enough resources to support cult-groups of this kind. Inasmuch as no active Shango worship is carried on, then, chapters dealing with the manifestations of Toco religious life will not include an examination of the Shango beliefs and rituals. But because it enters significantly into the matrix of Toco, no less than Trinidad Negro religion, even where it is not present in institutionalized form, those facts concerning its organization and beliefs that were obtained during brief discussions with one such group in Port-of-Spain, and descriptions of its rites that were observed, will be presented as an appendix to this volume.

In the chapters dealing with the religious life of Toco we shall first of all, then, review manifestations of religion that lie in the familiar Euro-American pattern, in terms of churches, preachers, and some of the customary activities of these groups and the individuals who comprise them. We shall then pass to a more detailed consideration of those humbler, yet all-pervasive forms of religious belief and practice that, lodging beneath the surface, or outside the canons of approved conduct, touch the lives of the communicants of all denominations. The latter portion of this chapter and the one that follows it will consequently be devoted to an exposition and analysis of the beliefs and rituals of the Shouters, and the succeeding one to that other aspect of the religious complex comprehended in the theory and practice of divination and magic.

3

The attitudes of the people toward the conventional churches show all willingness to leave to the minister or priest, who is the specialist in such matters, the task of mediating with Deity in a generalized way, on behalf of his flock. The need that is felt for affiliation with a church group is as much social as religious, for the churches, with the lodges, are the centers of social life in the community, and among a group where the goal is to be associated with all prestige-giving institutions, the dissenter is rarely met. Only two individuals were known to have no church affiliation, and one of these was the man having to do with the direction of bele and reel dances that are frowned upon by the clergy.

On Sunday morning, the Tocoan enjoys going to church in his best suit, his good shoes, a new-looking hat. These give him a feeling of well-being. He likes to sing the hymns, and the words move him deeply. He reads a special meaning into the hymns he prefers, translating his emotional response as a personal message for himself, as something of tangible efficacy for his own peculiar need. He delights in a good sermon. "When the parson talk, sometimes you feel the spirit come to you. It's like an injection. A shiver pass over the body. It happen if you are an Anglican. Happen if you a Catholic. But if the priest see you shiver, he not glad."

Pastors visit members of their congregations who are ailing, or in trouble, or are felt to be otherwise in need of spiritual consolation. A vicar or priest or pastor — Anglican, Catholic, Baptist, or Adventist — is called to bless a new house. The corners are sanctified, and there is a short "thanksgivin' " inside, after which there is a party where those invited are "served things like cake and wine." When a succession of infants of a family die, a saint is invoked to watch over one subsequently born. If the parents are not themselves Catholics, they seek out the advice of friends who are, and take "candles and good, sweet oil" to the priest, who puts the oil in the eternal lamp. "Carry it to

St. Joseph, or St. Peter, or the blessed Virgin. Call it after a
Saint. Call a girl St. Joseph, or St. Peter or St. Mary." The
day of the saint would thereafter be observed, and the child
would be dressed "to suit the Saint. Use the same colors as
the Saint. If the mother isn't Roman, they join the child
there. But not the whole family."

Special emphasis is placed on the christening rite because
of the belief that an infant who has not been presented to
the church is peculiarly vulnerable to mischief perpetrated
by workers of magic and the pranks of malicious supernatural powers. Furthermore, if death comes before this
rite, the soul of the child would not know its way to return
to God, but would wander in the forest as a *dwine* or *jab-
lesse* (*diablesse*), with the possibility of returning to claim
the companionship of other infants born to the family.

Confirmation rites, as practised among the Anglicans and
Catholics, differ from those of the evangelical groups, where
confirmation is more a matter of consecration and individual acceptance of dogma, at any age, than of the type of ritual wherein, at a stated period in the life of a young person,
he is received into the church. Even among Anglicans and
Catholics, however, the customary age of ten or twelve years
is not always observed. "Not everybody is confirmed, but
who likes to, who is able. Some people is confirmed when
they get big; they confirm themselves." A girl is given a
white dress, a slip, shoes, and veil for the rite. The Anglican
veil is "small as a kerchief" with a white or red cross on it.
"The minister's wife get it for a shilling." The Catholic veil
is, of course, larger. Boys wear white suits, or dark ones.
This clothing may be given by the grandparents or the godparents of the child. If the latter, the godfather provides the
shoes, the godmother the suit or dress, and some god-
mothers bake a cake for the child. "Some parents got to find
all that themselves — clothes, refreshments, cake, wine," to
celebrate the event. Any child, legitimate or illegitimate, is

admitted to confirmation without prejudice, though communion is not later given one who "is not married but is living with someone." Children confirmed in the Catholic faith take first communion before the ceremony.

The church marriage is viewed in the community as validating social status and ensuring economic opportunity insofar, as was stated, it is in the hands of priest or minister to further the chances of preferred employment with a favorable letter of recommendation. Those measures that involve supernatural favor for a successful marriage are associated with the rites for the ancestors, and only indirectly with the powers of the Church. Marriage may therefore be said to be viewed as the concern of families — that of the man and the woman — since the family dead, whose preoccupation is the welfare of the descendants, are particularly invoked for this purpose. Consequently, the formal religious complex that sanctions a marriage, which follows Euro-American patterns, need not be detailed here.

For the fishermen, of whatever faith, and the villagers, St. Peter's day is a festive occasion. The boats first go out to the fishing ground, if weather permits, to obtain fish to be given the poor. When they return to the jetty, the Anglican minister awaits them. It is a gay sight, the boats flying red, white, and blue flags, and people in their best clothes. As the boats are slowly rowed out to sea and back to shore, the minister prays and blesses the sea, and hymns are sung. "People cook, have rum. All kind of thing." They eat at the cove, and all who come are fed, while rum and food are "thrown away" in "all corners" and in the bay, also. "After they eat done, they take people for rides in the boats. Go out an' come back." If the fishermen are able to provide a "band," social dances are held. But after the minister leaves, "Then dance the bongo and bele dances," to honor the saint.

Good Friday is generally observed, though the most im-

pressive rituals of this day are those of the Anglicans and
Catholics. The former have a three-hour service; the latter
follow the stations of the cross, each one with his "piti bon
Dje" (*petit Bon Dieu*), preparatory to a principal service
that takes place in the afternoon. For the Baptists and other
Protestant sects, it is also a holy day.

In death, the offices of the church are not to be dispensed
with, though poverty may limit the elaborateness of the
rites. If the deceased is a Catholic, and a regular communicant, "extramotion" — extreme unction — would have
been accorded before death. The funeral procession would
go to the church, but the role of the priest, according to
local report, would depend upon the fee. "You got to pay
plenty for read, pray, candles. Then if there is an acolyte
with incense and pries' to follow to burial, that cost plenty."
For twenty-five dollars, one account had it, the bells toll and
the priest meets the coffin in front of the church, takes it inside, and goes to the cemetery. "Six shillings for tolling the
bells alone, with no service. If you can pay ten dollars, then
you get the service inside the church only. For forty dollars,
the priest comes to the house in his car. Then he leaves
to get into his vestments and meets the procession. . . .
But for fifty dollars he walks the whole way from the house
to the church and from the church to the cemetery." The
Anglican church asks the family of a dead communicant no
fee for the officiating minister's services; if not a communicant, a fee of eleven shillings is charged, plus a shilling for
tolling the bells. "But the Anglican minister would come
even if you're six months in arrears" with church dues.
The minister comes to the house and then goes to the cemetery, but he does not lead the funeral procession.

Moravians and Seventh Day Adventists have their funeral
services in the church, there being no rite at the home. Catholics and Anglicans bury their dead in the churchyard,
but Adventists, Baptists and Shouters use the public burial

ground. Participation of the Shouters resembles that of a lodge. They come to the house of the dead singing songs, the women wearing white, the men in black. They sing over the coffin, and when they close it, all who are not members of the group, except the family, must leave. The next remark discloses how this group is associated by the community with understanding and kindliness. "The other societies put out the family." If outsiders do not go, "They shakin' now, come over an' growl at you, tell you to get out." In the funeral procession, Shouters, both men and women, carry the coffin, "the men at the head, where it heaviest," and at the grave, the spirit may "come" to various members, in a manner to be described later.

Persons of all denominations have wakes, but only the Seventh Day Adventists do not "throw away" food for the dead. The Anglicans sometimes feed the ghost — "but many don' worry about it" — the Moravians "feed the dead more often than the Anglicans." As for the Catholics, "You can't beat them. There's too much business at a Catholic 'forty days'. They kill a goat and plenty fowl. Too much business." The attitudes of the clergy toward this practice vary. One Anglican minister, now dead, was particularly hostile. "He used to come in storming while the bongo was going on, and the body lay there. He so mad, say he won' bury. But the boys now, playing bongo used to raise the stick over his head [in defiance], beat the bongo strong. People to whom the dead belong say, 'Reverend, you don' bury, you just say a prayer. To bury we need friends, neighbors. If we insult them, tell them to go, who will follow the coffin? Who will bury? We can't quarrel with we people. Is they who carry, is they who bury. . . . After some little time, he got used to bongo. He bury just the same."

Though the influence of the churches of established denominations does not impinge appreciably on the ordering of the daily round of the people, we have nevertheless seen that church affiliation is not perfunctory, that its role is not negative. Discussion and observation soon make clear that though there are varying emphases placed on established ritual, certain of them, such as the christening rite or the rites of death, are viewed as indispensable. A denial of these rites signifies more than a defection in worldly prestige; it involves actual jeopardy to well-being, because of vulnerability to attack by supernatural forces. In the instances of christening, the danger of attack would come from the creatures of the forest, unbaptised themselves, with no means of redemption such as is had by those accepted into the human family by the powers of the Universe, in this instance the Saints or the Trinity. The rites of death are exigent because the dead are interpreted as continuing influential, for good or evil, in the lives of their descendants, and must on no account have withheld from them those ceremonies that are associated with prestige and grace.

The impulse to conform to other prescribed rites derives from more generalized motives, less deeply rooted in traditional or personal need. Not in these do the people find the satisfaction that comes from a sense of security built up by a conviction of living in tune with the forces that control the Universe, of being close to the forces, and of being able to call upon them as need arises to smooth a troublesome path, to resolve a difficult situation, or to assure success in a new undertaking. From the point of view of personal adjustment to the forces of the Universe, organized religion is regarded either as oblivious to, or removed from, many of life's experiences. Church affiliation, while in no way casual, is thus not so meaningful psychologically as if the conscious need for supernatural intervention in the lowly affairs of day-to-day existence were met.

From this same psychological point of view, it is equally evident that these people are deeply religious. Conversation with them does not need to be extended to demonstrate that they live by a system of values they feel to be sanctioned by the powers of the Universe, and that they are in accord with these powers, or have the means of achieving personal accord with them. This follows from the belief that each individual is bound by personal affinity to a Saint, or a member of the Trinity, and that with the guidance of tradition and individual insight, means can be found for performing special acts of devotion or propitiation to gain special favors. As the outer layers of this culture are finally penetrated, it becomes possible to assemble statements of these beliefs, and to discover humble rites that disclose the mechanisms whereby conviction is sustained.

4

Any attempt to understand the place of religion in the life of this community must take cognizance of the impulse to conform to the dominant practices that afford prestige. But no penetrating grasp of the drives that motivate purposeful living can be had if the compelling impulse to participation is ignored. For herein lies the key to the significance of the Shouters sect, and of all those practices that rest outside formal worship.

The degree of psychological participation may be related to the extent to which two factors enter into the situation. The first of these is that the Shouters, to the greatest degree, and to a somewhat lesser extent the Baptists and Adventists, operate in terms of an idiom — of which the Shango cult is the most complete expression — that is more congenial to the traditions of these people than do the other denominations. One need only cite such an aspect of worship as the emotionalism of spirit possession to make the point. For the restraints of the more formal Anglican, Catholic and Moravian rituals inhibit the release in motor behavior and verbal and vocal expression that is found in a kind of scale of increasing freedom in the Adventist, Baptist, Shouter and Shango rites.

The other factor concerns the nature of the controls that are operative in assuring the continuing and disciplined functioning of the congregation as a group. In a sense, the point under consideration here has to do with the degree of democracy found in the various churches, and the resulting feeling of participation in the ordering of its affairs that accrues to each member. The Anglicans, Catholics, and Moravians are therefore at a disadvantage in contrast to the other groups because they obey rules concerning dogma, ritual, and organization that are laid down far from Toco, regulations that communicants can only obey, and in the establishment or alteration of which they have no voice. This is also true, to a degree, of the Adventists, who from this point of view may be thought of in the same category as the other three, though outer regulation bears more lightly on the Adventist.

In addition to the factor of the local or outside nature of the controls exerted over these groups, the fact that Anglican and Catholic clergy are of different racial stock from their communicants tends to set off these churches in the minds of the members of their congregations, as well as those who belong to other sects. The non-Negro elements in the population of Toco are too small to permit of the existence of a race problem. Yet the climate of opinion in the Island is such that the Negroes are quite conscious of racial differences and their social implications. It is not difficult to see how the presence of a white vicar or priest functioning in a church that opposes modes of conduct which reveal too realistic an identification with the Trinity or the Saints, tends to set up barriers that stand in the way of the full and free emotional response that marks the worship of the groups where leadership is local, controls democratic, and racial homogeneity sanctions traditional means of self-expression.

5

The Shouters take their name from the possession-phenomenon that is termed "shouting" or "shaking," and distinguishes them from the other Christian denominations of Trinidad. This phenomenon consists of the familiar pattern whereby the personality of the devotee is displaced by what is believed to be the Spirit of the Holy Ghost, which causes the one under possession variously to sing, shout, dance, stamp, prophesy, or cure. Possession when witnessed, gives little hint of its disciplined character. This is one reason why it appears to the outsider as uncouth and hysterical, an impression which without doubt figured in the official action that culminated in the proscription of the cult. These seizures, however, are not regarded as at all unique to the setting of worship that marks this sect. This was evidenced by the comment of one devotee, who before baptism had been an Anglican, and was explaining why he could not attend services of that faith or those of the Roman Catholic or any other church, though he was sometimes tempted to do so. "The Power will be shakin' me after the hymn, and the pries' will say 'What's wrong there?' an' put me out."

The ordinance under which the activities of the Shouters sect were rendered illegal is known as the "Shouters Prohibition Ordinance, 1917." It was adopted by the Legislative Council of Trinidad and Tobago on the plea of the Attorney General that worship of this kind — which, according to his statement, had been introduced from the neighboring island of St. Vincent — was "an unmitigated nuisance" because the rites were noisy, and because other "practices which are indulged in are not such as should be tolerated in a well conducted community." *

Why the Toco Shouters are under a legal ban cannot but be a puzzling question to the student who is concerned with understanding the beliefs and rituals of this group, and particularly its place in a community such as Toco — a place that, as illustrated, is so disproportionate to its numbers and so striking when viewed in the light of its meagre resources and the humble station of its members. That the police are active in suppressing the cult is to be seen in the fact that in this village two charges against Shouters groups were lodged, and convictions were obtained, within a period of four months in 1939. The effect of the first, it was apparent, heightened the interest in the group felt by the villagers, while the heavy fines assessed against the head of the group, one of the converts, and the man on whose land the meeting had been held, served to create sympathy for them. This interest was, if anything, intensified by the second series of arrests and the resulting court case to be described in later pages, where again convictions aroused the sympathy of many whose own religious affiliation was with the approved denominations.

As one comes to know Shouters, both as organized into congregations and as individuals, it is clear that the interdictions under which they carry on their activities give them, as a group, an inner cohesion, and as individuals a depth of conviction that strengthens them in pitting their weakness in numbers and resources against the legal sanctions of the State. Sharing what little they own, meeting for the crucial rites of initiation and worship in secret, refusing to pay fines levied against them, choosing instead to "go to

* Because this action has been so important in determining attitudes toward various religious groups, no less than toward the Shouters, on the part of the Negroes, the text of the ordinance, the statements made preceding its adoption and excerpts from the Police Manual under which suppression is carried on, are given in full in Appendix II.

jail for Jesus," their convictions make a deep impression on their co-villagers.

Characteristically, these prosecutions give rise to gossip about the events that led to suppressed meetings, tales that are told and retold with a mixture of relish and sympathy. As a reflection of popular attitude and point of view, this gossip is included, as revealing how fantasy supplements or even supplants fact in order to weave more closely a new motif into the old pattern of grievance against discrimination. Thus gossip, recounted many times, had it that one of the local ministers had been responsible for the first series of arrests; that he had informed on this group of Shouters out of pique, because at a nearby settlement where he had gone to preach he had faced empty benches when his service chanced to coincide with one held by the Shouters. Similarly, after the second series of arrests, the story was at once bruited about that the police had been accompanied to the nearby village where the Shouters were alleged to be holding their forbidden baptismal rites by three laymen prominent in one of the recognized churches.

These tales, one soon learns, are particularized versions of other accounts, of broader implication, that purport to explain why the restrictive ordinance was passed in the first pace. Popular belief holds it to be demonstrated truth that it was the jealousy of the larger, wealthier denominations, that, taking advantage of the higher social standing of their members and the political influence they were in a position to wield, achieved the passage of the ordinance in order to suppress a dangerous rival in the quest for souls. Further, it is accepted as fact that the ordinance stays in the statutes, and the police are diligent in its enforcement, because of the continuing fear which these churches have of the appeal of the beliefs and ritual of the Shouters.

There are still wider associations evoked by the suppression of what, to the inhabitant of low socioeconomic position — ordinarily a neutral where the status of religious groups is involved — seems to be an honest and inoffensive mode of worship by folk of his own class. This, by extension, comes from the identification of the whole range of his own social and economic disabilities with those special restrictions that apply to the Shouters. Biblical citations having to do with the final triumph of the meek fall frequently and easily from his lips when he discusses the case of the Shouters. He moves from this to tell of the objectives of the Garvey movement or of the struggle of Haile Selassie against European powers, thus effecting a transfer to the broader, world-wide inter-racial situation. He hints darkly that the powers of the other church groups are derived from such apocryphal works as "The Book of the Maccabees" or "The Book of Moses" that are withheld from him, implying that with these powers the lower-class groups would be able to cope with the difficulties that hamper them.

Revealing, also, is the role of Herod in their thinking on religious matters. For the order issued by Herod to kill all the male infants in his kingdom, an order from which Jesus escaped, is frequently referred to as symbolizing the action of Government in suppressing the Shouters, and in justifying the subterfuges to which they must resort in order to go on with their worship. "It is so they persecute those who baptize," said one Shouter. Such stories as that of Salome, as expounded to explain the case brought against the first group of Shouters in Toco, are deeply revealing of the psychology that draws these broad conclusions from a specific instance of this suppression of their worship.

The point made as often as any other when Toco folk discuss the ban on the Shouters is the discrepancy between their practices as viewed by law and in actual fact. They are known for their trustworthiness in personal dealings, while they are nothing less than puritanical in their standards of moral conduct and in the values they live by. Their willing-

ness to aid one another also rouses admiration, for, as has
been stated, they share what little they have with each
other; while the discipline that orders all phases of their
existence, as evidenced in their obedience to the teacher,
or Father of the church, and the punishments they themselves exact of erring members, is similarly commented on
favorably.

When the point is raised with folk who are not Shouters
about the charge of disturbance that is levelled against the
group, the answer is that Shouters' churches are located
where few people live to be disturbed, and that the rule
against drums and dancing after ten o'clock, applicable to
all gatherings, could still apply to them if their existence
should receive legal sanction — as it is not applied, it was
emphasized, in the case of social dances. The evidence of internal order, of discipline, and good faith on the part of the
Shouters, that is brought forward in discussion, in contrast
to the reasons for suppressing this worship as given by the
authorities which the Tocoan often cites, makes for a cynical view in the community as a whole.

This leads to another, more subtle reason why the Shouters exert an influence on the religious life that is so disproportionate to their small number and their institutional
weakness. It is noted that though unremitting effort has
been made against them for more than two decades, they
have not only persisted, but are today as strong or stronger
than they ever were. This, to the average man or woman, is
proof that they wield a spiritual power that sustains them as
individuals, and maintains their sway as a group, against all
attempts made to stamp them out. "Not everyone knows
God's secrets," said one man. "There are things to speak
and things not to speak," he went on, citing the Bible, as
he indicated the power of the Shouters. This power is made
most manifest in the way police raiders are believed to be
turned away by the strength of the Shouters' words:

"Mother Margaret was a little ol' woman. You never think she have power like that. But when she live at San Fernando an' the police came, she just told them of her power in Jesus an' the Corporal say, 'I believe you,' and get in his car an' go right back to the station."

This spiritual power manifests itself, moreover, it is said, in ways that all can see and be benefited by, for it is the gift of the teacher to "heal by de power of Jesus Christ." One villager told how a leader of a Shouters group cured a woman of cancer; another related how this same leader, through the power of the Spirit, caused a man who was bewitched to walk. "Teacher pray, sing, give him oil-cake and boil it with lamp oil and *ratchet* (an evergreen with red flowers). That bring de man foot up. . . . Stan' up an' walk." If a "trick" is set against a man, he goes to a teacher of a Shouters group. "Healer sit, an' meditate. Close his eyes. Some see with open eyes. Will tell you everything." Or again, "If a man hurt you without you give him cause, the Shouters give a service for you. Then it goes back to the man who sent it." And, as a further comment on the fact that this power is for good, and not evil, it was said, "Natural Baptist (i.e., Shouters), can't cause harm. Can heal, can rescue. Can make evil against you turn back."

We may now summarize the reasons why the Shouters bulk so large in the religious thought of Toco — and, in fact, of the Negroes of the Island in general. In the first place, whatever their religious beliefs, Shouters and non-Shouters alike belong largely to the underprivileged group. The religious "persecution" of the Shouters, as it is termed, thus symbolizes for them the struggle all face in meeting the social and economic disabilities under which they live. The racial factor enters here, also, since the Shouters are almost exclusively Negroes, so that this further identification in racial terms is made. Great spiritual power is attributed to them, because, as discussed, their worship has survived two decades of attempts to suppress it. This has the further result of establishing psychologically the power of the Shouters to heal or to intervene in the solution of other problems of a supernatural nature. More than any other group on the Island except the Shango cult, the Shouters function in terms of some of the most deeply set traditional values in Negro societies. For they grant to each member a degree of actual and psychological participation that makes the individual worshipper feel that he or she is a useful, a necessary part of the world about him.

CHAPTER VIII

THE SHOUTERS

Shouters groups are small, and from the exterior their places of worship are hard to distinguish from nearby dwellings. One such "temple," as their churches are termed, situated atop a hill, was the center of a kind of compound where some of those who supported it also lived. It was a small rectangular building with mud walls, a dirt floor, and a thatched roof.

Inside, toward the rear was a series of benches, with an aisle down the center. Across the front of the small room a low rail ran along the outer edge of a shallow platform on which were chairs for the preacher or other church officials, and the altar. One cross hung against the wall, and another was attached to the railing on the left of the opening at its center. At the extreme right was a pulpit on which at night services a candle burned. Inserted at the base of the thatch was a flag of pale violet, while directly beneath the large cross was the altar, a table covered with a cloth, on which were a candle and four vases filled with white flowers.

Directly in line with the opening leading to the platform was the ritually-significant central post of the house. It was whitewashed, and at its base were a lighted candle, a large brass bell with a wooden handle, a Bible, and flowers in a jam jar, similar to those on the altar. Extending outward from the post to mark the cardinal points, four crosses were chalked on the dirt floor, with the long arm of each cross toward the post. Chalked designs appeared also in front of the entrances to the church. The plan of this church is as follows:

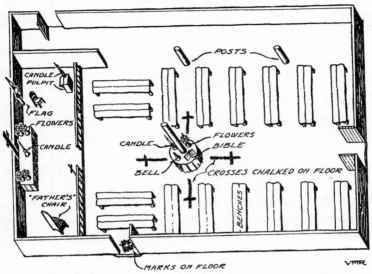

This particular "temple" was soon to be vacated, despite the fact that the rent paid by the group, one dollar a month, was twice the sum that would ordinarily be charged for it. The plot was owned jointly by a brother and sister, and though the woman had no objection to this congregation remaining there, her brother, a devout Catholic, would have no Shouters on his land. The group was therefore building a new "temple," on land owned by another man, where they were to be allowed to remain until they had accumulated the money to buy it.

Another "temple," in a locality some distance from Toco was situated on the periphery of the town. Here was to be observed a sizeable compound with a number of thatched houses in the clearing, on both sides of a path leading to the church. From these houses protruded poles, with flags of various colors on them, and there were at least two outdoor shrines, with candles burning in them. The "temple," or "tent," as the church itself was called, was much like its Toco counterpart, though more solidly built, with straw thatch of the finest workmanship and mud walls painted a blue-grey.

Since this second "temple," which serves a larger and more established congregation, probably was as elaborate as any Shouters' center to be found, it will be described in some detail. At each corner of the room was a semicircular altar, consisting of four steps, each top step holding a lighted candle and a vase of flowers. The principal altar, facing the entrance, had a great cross in low relief against the wall, and a smaller wooden cross on either side of it. Separating this altar from the rest of the church was a wooden railing similar to that in the Toco church. The central post was here set in a high circular altar consisting of seven steps on which rested a large bell, a candle, and flowers in a vase. The benches to accommodate worshippers and spectators were ranged behind the central post, facing the main altar, and along the side walls. Flags of many colors hung over the principal and subsidiary altars, and were attached to the central post.

2

Contrasting with the simplicity, and often poverty of the physical setting of this worship, is the richness in concept of identification of the worshipper with "the Spirit," with "Glory," with the "Holy Ghos'." The "Spirit" actually touches the worshipper with an unseen hand, and a shiver electrifies his body, causing him first to stiffen, then to begin to shake. The "Spirit" fills him with joy, causing him to dance, to speak in tongues, to prophesy, to "see." The worshipper sings a hymn of joy that had never before been sung, and thereafter there is a "spiritual hymn" that all will sing, as

> Give me wings,
> Let me fly to Glory;
> Only the pure of heart,
> Dear Jesus.

This will be sung to a melody so full of verve that it will lift the congregation to its feet dancing.

But entering into this identification are psychological factors which lie outside the mystic, other-worldly emotions. A worshipper who lives a good life has tangible symbols that can be looked to to achieve tangible benefits for his everyday well-being. More than this, from his mournin' experiences, which will be detailed in succeeding pages, he emerges with "gifts" which define for each humble worshipper in supernatural terms a specific task, or series of tasks in the fabric of church organization.

Baptism, proving, mournin', the phenomenon of possession by the "Spirit," the physical manifestations of such possession in the shaking, the dancing, the speaking in tongues, the bringing back of spiritual gifts are all at the core of the Shouters worship everywhere. The resemblances from group to group are significant, because each congregation is autonomous, and no supervisory body sees to it that in organization — or dogma — the separate churches maintain any degree of unity.

But while variations in pattern do occur everywhere, it is possible to draw generalizations about cult structure and practices in broad terms. Leadership and discipline are outstanding features of the worship, and leadership always vests in one who exerts his controls because of the supernatural powers that are his by endowment and continuous seeking. This individual may be a man or woman, may be termed "teacher" or "preacher," or "father" or "mother" of the

flock. Regardless of the strength of the personality of the
leader, he is responsible in varying degrees to his associates;
on the other hand, his congregation, depending largely on
his relationship with leaders of Shouting groups elsewhere,
may be self-sufficent or may have relatively close affiliations
with other churches, even where no inconsiderable distances separate them.

The most important functionaries, however, are always
the "father" or "mother," the "teacher," the "preacher,"
and the "prover." The franchise of these offices derives
from the quality of their visionary experiences, especially
as these manifest themselves in the mournin' ground, and
the continuing power they demonstrate as they fulfill their
tasks. The most inclusive list of "gifts" recorded was given
by a woman, herself "teacher" and head of her group, who
is reputed to be endowed with great spiritual power. This
list demonstrates how the proliferation of "gifts" serves
to integrate each church member into the organization of
worship as a purposeful unit in the play of forces that rule
the lives of men. In presenting this list, the "work" expected of each member endowed with a specific "gift" will
follow the version of this "teacher." Unless otherwise
stated, persons of either sex may be conceived as functioning in these duties:

preacher — one who preaches and, at times, "interprets"
    the Bible.
teacher — one who teaches the meanings of dreams and
    visions, and "sees things." "Some teachers don' know
    how to point proper, or don' want to point them cor-
    rect. I look at them, say, 'But I can see you in the spirit.
    You have a high call. As soon as I lay hands upon you,
    you are wise already.' "
prover — "He is there to prove the good from the bad in
    the church. You say you are a teacher, well, you've got

to write an' the prover proves it. To be a prover, you must say something about this writing, spiritual writing."

leader — "He leads the children to the water," where the one who is going to baptize new members awaits them. He may also preach in the church.

divine healer — "Heals everything, with the aid of divine power." In this list, he is differentiated from the

healer — who was set down as a person who merely "heals diseases," and whose title is synonymous with that of *doctor*.

captain — "He sails the camp," like the captain of a ship. "He begins everything, has everything fixed."

pastor — the father of the church.

shepherd — "Who takes care of the children."

shepherdess — "When you come to church, find you a seat, an' if there is anything you need they must let you have it. Shepherdess can also lead a prayer meeting." Just as there is an assistant teacher and a teacher, so there is a leader and a shepherd. "The shepherd must be very bright, yes? Can be brighter than the leader, can do mysterious things. The shepherdess, too."

pumper — "Help you when you go down to seek the spirit, to really bring something back. When the pumper pumps, sometimes he hear Mother Earth speak to him and tell him what to do." The explanation went further: "That is about spiritual work of the church. Not about curing."

diver — "Anything that down, he would get up. It's when the spirit leaves them and goes away (i.e., among members of the church)." Or, "The spirit takes them away and he brings it up." It was made clear that this did not involve curing in the sense of recovering the soul of a person that has been "taken away" by the black magic set by an enemy.

prophet — one who prophesies things "of the past and the future."

apostle — "Jesus' messengers, who saw his miracles." They prophesy, teach, "an' heal, too. They're higher than the prophet."

queen — "She can be queen of teachers, queen over the spirits. I mean they have got to take orders from her so. She can prove, too."

fortune-teller — "Tell you things of the spirit, an' many different things, also. It's like an astronomer." A fortune-teller, however, it was explained, cannot prophesy the "things of heaven," or read the stars and the moon. A prophet is higher than a fortune-teller. "Fortune-teller read you, the man. Prophet read the writing in the sky."

surveyra — surveys the camp where mournin' is held, and designates the water for baptism. "What does it mean to survey the camp? It's the four corners you want, for you have to know the center. When the leader wants to do his work, he must know the center. If a strange Baptis' visit you, you make your sign inside, he makes it outside. Then you see if he is a good man and know the Baptis' secret. Then you shake hands, you glad." The "surveyra" also keeps out the evil being called *sukuyan,* or vampire.

judge — "Higher than prover, but something like him. If you are wrong in doing spiritual things, then the judge is higher than everything — than teacher, or leader or preacher. If the judge calls another, an' he don' come, he'll suspend him, an' then put a penalty. He mus' fast, an' then gets a pardon." His powers go farther. "He can flog even a teacher. But he does this at a particular (secret) meeting. The children (the congregation) won' be there, won' hear about it."

nurse — "That's a woman alone. She cleans the church, puts flowers around." During the services it is she who, in accordance with the instructions given by the "mother" of the church, goes to each corner, "watering the field."

Such are some of the "gifts," or "vocations," or "spiritual tasks" as these are variously called, that are found in different Shouters groups. This list does not exhaust the tale of the gifts named by persons affiliated with other groups, a few of which may be mentioned. These would include the gift of the *philosopher,* "who tells of something expected to come," or the *artist,* "who draws the signs" made in white on the floor of a church, or the *revealer,* "who reveals things in the Bible," or the *searching warrant,* "who can tell you when the spirit of God is coming; lays hands on a mischievous person. Anything secret he will put his hands on it; and when there's a bashfulness toward the spirit of God, he comes to you and the bashfulness leaves you."

Outsiders who discuss the Shouters mention their discipline as often as their spiritual power. Not only religious behavior, but everyday conduct of those within the community is scrutinized and regularized. "Baptists don' like cards. Don' like too much rum. Don' like running around with women. Livin' is all right, but steady. If he married and wrangle, don' like it. Better livin' steady and nice with another, because marry not sustain always. That's why a young man work to become a member, we ask, 'You married? Livin' with woman? Intend to begin livin'?'" If he say 'No,' we won't have him. Say, 'You is gentleman in the day. What you doin' at night?' Same with woman. Say, 'You not old. You a human being, what you doing then?'"

Several persons spoke of an officer of the Shouters groups called a watchman, whose task is to know what is "going on" among the members, and particularly to learn and verify gossip about wrong-doing. "They chastise you in open church for it," it was stated. "You have to kneel down and then they chastise." At times, too, the spirit will come to a member who will testify, "Sister Mary or Brother John is living in sin." To accept chastisement when guilty is regarded as a test of willingness to live in accordance with the principles of the sect, for one who is "a frivolous person" will, under these circumstances, leave the church before permitting himself to be flogged or otherwise humbled.

The office of *"prover"* is another cited by outsiders discussing the strictness with which Shouters hold their members in line, and see that the tenets of the good life are not violated. One person even maintained that there is a head prover to test the provers — something not borne out by the statements of Shouters themselves, but indicative of opinions held by others concerning Shouter discipline. The *prover* has a wand which, "have something in it. Say it's the spirit." It is put to the head of each member three times. "You begin to shake. If you fall down, a sister call out, 'Prover, flog her, she fall from grace.'" They "prove" the entire membership, and perhaps find one or two of these who, after their punishment, are termed penitents. For a time, penitents sit alone in the church, and wear special clothes. "If they're women, they wears a blue dress with a white collar, like a nurse." Then, later, at a meeting in the "teacher's" house, they are questioned. "Then they have to tell, an' promise not to do it again."

As a consequence of this discipline, and the impression made on the community by the retelling of incidents that come to popular attention, the Shouters enjoy a reputation of great probity. "Wednesday night meeting flog you self, till you bawl (if you have done wrong). Outsiders see it, yes? But if they're seeing it too much, then they shut the windows. Member get three chances; then if they do wrong again, cut him off." Inner controls, as described by a "teacher," reinforce this reputation of discipline and rectitude by intervening officially in internal feuds that might bring members before the law. For "the church judge things between members. Don' like court at all; try to settle things between ourselves. I'm strict, yes! If I say, they do so." The view of the younger men and women was that the flesh is too weak at their age to live in such grace as this worship demands, but that it is a way of life they hoped one day to attain.

3

Most Shouters come to seek membership in the church as the result of a dream-experience. Two of these experiences may be given here. One man, the "father" of a Toco Shouting church, had come to Trinidad from St. Vincent some four decades before. There he was a Wesleyan (Methodist), but because this denomination was not represented in Toco, he attended the Anglican services. "Say we all was sinners. It was like they beat me. I couldn't go there." So he "stayed at home, studied, studied. All the different churches, all say they tell the true word. I study, say, 'Lord, I want to serve you. Which you true children?' "

"One day," his tale continued, "I dream. A white man come hol' up two fingers. A fine lookin' man. I look at his face an' down to his feet, then I begin to look from the feet up. When I come to about here (showing his side) , I know it the Savior. I say, 'Lord, which one has the true word?' He show the two fingers, say, 'They there.' Say, 'Which one, Lord?' He say 'Choose.' I choose, and then I know it's the Baptis', the spiritual." And since then, his search for the truth having been successful, he like St. John "bring the light." He added that his religion made him happy, that it filled him with joy. "When the body is fill with joy, it move, it shake. If I got up one mornin' an' didn't feel like shoutin', then I know the Lord is not with me. I would know something was wrong."

To another man, who had lived earlier in Tobago, the call likewise came in a dream. He had had many conversations with the leader of a Shouters' group, and one day, while ill, he dreamed he was thrown out of a boat in which he was sailing. "The sea was dry and level. You could see everywhere, to Port-of-Spain, even to London." He was on shore near the Galera light-house, east of Toco, where many people stood in line, moving out over the sea until they reached Christ, "the place of Glory." Some went to the right, some to the left, "But glory be, when I got there I go to the right-hand, not to the lef'. Go to glory with Jesus." Those who went to the left are "gone to the devil-imps, an' burn night an' day." So he knew he was among the saved.

Let us follow the subsequent behavior of this man. Next morning he packed his clothes and followed his mentor to a house in the country, some distance from Toco, "though he didn't wan' to take me." However, after some urging "He take me. We trottin', goin' an' when we meet the house, he wife get some 'dust grass' put it in the water," and then tied it about his aching feet, which had "come big, boy! It swell wit' the distance." After he had rested, he began to work for his teacher — "clean the yard, draw water, work in the estate" — until, since his visions continued, he was taken to be baptized. After this, he went to mournin' groun', thus becoming a full member of the group, and returned to Toco, where he has been active in Shouter circles ever since, though it was bruited about he was falling from grace for being unfaithful to his keeper.

The decision to be baptized may thus come to a person as the result of a dream or vision. Baptism is the first step in the chain of rituals that are to be thought of as a process of initiation into the Shouters sect, an image that becomes the more apt when it is pointed out that for the community as a whole the Shouters are regarded as "an order like the Rose of Sharon" or other secret societies.

Dreams and visions are said by some to be of equal weight in this process, while others hold them to be of different quality, though of equal importance. "There can be dreams and visions, though children only have dreams. Dreams mean something, but God sends visions so you know what to do." God sent the vision that led to the baptism of the man who volunteered these opinions. "When you get a vision like this, you got to baptize. You got to obey." Otherwise God punishes with sickness. "Is the Angel self speak to you, the Angel of Christ! He show you the spot where you are to baptize even, whether fresh river or the sea." Rivers were likened to the Jordan — "Any river is the Jordan. You have to be born again. Born again mean remerge. Remerge mean baptize." Sometimes, according to a statement by another cult-member, the teacher may have the vision, and inform the candidate, or the candidate may have a dream and the teacher interprets it in the manner in which dreams sometimes have to be interpreted. In any event, the importance of prior interest in the cult is recognized. "If Baptist appeal to you, it's a voice inside you speaking to you. It's the voice of God. We calls it getting converted."

When a man or woman comes to the teacher with his vision or dream, and offers himself as a candidate for baptism, he undergoes a period of instruction that some say lasts for three months, others three weeks, a month, or longer, depending on the candidate. During this time he goes to the teacher every other night, and must lead a life worthy of his new calling. "If he's single, can't live in fornication, but if he's married, goes on livin'." The teacher gives him a chapter, or part of a chapter of the Bible, or a psalm to read "all by himself." The Spirit of God may come while he is reading, and he begins to pray.

This is an important — probably the most important — aspect of the pre-baptismal training, for "everyone who receives baptism has a *hymn*, a *psalm* and a *chapter* that is his

. . ." which cause him to "receive the spirit, and when he testify with a candle, he start with that hymn." For to the question, "Why do some shake and others don't, when a hymn is sung?" the answer came, "If my hymn is sung, I'm happy. If another hymn is sung, if it's connected with mine, it would move me. But if it wasn't either of these, I wouldn't feel it." The speaker added, "Sometimes a hymn move everybody. We say 'Spirit of God come like a wind.'" It is recognized also that individual differences may not be disregarded at any stage in affiliation. "When members are deeper down, it's easier for them to get the Spirit. But some are self-starters, while some need corkin' up," and some, "Oh, the spirit love them too much, come too quick, rush to them!"

The baptismal meeting begins at the church or the home of a member. It is usually held on a Saturday, and lasts the entire night. The eyes of the candidates are bound early in the proceedings, about nine or ten o'clock, "to prevent them from looking around." There are prayers and hymns, and the teacher addresses them, exhorting them to give their hearts to God, and to pray sincerely; which they do while the congregation sings softly in accompaniment. Coffee and refreshments are served to all about midnight, and there is a recess of an hour or two. "Let them cool off now. Some teachers let them sleep, but others only let them rest. Prayin' is quieted down now, too."

At about this stage the baptismal rite which occasioned the series of arrests and subsequent trial of Shouters shortly before the period of this research, was interrupted by the police. The testimony of one of the officers, as given before the court, may be quoted here from the transcript as a first-hand account of the nature of the proceeding in the ceremonies immediately before the arrests were made: "I heard singing and shouting. . . . I noticed a woman serving coffee, some drinking coffee and some singing. I saw five persons sitting on a bench. Their eyes and heads were bandaged with white cloth and they had lighted candles in their hands. They were moving their bodies from side to side and grunting. I noticed . . . [the leader] . . . reading from a paper in her hand and holding a woman in one hand who was jumping. I noticed . . . [one of her assistants] . . . with a small stick making signs and touching the heads of the persons sitting on the bench. . . ."

At about four o'clock the group start their march to the river, or the spot on the sea-shore where the baptizing — which must always take place in "living" water — is to be carried out. They take the bands off the eyes of the candidates, and all "march singin'," the leader first, staff in hand. Attendants greatly outnumber candidates. The "surveyra" tries the depth of the water, and plants a cross there, while the teacher enters to consecrate the water, as all sing and pray. Then, shortly before dawn, baptizing begins. Each candidate, holding a lighted candle, is immersed three times. "There are miracles, yes? Some go in with it lighted, come up with it lighted." But to all, the Spirit comes. The elder who performs the rite, it was pointed out, gives nothing when he baptizes. "It's Christ who gives, for the Bible say, 'A sign shall follow you,' an' that sign is the power of the Holy Ghos'. If you heart clean, you get the power clean, if not, you get it partly. But after you receive the Holy Ghos', you cannot keep still at all. You feel a j'y (joy) within you, an' at the mention of God, the power shake you."

Afterwards, the candidates are taken to the "tent" — a thatched shelter — to rest and partake of fruit and other refreshments before returning to the church, and to "give thanks." Later that morning, at the church, they sleep, and some of them may have further visions that often tell them they must undertake the next step, the rites of the mournin' groun', specifying also the period they must spend there to obtain the "gift" they are destined to receive.

Should those having undergone the rite of baptism feel hunger, they are fed during the day, but many of them go without food, resting while they await their consecration at the seven o'clock services. At that time their heads, hands, and feet are washed, the face, head, palms of the hands and soles of the feet are anointed with oil, and they are given sacred water to drink. "They read the orders to them: Remember the Baptism morning; remember the Baptism, remember the three drops of water (symbolizing Father, Son and Holy Ghost) given you." Then, the day's services over, they are free to return to their homes.

4

Mournin' groun' is the term used to designate a kind of retreat either literally or figuratively "in de bush," at which Shouters are initiated into the mysteries of their faith, obtain and later renew the power of their "gifts," or receive higher powers. "We call it mournin' because they fast there. Don' wash," said one teacher; and another, "We mourn for sins. Go there, and ol' person die, new person born in Christ." It was also said, "Long time ago people they call 'converted' had mourning, but didn't baptize. That was dangerous. On their way [to Glory] they saw too many things, met too many things. It hurt them sometimes too much after they got back."

The period of time required varies with the individual. "They do what they're told by the Spirit, but sometimes the Spirit says they must stay longer than they plan, fourteen days and not seven, or even twenty-one." Where there are no special instructions from a spirit to follow, mourning begins at night. At midnight, "you set them," putting bands about the eyes of those in mourning, and causing them to lie on pallets of straw, or banana or bread-fruit or bamboo leaves. "Wash today an' band them. Then they don' get washing till the bands are off. They are bathe' right through with consecrated water. Some don' sleep at all," during the days of retreat.

When they tire of lying, they are placed on their knees, or are brought to a sitting position, and their arms are rubbed to help the circulation. "The mother of the church must be there to help," and women with the gift of nurse, who look after those mourning as they would after children. "There's a bell to ring if you want to ease yourself, but you must do this inside, an' not go out." The leader is in the same house. "He know your thoughts, an' if your spirit isn't going beating the pass (path) to the other world he may flog you." Another person commented, "If you do something wrong, the Spirit lick you. Spirit bound to lick you before you get it. . . . Spirit send some to Africa, learn to talk language, African language. Some to India, learn to talk like Indian. Some to China, learn to talk Chinese." But in answer to a question as to whether the Spirit is Jesus, or St. John, or the Virgin, the only answer was "No, it's another spirit."

Each morning those in retreat are "called up for prayer." They are given milk and a little sweet rice to eat. "When an African spirit get to them they ask for *kuku* (an African dish made of cassava). Sometimes spirit don' allow them to use a plate. Have a calabash. They eat and drink out of it. Have a spoon — they bring spoon, fork, plate, glass, towel — but don' use it. At times the spirit ask for a knife put under their head. Then, when they travellin', there's three people then, not one. The knife, fork, an' spoon are not to eat with. The knife cuts away the path, the fork clears it, the spoon digs." There are continuous prayers and instruction. Each Saint who appears to a mourner tells "what things he don' like to eat. Some don' like smoke, some other things."

"Spiritual tasks" are shown them. "Reading, not the

Bible, but religious books" that pertain to the Bible, such
as "The Manual of Devotion," "The Guide to God," "Pil-
grim's Progress," "The Prince of the House of David," and
the "chapter of the Bible with wisdom, called Book of Maccabees." Those mourning are conceived as "travelling a
path" to Glory, as many of the images already quoted indicate. From their travels, they "bring the psalms they want
read, new hymns, chapters (of the Bible) . The members of-
the congregation come there to build them up, help them
in prayin'." Sometimes a message for the teacher, or the
church, or for things to be done for them is brought back
from this journey to "Glory," and "They call what they
see," as they kneel, or sit or lie.

At the end of the period, most of them know such "gifts"
as it is their lot to possess — if it is their first time in the
mournin' groun' — or, if they had been through mourning
before, the higher gift which gives them greater status in
the church. One teacher compared the gifts that are acquired to the education of a child. "There are seven standards in the spiritual world. After each mournin', you get
higher gift." One man, the Father of his church, held a different conception of the purpose of repeating the mourning
experience. "If you been to mournin' before the 'power'
gets cold; [after a time] you got to go again to hear what the
spirit will tell." Still another view made the point that it is
possible to return from a second or third visit to the mourning ground reduced in spiritual powers rather than aug-
mented. This would result only, however, "if your life is
not correct."

Not all are successful. "Some mourn and bring nothin'.
Mistress Small mourn *six* times. Bring nothin'. They flogs
her enough." Others who have had the same experience are
not so persevering. "Mistress Brooks went once, come back
with nothin'. Don' mourn again, just stop being member."
The gifts they bring back have to be "sealed in writing."

Members who go in more than once "come out of each mournin' with a new name for each new gift. They have saints' names — John, Joseph — even for a woman."

When the mourners emerge from their retreat, they are received back into the church in an important ceremony. First of all they are bathed by the teachers and "nurse," and are fed. Each then is told the head-bands to be worn — bands assigned by the teacher in accordance with the dreams and visions she, or the mourner, or both have had. These bands differ in color in accordance with the quality of a person's spirit. Over all of them, however, is worn the "baptism band," of white, that covered the eyes during the rituals when the member was baptized, so that outsiders do not know of the three or seven colored bands each mourner may wear. Three bands are worn at the ceremony of emergence.

Symbolic significance of the bands associates white with purity; yellow with glory; red with power — "It's the blood of Jesus" — green with peace; blue and pink with truth; mauve with mystery; and black and brown with "power, air power, African."

The color symbolism was further developed by one teacher as representing specific relationships to specific saints of the church. It was not possible to obtain from other sources corroboration of so close an association of the saints with the "spiritual Baptist" worship, lacking which it is offered as an extreme deviant from orthodox Baptist or other Protestant practice. The list which appears below is therefore given as it was detailed by this teacher.

COLOR	FEMALE	MALE
brown	St. Mount Carmel	St. Joseph, St. Michael, St. Anthony
green	Lady St. Anne	St. Patrick
red	St. Catherine	St. John

COLOR	FEMALE	MALE
yellow	Mysteries of God, Glory	Ascension
blue	Immaculate Conception, St. Mary, Mother of Christ, St. Theresa	Ezekiel
white	purity — the dove purity — the Holy Spirit	
black	"I forget the name of the Saint in black."	Resurrection, Death

With each mourner wearing three bands, then, the white on top, "like batteries of a torch (flashlight) — three batteries, but only one light," and carrying two bouquets, each with five candles for the Virgin, they march in procession three times about the church. The standard bearer, the shepherd, and the leader are first, then comes the priest. Those who have been in the mourning ground are next, followed by the teacher, the congregation, and finally the pastor. The church is decorated this Sunday night, for it is a festive occasion. "Have same as bride." This was elaborated: "If man come for king and has money, get fine things for him, and a crown."

When prayers are over, the mourners who are seated at the altar are called upon in turn "to give their tracts." Each, addressed by his new name which he has brought back from mournin', stands before the congregation and says in salutation, "Good night, brothers and sisters. Good night, teacher." The band on the forehead protects the eyes, now, from the unaccustomed light. The mourner sings or speaks, as he is impelled to do by his spirit. "If he must give a hymn first, he gives it." But before he speaks or sings, he is anointed by the "priest." "They get oil that smells nice. And when they are consecrated, they smoke incense for them." Sometimes when a tract is given — that is, a sermon is preached or a testimonial offered — "the spirit is manifest in the camp." Then all rejoice at the power this mourner has brought back, and though happenings of this kind prolong the ceremony — "sometimes it last till two o'clock" — none of those who have emerged from the mournin' groun' may forego this rite.

Before the newly emerged mourners are ready to resume the secular tasks of their daily lives, they must be protected from the ill effects of a too hurried transition from the trance-like state of mournin', and consequently they remain secluded for several days more — three, if there are people at home to care for them, otherwise nine days. "They mustn't handle a knife or cutlass, or spend money. It would hurt their sight."

5

Because the Shouters sect is proscribed by law, it is understandably not easy for an outsider to attain a position of confidence which permits him to be present at services where possession occurs. Except for minor deviations from conventional patterns, notably the chalked symbols found on the church floor, and the pouring of water in the four corners, nothing in the regular Sunday or Wednesday services differentiates them from services held at any legally approved Baptist church. The decorous behavior of the congregation, the nature of the sermon, the type of prayers offered at such services are, as a matter of fact, far closer to European conventions of religious behavior than that of the American Negro "shouting" churches, North or South.

The music heard at such a service illustrates this point. Shouters, like those of other evangelical denominations, sing and enjoy singing what they term "Sankeys," — the hymns from the well-known Sankey and Moody hymn-book.

These songs are sung as written, but the manner of singing emphasizes a certain lugubrious quality by means of drawn notes and slurs from one tone to another, rendered at full voice, and with a kind of paradoxical enthusiasm by the singers.

The memory of the song-leaders — the more important officials of the congregation — is prodigious, for in each rendition, every verse of the hymn being sung is exacted, and the volume of sound increases from verse to verse as the congregation solidifies its attack on the melody. A passage from the diary kept during this field research may be cited to illustrate the perplexing question which this singing posed when the setting of the dimly lit bare church with its earthen floor brought to mind services in equally humble settings in the United States: "What is baffling is the miracle that produced the American spirituals, and the historical reasons for the acceptance by the folk in these islands of the hymns just as the Whites sing them."

But just as the essential rites of the cult are carried on beneath an overlay of conventionalized decorum, so these "Sankeys" also mask more vigorous musical forms. This was disclosed when a recording was being made of the hymn "Jesus, Lover of My Soul," as part of a collection of songs which had as its object to cover the total range of Toco music, in which the Sankeys, whatever their derivation and affiliation, are of such importance. After two verses, the singers, continuing the melody, began to change their rhythm, introducing hand-clapping as the tempo became faster, until the hymn was transmuted into a swing idiom which in the proper setting would result in the spirit possession that was simulated in the sounds made by the singers on the record. All this is apparent in the transcription of the song, as given here:

Jesus, Lover of My Soul

Also to be encountered on closer acquaintance are the "spiritual" hymns that, as mentioned, are improvisations dictated by "the spirit." It is told, "The spiritual hymns are the shoutin' hymns. It's the spirit sing it, give the words, the lure." A few examples of the verses will show the nature of these improvisations:

> "Where are you been
> When de firs' trumpet soun'?
> Where are you been
> An' it soun' so loud,
> An' it soun' so hard,

As to wake up de dead?
Where are you been
When de firs' trumpet soun'? "

"We shall wear a starry crown,
In the mornin', praise the Lord!
We shall wear a crown,
A hallelujah crown,
Oh, yes!"

"Me mother (brother, sister) dis mornin'
She gone along home.
She gone away to Glory,
She gone along home."

In the rituals of the sect, as well, the restraints that impress on initial acquaintance are found to give way to vigorous, energetic forms of worship that, as has been pointed out, have an emotional appeal even for those not themselves Shouters, because its expression is in an idiom that flows out of the beliefs of the membership, and is equally understandable to those who come as spectators.

Descriptions may now be given of some of the services that were witnessed — a Sunday-night prayer-meeting, a Sunday morning "preachin'," the dedication of the site for a new "temple," and a Sunday night service where the full range of Shouters rituals was present.

The evening prayer and testimonial meeting that constituted the first contact with any Shouters group, was inordinately subdued, with barely audible interpolations from the congregation to punctuate the pauses in sermon and testimonials, and the singing of the Sankeys giving forth a heavy, doleful, dragging effect. On this occasion, there were some fifteen to eighteen people present. The vigor of the singing and the excellence of the voices were the only distinguishing things about the rendition of the six hymns that were sung. Singing was always done standing up; when there was a prayer, everyone knelt facing the altar. All were barefooted, and most of the women wore white kerchiefs.

Prayers and testimonials gave the same quotations from the Bible heard in American Negro churches. The rambling discourse laid emphasis on being saved and, as a distinctive turn, emphasized how Jesus was as poor as they were, but that their poverty would not stand in their way of attaining grace. The preacher testified first; then there was a hymn; then the "Father" of the church spoke, an able speaker, and a moving one, describing their poverty and their persecution, with obvious reference to the court action taken recently against the Shouters. Next the stout teacher who sat with her back to the altar, facing the congregation "testified"; then a hymn; then a prayer by a lad who knelt and held a candle as he half-chanted his rhythmic and almost metered plea; then a hymn; and finally another half-chanted benediction by the "Mother" of the church. There was no collection, and no request for offerings.

At the Sunday morning "preachin'" and the dedication later that day there was at least an approach to "shaking." Somewhat greater confidence in the presence of outsiders, and the participation of a visiting preacher of some renown in Shouting circles, perhaps accounted for this. At eleven o'clock, when the service was to begin, the people were just assembling. The women, who came in white dresses and hats, went behind the little church-building to change their hats for white head-kerchiefs, while most of them put white aprons over their dresses. The men wore clean clothing, in most cases white coats. Two of the women wore lavender dresses, one was in a brown dress, and two wore blue nurse-maid uniforms. "Naked red they don' wear," was said of the dress of these churchgoers, "but white with red flowers they love too much."

As the services began, shoes were removed, but not stockings or socks, and in kneeling to pray, a handkerchief was spread on the ground to protect the clean clothing. The church was spotlessly clean, with freshly laundered cloths on tables and altar. What had appeared a white flag over the altar turned out to be pale violet in daylight; the crosses about the center pole and the designs at the doors were not newly chalked for the occasion. At the base of the center pole was a jam jar filled with flowers, the bell, and an unlighted candle, but not the Bible that had been lying behind it the other evening. A lighted candle stood on the altar, that had its four vases of flowers.

The visiting preacher, who with the Father of the church appeared at about 11:15, was from a town near San Fernando. He changed into a clean white gown, with a white cord which was knotted several times with the ends hanging down the side. As the services opened there were fourteen people present, but the little place filled somewhat as the ritual went on, and at the end there were at least twenty-five adults and about ten children, who comported themselves much as they pleased, though noiselessly, while several of them slept.

An invocation was followed by a hymn — the preacher reading the entire text, then lining out the first half of every stanza. Several prayers by women, each followed by a hymn, preceded the prayer by the Father of the church. His "Thank you's" for blessings received, were in a quiet, conversational manner, as if the beings he addressed were close at hand and asked for neither rhetoric nor oratory. After the next hymn, the congregation remained standing while the Gloria, in English, was repeated by all.

Seats were resumed for the first scripture reading, which concerned the law (Exodus 21:5, 6) that a Hebrew servant must go free after six years of service; but that if his master had given him a wife who had borne him children, and he wished to remain with his family, he must be taken before the judges, and say "I will serve my master, I will not go free," whereupon a hole is to be bored in his ear with an awl "and he shall serve him forever." Again a hymn marked the interval between the first and the second scripture reading, this time from Paul's Epistles, then followed the Credo, in English, recited by all standing, and yet another hymn.

Sermon, hymn, benediction, and collection succeeded each other in orderly sequence, both preacher and congregation restrained, with but one emotional passage where allusion was made to the persecution of the group. The only observable evidences of nervousness were that one woman who entered the church while a hymn was in progress, knelt down in the aisle and began to "jerk," but quickly controlled herself; while another began to pat the ground; doubling the time of a hymn, and then quieting down. Services were over at 12:55, an early dismissal for this group, called for by reason of the scheduled rite of consecration of the site for their new church, at half-past three.

The visiting preacher also officiated at the dedication of the new "temple" being built by this group. The site was up a bypath, removed from the main road, on a sharply sloping hill, so that one side of it was a deep trench, behind a central mound of earth yet to be excavated. At the northwest corner a post hole had been dug, and at about the center of the north side was a small table, covered with a clean white cloth on which were a jar with water and flowers, and the bell; behind this stood the preacher as he began the services. The Father stood near the post hole; the members of the congregation, more numerous than at the morning service, stood grouped nearby. A number of playing children were about including a little boy not yet four years old, who was responding with the "Amens" and "Hallelujahs" during the prayers, and repeating the Lord's Prayer after the preacher, with all the assurance of a full-fledged member of the group.

The service began at 3:40 with the customary alternation of hymns, prayers, hymns, then the reading of the psalms, followed by another hymn, and a discourse by the preacher, based on the concept that consecrating ground must be secondary to consecrating people. With lighted white candle in one hand, and the bell in the other, the stout teacher next accompanied the Mother of the church to the four corners of the excavation, where she rang the bell three times as the Mother three times poured water from the jam jar holding the flowers. The preacher accompanied by four additional persons proceeded to dedicate the same four corners, reading a psalm, and offering up a prayer at each corner.

Emotion was shown when the Mother, praying at the southeastern corner, came to ask God's favor for the Father of the church. Her voice broke and she cried out "Oh, Father! Oh! Father . . . !" but the embankment intervened so that it was not possible to see whether she "shook" or not. Similarly, after making the tour of the four corners, the preacher stood just west of the unexcavated mound of earth, saying, "I shall take this for the center," and the Father himself prayed. Deeply moved, his shaking threw him from a kneeling to a sitting position, but he recovered quickly and continued with his prayer.

A number of details were recorded. Only those who offered up prayers knelt, and no shoes were removed. Care was taken to observe what offerings would be put into the hole with the "cornerstone," which was a block of wood, but the only one observed was a threepenny piece, tossed into the hole by one of the men present who stepped up just before the four-by-four post was lowered. The benediction was at 4:45, and as it ended and the handshaking with the preacher began, the shouting hymn, "Of the Church and

the Chapel" was started. This was the accompaniment to the
ritual handshake exchanged with everyone present, three
downward shakes of the right hand, then the hands elevated
above the head, the touching of the left breast of first one
and then the other party to the handshake, and a final downward shake.

6

To have pressed the Toco Shouters for permission to visit
those ceremonies where they worship their God in a manner proscribed by law would have been unfair. It is enough
to say here that for these rites they go elsewhere, carrying
out the services where "shouting," properly speaking, can
be indulged in, as is not possible in their own "temple,"
situated in so small a community and so close to a main
road.

The description of the Shouting service which follows,
therefore, recounts the worship of a group in another town
not far from Toco. This congregation, like others in the
area, has liaison with Shouters of the whole northeastern
portion of the Island; acquaintance with a number of its
members and officers, made and renewed in Toco itself,
made possible attendance at this ritual. It is worthy of note
that, despite the remoteness of the "temple" from a main
road, an efficient watch-dog gave notice during the services,
when anyone approached, while along the path leading to
the compound where the "temple" was situated, watchers
were stationed.

At 6:30, the beginning of the service, the teacher chalked
a design on the floor inside the entrance door. At the same
time she started a hymn. Candles were lighted and passed
around to those who needed them to read their hymn-books,
and as the singing went on and more people began to drift
in, all possible places were "consecrated" — the four corner

altars, the principal altar and the one at the base of the central post, the doors and windows — by pouring water from the flower-glass three times at each place, and ringing the big bell three times. Water was also thrown on the floor about the central altar at each cardinal point of the compass, and in front of the subsidiary altars. Song succeeded song — all slow Sankeys — with the group becoming steadily larger and the teacher supervising quietly and efficiently.

A singer went down on his knees and gave the first prayer, interspersed with songs and following the pattern, by now familiar, of using verses from hymns to fill in or, in the instance of one or two younger men, to give them an interval to overcome reserve. When the singer rose, candle and flowers in hand, he went over to a young woman in a grey dress who proved to be the teacher's most gifted disciple, herself leader of a church. With her, and later with the teacher and one or two others, this man shook hands, in the ceremonial "proving" manner, already described, and from this woman in grey he received a curtsy as he finished. It should be added that during the period of preparation the teacher did "writing" along a candle, which was used by all those later possessed by the "spirit."

The singing was not so "warm" as the leader wished it to be, and she called out "Sing, children!" telling the song leader not to "do any cold turkey." This had the immediate effect of producing singing of such fervor, that the leader for a moment began to shake. By this time the room had filled. Among those present were a Hindu woman and her daughter, who did not participate in the service except by joining in the hymn-singing from time to time, and who left early.

At about eight o'clock, the teacher herself began to pray. The singer had been succeeded by one of the other men, who carried on effectively in a soft voice that rarely went up in volume. Taking the candle and flowers from him after the approved handshaking, putting out the light and re-lighting the candle from the "eternal light" at the central altar, the teacher went to the door where her shepherd's crook — full size, and beautifully made of dark wood — was hanging, and took a place in front of the railing at the extreme right, where she had a seat and from which she thenceforth directed proceedings. Kneeling in this corner, facing the central altar, she offered up one of the rambling prayers characteristic of these meetings, punctuated with song in which the members joined, and dropping into "tongues" several times for some minutes at a time.

Her manner of praying was quiet, and with no apparent effort she roused her congregation to a high pitch of excite-ment. When her prayer, which took about fifteen minutes — not much longer than that of the others — was ended, and the song that followed it was in progress, she walked to the central altar and rang the bell there three times. Next the flowers and candle went to her disciple, who prayed in a loud voice for some time, and also stimulated some spirited singing. Then she, too, rang the bell at the central altar three times, and returned the candle to the teacher who handed it to a young lad who was quite aroused — his hand went backward and forward constantly in a sidewise mo-tion. The congregation of perhaps fifty sang the hymns that punctuated his prayer with an enthusiasm thus far not equalled.

At this time, too, the "jazzing" of a Sankey hymn at an actual service was first heard — the people here carrying the melodic line sung slightly faster, while the song-leader and a few others ornamented it with harmonized "ram-bam-bam, bam, bam, ram-a-bam," simulating drums and mak-ing the song irresistible to patting feet, and hand-clapping. It was sung toward the end of this youth's "testimony," when, overcome by the spirit, he danced on his knees, mov-ing backward and forward in a kind of body-swing while he also "danced" the candle and glass with flowers which he held.

He staggered to his feet, drenched with perspiration. After his handshakes, the teacher gave the candle and glass to an elderly man, also a teacher, who moved to one side to pray facing the main altar, first inspecting the maroon flag. Since he had forgotten to remove his shoes, this was done for him as he knelt. His disjointed effort did not stimulate the group as had the prayer that preceded it, but the hymns that he introduced were well sung.

The teacher now gave candle and flowers to a tall young man at the other end of the church, who began in a halting, hesitant manner, with words issuing forth with difficulty. He went over the words of several songs before he could speak, until "he catch de spirit," it was whispered; as he went on, his rising eloquence caused the choruses of response to swell. The hymn on which he ended was sung over and over until it gradually fell into a swinging dance rhythm, and brought about the second possession of the evening. The youth who had prayed and afterwards knelt and danced, now danced again, as did some of the men who had been sitting on the bench along the side wall.

One man in particular, who from time to time had shown signs of possession, and had shaken violently but had been restrained by the teacher, was now allowed to dance part way down the west side of the church toward the other possessed young man, while the song leader shook a bit and did a kind of foot-patting dance that gave a further basic rhythm to the massed song. The teacher also began to shake, and danced toward the other end of the church, but all evening her "possessions" in which she shook and threw herself from one foot to another, hopping to regain her balance, seemed to rob her of none of her awareness of the things about her — an awareness that was not present in any of the others except, on one occasion, perhaps, that of the song leader. It was almost 8:45, and the teacher passed the flowers in their glass and the candle to her disciple, who now held a Bible, and who was to "read the lesson," which was the chapter that set forth the miracle of the loaves and fishes.

Before she began, the leader handed her the bell, which she held with one hand on top of the Bible; the candle and flowers were in the other. She read well, though the reading dropped into Negro-English often enough, and then she preached for about twenty minutes. Her discourse was made up of the customary weaving together of quotations from the Bible and the words of hymns, and contained many requests for remission of sin. Once or twice she "talked tongues."

As she finished, she knelt in front of the central altar and began to pray. The singing became hotter and hotter, and the young man who had been dancing earlier resumed his dance. This time the response from the congregation was electric. The men on the side bench were dancing; one of them, like the teacher herself, went shaking clear around the central altar, hopping on one foot, until he settled into his dance step. The singer shook and danced alternately; two women in white danced and shook in place; while a church assistant in training, her head bound with a kerchief, who watched the door, also shook in place — hands clenched, arms half-raised, her angular frame shaken by a continuous quivering of the arms that extended itself to the entire body. What happened to the hymn that "bring a strong spirit to rejoice everybody" was as interesting musically as the dancing was dramatically, for it almost disappeared in the "ram-bam-i-bam-bam" of the full-throated song leader.

After a time, most of the dancers began to quiet down, but one of them continued to grow more and more excited, and "got the spirit" strongly, continuing to cry in the rhythm of the song that was no longer being sung, as it had been succeeded by another prayer, intended as a final one. The visiting male teacher got him to kneel while he was still shaking and crying out, and then forced a Bible into his hands. Gradually the possessed man calmed down sufficiently to be able to testify when the candle and flowers were handed him by the teacher. His intense possession at an hour so late in the service presented a special problem, for since the spirit had entered him, he had to testify no matter what the time, and the ten o'clock deadline of the law had already passed.

This last prayer, though an anticlimax to the dance of a few moments before, proved to be the most moving incident of the entire evening. The man could barely speak, and the candle shook in his hand causing the hot wax to drop on his upper arm and on the floor. He seemed obsessed by a sense of guilt, and his broken pleas for forgiveness were more coherent, more marked, and far less a matter of phrases than those of any of the others. As he prayed the teacher began a hymn, softly, so that the sound of his words was progressively blurred by the voices of the congregation repeating the hymn again and again in a sustained crescendo that finally drowned the voice of the supplicant, until he arose and gave his hand in the "proving" handshake that must end any possession. Again, he was barely able to control his shaking, though the teacher's caressing gestures did much to help him regain control of himself. After "proving" the disciple and several other members, his state of possession passed completely, and the services were brought to a close, at about 10:30, with the recital of the Credo and some other liturgical passages.

CHAPTER IX

DIVINATION AND MAGIC

THAT THE DESTINY that rules the lives of men can be read
by those who have "sight," is a fundamental conviction of
the Tocoan. Equally forceful is the belief that such reading
can be enlisted in behalf of the individual to give him security in his daily pursuits, and power to enhance his personal fortunes, whether these be keyed to economic goals,
or to amorous ends. The specific manner of achieving this
security finds expression in diverse forms, but may be said
to be met chiefly in the category of magic called the "guard,"
while the powers that enable the individual to pursue ends
of personal aggrandizement derive from the opposing category, known as the "trick." These two magical categories
must, however, be supplemented by the range of practices
that enter into the curing complex of all those illnesses that
are diagnosed by those with "sight" as caused by supernatural rather than natural agents. "It be sickness doctor can'
cure."

Those with "sight," the diviners, are generally called
lookmen, but sometimes the proscribed name obiaman is
used. A practitioner who is one of the "church people" is
called a teacher. To these may be added the "bucks" or
"Warahun," inhabitants of the Venezuelan shore, who are
said to be exceedingly small of stature, appearing for their
"work" in loin-cloths, harpoon in hand. They are reputed
to be among the most powerful workers of magic, and a

lore has sprung up about their cures. Akin to these "bucks" is the occasional visiting *Kpanyol* (Venezuelan of Spanish descent) , one of whom was induced to explain at length his oraisons, and their effectiveness in protecting against evil.

Before examining the differences in method, if not in function, that may exist between types of professional workers of magic, we may indicate their common activities. All those who "look," who divine, not only diagnose an illness, but see to its cure; not only interpret a dream, but direct the steps to be taken to fulfill the wish of the supernatural agent who sent the dream; or fashion the guard to ward off the evil that a vigilant ancestor had warned of in the dream as impending. They also use their powers, after they have "seen" obstacles in the way of the fulfilment of a desired end, to clear these from the path of ambition by providing the consultant with a trick.

How do the Tocoans differentiate a lookman, an obiaman, and a teacher who "looks"? "Is the same work they do. But when you speak about teacher, you careful. Don' say 'Lookman'. Say, 'You mean the Baptist woman that does look?' " Another comment was, "Lookman and obiaman the same thing. Don't talk about obia much. The law is against it. Is against look, too, but obiaman is name they use behin' man's back." Nonetheless, obia, it was explained, performs good and evil. It cures as well as harms, depending upon what the powers that actuate it are asked to do. "Obia, m'lord, is the signature of roots according to the planets," observed one of the erudite practitioners, who had read many books on magic, including Albertus Magnus, the "Eminence of God," the Master Key, and the Lesser Key, as well as the brochures of de Laurence of Chicago.

An obiaman or lookman works with a familiar, it is said. "All obiamen keep snakes. Snake is the spirit of a dead person, a dead person who was cast out. That's why it know everything. Obiaman can work with fowl-cock, too; can work with man. The dead does manifest themselves in different ways to work for those who command them." A teacher, who can be either a man or a woman, is usually of the Shouters' group. "Baptists get visions. They sit back meditating, and that's how visions come," it was stated; or, again, "A teacher sit back, meditate, then begin to shake. It's the spirit. Then she talk." Sometimes, after the meditation, the teacher will open at random to a page in the Bible, and there will find lines telling of the trials that the consultant is about to undergo, or the means to rid himself of them.

One of the teachers was asked, "How does this spirit that comes in the mourning ground and teaches in a dream or a vision what bush to take to heal, or what danger is impending, differ from the spirit that comes to a lookman and tells him the same thing?" The answer was thoughtful, and given with humility. "You're asking m'lord, something that is not clear to me, too. I seen a man lying so sick he couldn' lif' a hand; so sick, he was almost dead. Then the lookman came, and he brought a man with a fiddle and another with a tambourine, and they play, play. Sweet music the fiddle makes, yes?" With the power of this sweet music and what rites this lookman had performed in privacy, the man arose and danced, and before long he was cured. "The power we get comes from the Holy Ghost," was added in conclusion, "but the lookman keeps a familiar."

Still probing the beliefs that accompany this differentiation, he was asked, "What is the familiar? Is it the soul?" The reply was emphatic, "No, m'lord, the soul belong to God." Was it then the shadow? Again the answer was unhesitant, "What is the shadow? It's like a viper, or like the wind. It's here, it's there and it's gone. The familiar is the spirit part of a person. What part is it? Well, if the Devil make a familiar out of me, will it be Johnson? Look like

Johnson, yes, but it's him, the Devil, taking the face of somebody that die!"

According to a villager of experience, who as a man of property, and being actuated by curiosity as well as need, had delved into the matter of magic, the role of Satan was clear. "Obia itself, and the jumby that is the messenger who carries out the instructions of the worker of magic, come from the Devil." But Satan, it was stressed, can do good as well as evil. "Even Jesus used Beelzebub, you know," was given as an illustration of the point. The dead, the real dead, he continued, even if they "are bad, bad people" lie quietly in their graves awaiting judgment day, whereas the manifestation that emerges in answer to the summons issued through the use of magic books or traditional methods is that of Satan.

An obiaman, one of the most prosperous of the region, who during the first few visits pointedly denied that his form of healing had anything to do with obia, also maintained that Satan is the source of obia. "Even when there is a cure, it is Satan trying you out, luring you," he said. The power to effect real cures lay in the elements, for all things are either fire, water, earth, or air. "I use the elements when I cure, and it is always something that no doctor could cure. They come to me, after they have tried many doctors." When he cured with a stone, for example, a blue-veined stone with a cross in the center, part of the power was in the stone and the other in the belief of the sick. As for himself, he liked best to cure with the aid of a medium. "What I know came down to me from my family, and what I have learned since;" but he added, speaking with the candor of a confederate, when talking about cures and other miracles that are performed with the right knowledge, it is important to talk about "natural science," for if it were claimed that these involved supernatural aids, "there would be trouble with the law."

Another distinction was made between the lookman or obiaman on the one hand, and the teacher who "looks" on the other. "The lookman work for you for an agreed amount. If you don' have cash, pay with a pig, or a goat, and some cash you have. Sometimes credit you for the balance. But if you don' pay, he spoil you. You afraid not to pay." In contradistinction the teacher often declares that he does not wish payment, saying that the power to read the "unknown" comes from the "spirit." Nevertheless, "If they really help you now, you only too glad to give. You give them first two shilling, and say that this will help buy cyandles for the altar. Nex' week you give egg, give fowl. You progressing now, earning something, you come and give a dollar, and say that is for sweet oil." In the end the teacher receives more than the lookman. "If everything goin' fine, you only too glad."

Whether a man goes to a lookman, or an obiaman, or a teacher will depend upon the importance of the errand and the reputed skill of the practitioner for the particular problem facing him. For while it may be assumed that Shouters, for example, will visit a teacher, those of the much larger group who have other church affiliations choose among all the practitioners. Many examples, met at first hand, show clearly that selection is based on reputation of competence, and the person's ability to pay a required fee. In important decisions, or on occasions in which secrecy is a special factor, Tocoans often go to the capital to consult practitioners of the Shango groups. In one instance, an Anglican communicant said, "I lookin', lookin' for a good obiaman right now. If you are a mother, you want to know what will happen to your daughter. Even if she not marry, you want to know if the keeper and she going to live good, or he go leave her in two, three month . . ."

Among the older men who, as non-professionals, are concerned with magical practices, great interest was expressed

in the books of de Laurence who furnishes tracts on healing, and magic formulae of various kinds. "The work that
de Laurence does is a correct Baptist work. They are taught
in the spirit," and one man illustrated by showing some
symbols that were in his house:

The drawing meant prosperity, but it was also interpreted
as signifying "God the Father, God the Son, God the Holy
Ghost." While de Laurence's publications are held to incorporate both the wisdom of the ancients and more recent
occult discoveries, the Petit and Grand Albert, and the
volumes already mentioned, such as "Man, Know Thyself,"
and "The Eminence of God," and the "Greater Key" and
"Lesser Key," as well as the Apocrypha, are studied by
groups of three or four men who form a "little society" and
share the cost of buying these publications.

2

Among the principal causes for seeking out a diviner, of
whatever category, is that of ill health, when, "You try
many things and don' get better." Failure of home remedies,
the doctor's prescription, and the clinic to effect a cure
would indicate that the cause and cure must be sought in
supernatural terms. If, as a modest beginning, some offerings were given to the ancestors, and no help had come, the
suspicion that some "powerful workman" had been set
against the unfortunate patient would merely be verified.
Steps would then be taken in haste to ascertain the nature
of this enemy, and the way to overcome his power. Another
cause for a visit to a lookman would be to get "luck for a

job, or for a journey." A mother, anxious for her daughter
to marry an acceptable young man, would go to a diviner.
She would wish to discover, first of all, whether this would
be a "good marriage" for her daughter, unopposed by ancestors; at the same time she would seek to provide herself
with special aids to assure its consummation. "If you have
a case in court, you always sees a lookman first," was said,
while if a man had an important business transaction to conclude, such as a contract to sign, or land to buy, he would
wish to make certain that the undertaking would be profitable and without mishap.

A woman would consult a diviner on how to keep her
husband, if he had shown unduly wayward tendencies. She
would also ask advice of a diviner if her husband had been
taken away from her by another woman. In such a case she
would seek means either to compel him to return to her, or
to revenge herself against her rival. A man jilted by a
woman in favor of a more prosperous rival, and knowing
that the step was taken not because of loss of affection for
him, would go to a diviner and ask for revenge against the
man and the faithless girl. Anyone who harbored a grudge
against another would go to a practitioner of magic, as
would a person who suspected the existence of such a
grudge, since he would wish to secure a special guard to
ward off the machinations of the enemy, because "He afraid
now that the enemy is trying to keep him down. Afraid his
luck will go, if he doing well."

We have but to recall, as additional instances, the cultivator who acquires new land on which is found a silk-cotton tree, or an ant-hill, or through whose land, newly to be
put under cultivation, a brook flows. To these may be
added protection in the form of a specially prepared guard
against the pilfering of his crops, or to render harmless the
evil eye of the envious as they pass a finely bearing
field.

The several consultations that precede marriage are a commonplace. Later there are visits for a first pregnancy, and if parturition proves difficult, the diviner is summoned, that he may supplement the efforts of doctor and midwife. A breech presentation, even where there are no serious consequences to the health of the mother, calls for a visit to the lookman, who advises what enemy power caused this abnormal occurrence. When successive children are short-lived, the diviner determines the cause, and takes measures that there be no repetition. Certain children's ailments, if recognized as not falling in the group for which there are home remedies or "things in the doctor-shop," are also referred to the healer who is a specialist in diagnosing supernatural sicknesses, and providing for their cure.

Significant is the fact that in all discussions of the work of these professional diviners and healers, no skepticism was heard about the general principle of the ability of those who have "sight" to reveal the ways of Destiny. Nor was there any doubt that such knowledge makes possible the effecting of miraculous cures, and as miraculously the circumventing of impending danger, or the favoring with the good things of the earth those who do the bidding of the supernatural agents that these specialists control.

Failure of an individual practitioner in a specific case is attributed to his losing strength because of abuse of his powers for pecuniary ends. "The spirit don' be glad to do bad." Or if the tales of feats performed by the adepts of earlier days reflect discredit on the lookmen of today, this is explained as being due to the reluctance of these earlier lookmen to disclose their secret knowledge to their successors.

"Old ones don' tell their children much. If they asked, say, they tell someday, when child more ripe (mature). Then they die." This was held to be the reason, too, why these knowledgeable dead appear in dreams to counsel their

descendants, or appear as strangers during a healing ceremony to assist the obiaman engaged for the occasion. This
is interpreted as though in death they felt compelled to continue their solicitude for the well being of the living, because in life they had failed to transfer their powers to a
successor.

3

The favored hour for consultations is either noon or midnight. Another person is customarily brought along when
calling on a diviner. Each practitioner has his individual
method of "looking." One man, the report tells, puts on a
round black cap over a red cloth that reaches below the eyes
as it hangs loosely about the head, while others tie the head
with a large black cloth, the ends hanging down in back,
and wear a black cloak. "Goin' to work with you now," was
the interpolation. He wears a necklace of beads, with a large
wooden cross suspended from it. "That cross have a little
Jesus on it." About his wrist is "a thing plaited with twine,
like little tassels. You knot the thing to look like that."

He may have an iron armband on his upper arm, or an
armband of cord, and anklets of woven palm, but consultants do not see whether he wears a charm about his waist.
"You there in the room, sitting down, and the lookman
talk, and he goin' in and out a nex' room. Must be some
other person there. You hear a voice comes out, and he
speaks 'language,' and you only catch a word. You don' go
in that room at all. Only he comin' out." The reference to
"language" is to some unknown tongue, which the lookman interprets as he returns to the room where the consultant is seated.

Some lookmen use "thunder-stones" both when they
divine and when they cure. "They have round stones, and I
saw one was black and flat, and two had the points sharp,

sharp, and very pretty and shiny," one woman described her latest visit. The obiaman had told her, "I know where to find these stones after the thunder pass." Divining is done also by peering into a water jug, or by watching a candle as it burns in the centre of a white plate.

A usual initial fee is two shillings, but "When he start to work you got to pay him." If he comes to the consultant's house this fee might be as high as two dollars. In one instance, the consultant had been told to have on hand a pint of rum, a pound of very white onions, and a pint of molasses, to be cooked together. The lookman lay flat on his back on a cot in the room next to the one of the woman he was treating, a bowl of water beside him, and in his hand an egg. From the cot in the adjoining room, he spoke, telling the nature of the spirit that had been sent to the woman, telling whether it had been sent by a man or woman, and the reason it was sent. "Then he come in, he shaking now. Then he throw the egg at me. It must break on person, not on the ground."

He next added herbs to some water and "bathed" the patient with this, and before leaving he had the mixture of rum, onions, molasses, and other ingredients which he himself had furnished, pounded and put into a bottle. He sprinkled this about the house, and gave instructions to repeat this every night for three nights. "When I go back now, he ask how I feel, and say spirit is coming together." He then named the price for exorcising the spirit, and asked for rice and a fowl, among other things. "When he have all this, he catch spirit in a bottle. He throw the food from the house to the road calling names, especially in the Congo language. He call

> Kwaka adja ma hambe Brebna
> Me Joe-Peter, me Congo Brown
> Me come out a Guinea."

At midnight, with the utmost secrecy, as the four men who assisted him in his exorcism rowed out to sea, the bottle was thrown into the water. "Then they call the dead, the proper workmen, but they dead. There is plenty rum, you know." When they return to the patient's house, they beat a drum; but softly, so that if by good fortune they had not been observed, there would be no gossip, and above all that the "law" would not be apprised of the proceedings. "They buil' a little fire," on the earthen floor, "and drum softly, softly, and sing

> Me Congo Brown,
> Me a go home morning time,
> Me a come tonight."

The concluding treatment, and the exorcising rite, cost the patient five dollars, and might have been more. "But I cured now," said the teller of this account, and explained that the lookman had left her a guard to ward off future recurrences of spirit mischief.

It would seem profitable at this point to explore more fully the concept that a "spirit" can be responsible for illnesses and mishaps, or that the dead are "proper workmen" when a healing ceremony takes place. In this region, as, in fact, in the entire Carribean area, a generic name for such a spirit is *jumby*. We have seen that there are differences of opinion as to what type of spirit the jumby represents. It was held, for example, that a jumby is the spirit of a dead person who is diverted from peaceful rest in the grave by the machinations of a practitioner of magic, and is put to work as an agent of such a practitioner in his profession, doing his bidding, unseen, and, until the mischief is done, unperceived by the victim.

Similarly, the view was expressed that a jumby is the spirit of a dead person, but one who had in life been evil, or of a restless man, who neither in life nor death could achieve tranquility, or of an angered dead, who had not received from his family a fitting burial, or of one who had been the victim of malpractices at the hands of a man more powerful than himself. It is even stated that when important "work" is to be done, a practitioner of magic will provide a spirit for the exclusive use of the consultant. This might be one that the practitioner has on hand, or someone, not too long dead, from the man's own family — "somebody bright" whom he summons. Then again, there is the opinion that the jumby is not a manifestation of someone dead but an emanation from Satan, made corporeal by assuming the features of some human being who had lived in the region. This is held to be logically possible, for Satan is both one and many, and his power is everywhere just as is that of God.

The divergence of opinion, however, is not on the existence of the jumby, but its source of origin; not on its role in the execution of the will of the practitioner of magic, but whether there is any self-determination in the work it does. The long discussions heard on these points were pursued as much for the pleasure of the theme itself, as for any desire to arrive at a solution. Of interest, as illuminating the world-view of the community, is the unanimity of belief that no magic formula, however potent, and no compounding of ingredients, however effective, will of themselves achieve the desired result. "Something that have understanding," must be employed, it is said, something that has had life, and can be made to move, to enter unseen habitations, and otherwise to place into actual contact the person who is the object of attack, and the attacking materials.

This would suggest that the concept of the jumby is associated with the trick, the aggressive magic, or the evil magic as it is often called. But here we must recall the qualification made by the Tocoan that even Satan can do good work as well as evil. The jumby is, indeed, the agent that is at the core of the trick. But a jumby, as familiar of the healer, may exorcise the rival jumby sent with the trick, just as this same jumby may prompt at divination sessions, or enter the body of the lookman and through him choose the herbs that effect a cure, the roots for the sacred baths, the materials for the guards to fend off the approach of enemy magic.

The phenomenon of the power of one jumby in combat with that of another provides the villagers with subject matter for dramatic recitals. It seemed at times as if it were this love of the great climaxes, whole cycles of tales — all, incidentally, following a pattern so alike as to make of them traditional legend — that not only helped to turn the long, dull evenings, the spare supper, and the leaking roof into things of lesser relevance, but was an active force in perpetuating the place of magic in the community. There was the most recent tale of the woman who had taken another woman's keeper from her. "The two women wrastling with lookman, up and down," it was told, which meant that each woman with her own lookman was pitted against the other. "Happen now this week here. Woman take man away clean from the other. So she lookman mus' be stronges'." The well-known proverb was again invoked, "Who have more mouth water, soak more farine."

Just as the jumby is assigned the dual role of the emissary of evil, and the force that exorcises and cures the evil, so when an attempt is made to examine the situations that call forth the use of the guard and the trick, and the motives for their uses, it is again difficult to classify in absolute terms the one as serving the ends of good, the other of evil. Thus both guards and tricks are used by men and women in affairs of the heart. A woman, let us say, who is enamored of a man will go to a lookman for advice how to win his affections. She will be given various things to put into his food, some liquid to pour into the refreshments she may offer him on a visit, or a few grains of a crushed herb, especially treated, to put into his tea. From the point of view of the man, this is, of course, a trick. If we assume that she has had some success with this method, and now wishes him to propose marriage, she will visit the lookman again; this time he will give her a ring to wear — a special ring, "with things inside it." Such ring is clearly regarded as a trick. "It's there to draw a next one, a wedding ring. Something has been put in the ring by the lookman, yes?" When the man calls again, she will turn and turn the ring on her finger, and to herself repeat the formula given her. "I hope you is not in vain. I hope you will do your work." This is a trick, but its use does not mean that the girl is not a "good girl." For she means no harm to the man but, on the contrary, would "go through fire" for him.

Another method of winning a young man, a trick, but in the psychology of the women of Toco, at least, not too reprehensible, since it was in the interest of requiting honest love, was described as consisting of a bush ground up, and put into a flower pot. "You might do it with a Congo lale bush. The girl mother put the chairs so he sitting nex' to flower pot, looking at she. He play with it now, and the trick inside. Flower might be bush called 'zalea, that bear flower. That is a flower trick. That door the flower pot stand by, he mus' pass come, mus' pass go. So when he come again, he ask for marry. Thing behin' that trick strong. He have to come and ask."

Some lookmen prepare powdered rice, which they mix with "essence," to be sprinkled where the man must walk. As he passes over it, "he mash it," and the result is then apparently accomplished. There are women who take, "hot, hot bread, put it under the arm. It hot till it burn them, but they ain' min'. Then butter the bread well, give man this, give him the bread to eat." But no man, however much he reciprocates the girl's feelings, or however unworldly, will have the temerity to accept a cup of chocolate "from any female except he mother. Put too many thing in chocolate!" All these uses of tricks are known, and although they are looked upon with less tolerance by mothers of sons than of daughters, are more often the subject of light banter than of criticism. "What do men do to get a girl they want? Men is terrible when they want a girl bad. They throw something on the house, like powder. Don't know what they get, but girl crazy when she don' see him. Follow him anywhere. Don' hear what she mother say."

Not all tricks that enter into the relationships of men and women, however, have such amiable ends in view. A woman who is married, or who has formed a keepers relationship with a man takes steps upon the advice of her family, or at the instance of gossip to keep her mate faithful. A number of the more widely recognized practices to insure fidelity include cooking food, and "sweating it with herself"; or more effectively, she might "tie" him. The process of tying must be done with the utmost sureness of touch, and so lightly that the man will not awaken, for it is done at night while he is asleep. Having at hand all that she needs, the woman gets up softly. She takes a piece of twine, measures him from head to foot, and calls his name three times. She calls and makes a knot, calls for the second time and makes another, calls for the third time and knots, then ties the twine about her waist, calling his name again as she does this. "She say, 'Never leave me, Andrew, to follow the nex' woman.' " If this should prove of no immediate avail, she will repeat the tying ritual, but this second time will take care to bury the string at the door leading to the street. Another way of tying is to rip open the pillow on which the man sleeps and put the twine inside it, saying, "I tie you down there. I fasten you there. You mus' never get out."

But men are not unaware of these practices. "Men get

guard, yes? Wear the guard around the waist. Some men is skilful more than others. Mothers tell them as they come to manhood." When a man has a proper guard, "what girl trying to do, his guard would know." Then the man would be sure to waken while this tying was in progress. "Man jump up, say now, 'You playing me trick!' Beat her plenty for it."

Men practice tying as well as do women. "Man does tie a woman too much time. They would fall out, but she would have to come back. That happen here. A man does take woman towel, soiled one, and carry it to lookman. He make something for tie. Woman cyan' get away from it. That's why every woman count the towels carefully when she washes, and if one is missing she start to fret." She, in her turn, would go to a lookman to find out who had taken it, suspecting at once that it would be put to no innocent use. "They livin' together, and she cyan' leave him, because she tie. But always quarreling, never have peace."

A further discussion of tying brought forth this advice. "People does tie you. If someone call you, you must never answer the first time, because if you answer the first time and they make a knot, they got you. If they call a second time, a third time, then all right, they cyan' catch you to tie." The question was asked whether one showed such caution while with enemies, and the reply was cynical. "Friends, friends. Enemies, you don' have business with. No trouble. It's your friends do it. They call you and tie. Like me and Doris here going to work. I ahead. She walk behin', she call, and I answer. So she tie me. Then I cyan' get on at all. She ahead now. I have to go home and do things. By that time, she loose me, yes?"

The most successful method of tying, by general consensus of opinion, is through the use of food. "Food is as smooth as water." The other forms were pronounced as involving decided risks for the woman, for "if man now find out, he licks the skin, licks the skin, till she mus' untie him. Or he leave her."

More serious consequences may result than quarrels or separation. There was the trick that a woman got from a lookman to put into her husband's food. He was "wild, and she want him to stay home," and none found her at fault for trying to change him. But while the lookman had told her to pour three drops into her husband's food at breakfast, she was so anxious to have him mend his ways that she put in more. She continued this for several days until, one morning, "The man (a blacksmith) goin' to shoe a horse, and he fall down. People carry him to a doctor. Doctor say cyan' find out his complaint. They carry him back home, and the wife start for said lookman." When the woman arrived, the lookman told her he was expecting her, and that he knew her errand, but that he could do nothing for her. "He goin' to die. No cure again. You didn' do by instruction, so you kill him." The man died two days later, and there was much gossip. "His mother and all talk, but don' take her to court, because they say she didn' mean to kill him. Woman herself die a little while after."

A woman who has taken a man from another, and is about to have a child, will get for herself all the protection that she can. Otherwise, at some critical moment either during parturition or when the child is little, the rival's vengeance may strike. "She don' leave she little baby alone in the house, or somebody come behin' now, take the shadow." The child must at least be christened before it will be left for an instant; but even after baptism, a mother who has cause to be anxious about a rival will take steps to guard her child. "They do something to catch the baby shadow in a bottle. Some bad people does it."

When the child sickens, the mother goes to a lookman, who works to bring the shadow back, though if the mother comes for advice three days after the illness had begun there is no help. "If the shadow gone, it's no good to take the baby to a doctor. The shadow is in a bottle with other things all corked up. The doctor can't bust the cork." Only a man as strong as the one who had taken the shadow away can free it. When, as the child grows, it becomes necessary to leave the house where it lies asleep, an open Bible, or a prayer book, the first preferably open to a psalm, and the second to the twenty-third psalm — "The Lord is my Shepherd" — is laid near its pillow, or under it, while on top of the open pages is placed a pair of scissors with "points sharp, sharp." Anyone who came for the baby's shadow, "scissors juke (stab) him."

As a safeguard against tricks it is a good idea to have a "sensa fowl" — a chicken whose feathers grow erect — in the yard, and still more foresighted to take the fowl to a lookman and "have him fix it for you." When that is done, the fowl will scratch up any trick buried in the yard, or under the house. "Nothin' at all can come across, no matter what dey buries." But even a sensa fowl that is not especially prepared will generally be effective enough, for "dat fowl dig, dig all de time, come on anyt'ing de."

It is equally necessary to be alert when out with companions. An incident in a rum shop may bring danger. There are men with long finger-nails that can harbor poison, and a finger-nail casually allowed to dip into another's glass may have fatal results. "Anyone that is sensible change the glass when drinking," if anything is suspected. Warnings of poisoned drinks have come to men in their dreams, or the guards they wore caused them discomfort, and in this way saved their lives. They say, "Groun' glass is quick p'izen, cut you all up inside," and is easy to introduce into a drink. Such tricks are the work of bad men "who have vindicted feelin's against another."

Other precautions must be observed. Sometimes an illness may unwittingly be picked up along the road, and children are particularly warned to touch nothing they see lying about where they pass; and whatever the temptation, to take nothing that is at the crossroads. "We tells them they mus' never pick up money wrapped with bush (in leaves) in the road, especially at the crossroad. That is put there by somebody who have jumby, pay to get rid of it." The same advice about not touching the things lying about at crossroads, or anywhere along the road, in fact, was repeated often. "People not glad to pick up money they find. They afraid. You have children, then you warn them, warn them." The urgency of these warnings are less felt at the present time, however, for "with motor car· an' all, crossroad come open now. Motor car mash the thing in the road. Even our crossroad come open now." This was a reference to a junction of three important roads where formerly it was reputed "they make plenty jumby bring there."

In former years money was likewise found on graves in the cemetery. This was the offering for "grave-dirt," used to sprinkle in the yard of an enemy. "Grave-dirt sprinkled in your yard, but you don' know it, so you walk on it, mash it. Then someone come with clearer eyes than yours, say, 'A spirit here.' So you go get a lookman to give you a guard against the spirit, and that cure you."

4

The dichotomy between the guard as protective magic and the trick as an aggressive and ill-intentioned force is not clearly sustained, for there is much overlapping between the two. At times the worker of magic achieves a blend of a guard and a trick. When this is done as protection against thieves, the charm, whether hung above a doorway, or buried under a doorstep, or in the center of a field to protect a harvest, or placed on top of a buried money jar, is intended primarily to frustrate the ability of the thief to act.

But if, because of a trick the thief holds, he succeeds in stealing despite the power in the guard, then the trick, or punishing element that is associated with the guard will either expose him, or exact whatever penalty the maker of the combined guard and trick has set.

Some of these penalties are not lacking in entertaining detail, and are told with hilarious appreciation, though others are grim enough. For instance, to protect fowl running about the yard, various devices are employed, such as feeding them especially prepared food so that if they are stolen and eaten, the thief will raise his arms and crow, betraying the act. One such case was reported from Port-of-Spain, where, the story runs, at mid-day a man always raises his arms and crows, regardless of where he may be, and much to the delight of his ever-changing audience. The story is also told of one such combination guard and trick that was made by a practitioner in the capital after copra had several times been stolen from a man's drying-shed. Upon his return to Toco the owner of the shed, in accordance with the lookman's instructions, visited the priest. "Then he give oil, put candles to burn, come home say, 'In nine days, who took it will go stark mad.' In nine days Anne's husban' go mad, and he is still in the asylum. They are trying things now, working, working. But he still there."

The question was raised, particularly in connection with this case, as to what happens when the same lookman is visited by both parties to an enmity. The ethics of the profession were described as requiring the lookman to tell the second in any one of various possible combinations of visitors that, "Someone far in front of you. He gone before you, man. Can't catch him." He does this principally because he does not wish to hurt his reputation. "Because the first man would see his trick no good, and wouldn't give him good name." Some lookmen, however, would get from the second visitor all the information they could, so that this might be put to use in behalf of the client for whom they were working. For this reason it is held that, "You has to be careful whom you go to. That's why you always look for one in another place. If you have money you go far, go to Tobago, get man from Demerara who is visiting, get a *Kpanyol,* go to Port-of-Spain." But if a practitioner considers a man one of his regular clients, "He won't spoil you for nex' one, not if he have you already." This would be true even where a larger fee from the second consultant was in view; and here, rather than the pragmatic end of not impairing one's reputation, a more subtle, more effective factor is put into play. "You own spirit working for you will spoil you, if you work for both sides. The dead lookman self come spoil you."

If a man is the owner of an ordinary guard, one of a generalized type to be obtained as preventative against all forms of envy, or malice, or evil design, then toward the close of the year "if you have a little trouble," or even if there was no trouble at all, "you look back to the man who gave it, and have him strengthen it." Since all guards and tricks must be removed during intercourse, and many of these bear in addition individual taboos — such as prohibitions on given foods while wearing them, or taboos against touching the ground — it is not difficult to see that there is need to be assured that nothing had been done during the year to render them ineffective. To reactivate a guard or trick involves bathing the consultant with special herbs to ward off ills that might be about, and those of the future; and, of course, a "present" to the practitioner in appreciation of his services.

An important trick, provided a man to give him advantages in his work, or his trading enterprises, or his fishing, will require a visit from the practitioner to the house of his client. For the renewal of the power of the trick, or guard, if of importance in keeping a man at employment that is coveted by others, let us say, the work is done at night. "Bound to have a little drum for this. Neighbors hear it beating in the night. It's when lookman is bathing the person, calling the dead to come and help." There is gossip about this the next morning, and speculation about where the ceremony was held. "What I hear is really drum," the neighbors say, "Look at the food in the road. Take a care you don' mash the food." Report has it that one family has their lookman visit them for three or four days each year. "He come at night, and leave at night, and all the time he working, working for them. The boys (of this family) keep their job, keep it, you can't loose them with a cutlash. It's the work said lookman does every year. The man comes from far away."

Special rites that renew the strength of some tricks must be performed, at much more frequent intervals than once a year. These intervals may be monthly, or weekly, and involve no more than "throwing" some rum. This should be done at noon, when the owner of the trick pours some rum out of each window of his house, then out of the door, and makes the tour of the outside of his house. In pouring ceremonially, three gestures of dropping the liquid on the ground is mandatory. Once inside the house again, he washes his hands and face in the same rum, and during all of this operation, he speaks a formula given him by the lookman voicelessly, or in whispered syllables. In addition to this, or at times in place of it, there are two "feedings" of the important trick annually, usually on a Friday in the months of June and December.

"When you have thing at house, lookman bathe you and give you some of the bath to drink," that is to say, some of the mixture of herbs and water is set aside for internal use. "Then he sing praise on you." This "praise" consists of church prayers. "On such a day, you stay away from work. The bed is changed, everything." An animal is killed, and the blood of the sacrifice is poured over the guard or trick. The preferred animal is a young goat, but under special circumstances the lookman calls for a sheep, though this occurs only rarely, and a white cock can be used when no goat is available.

"Some people when they get a trick, they only pays part." The lookman promises to keep the trick effective and the recipient agrees to reward him at stated times for this service. "Once you go up," that is, when a man is successful in his undertakings, "if you forget to take care of the lookman, the trick spoil, and you can't get back the power for anything." But since a compact broken with a man who controls supernatural spirits is understandably dangerous, the Tocoan points out that only a witless person would dare to do this.

Yet the fate of the practitioner can have its ironic twists, as the life of the lookman Martin illustrates. "This man had watch and chain, heavy, you know, and all gol' rings all the way up the fingers. Big letters come to him. People come from Matelot, from Gran' Riviere, from Port-of-Spain. But he die in the poor-house." No one noticed how this change in his fortunes came about, it had developed so gradually. As he grew old, people no longer felt his power to be what it had been at the height of his career, and fewer and fewer consultants came. When he himself fell ill, his clients came to him no longer. "Now there's Andrew take his place. He ain' fail yet. Still goin' strong. People say, 'He good, self.' I don' use him." Then, in further explanation, 'He used to have a trade. I don' know what make he come lookman."

The weakening of loyalty toward a practitioner, or a sense of being free from the need of his services, does not give one a free hand with the guard or trick he had fashioned. The story was told of a woman, who after having had a guard for a period of years and feeling no further use for it, was overcome by curiosity to examine its contents. She thereupon cut open the little black bag and found two nails, some nail-parings, human hair, and three grains of a plant she could not identify. This was done in the presence of the neighbor who had been at the original divining session at which time this guard was given, and the cure that had followed it. The neighbor did not at all relish witnessing this and reprimanded the woman for her frivolousness. "But she only laugh, and sew it back, and put it around she neck again."

The following morning early, this neighbor heard herself called from the house next door. She found the woman feverish, the guard missing from her neck. "She dream that night a man come and shake his finger at she. He be vex, vex. He say, 'You playin' with my work.'" He repeated this three times, each time speaking louder. When she awoke the guard was lying in "de corner." She sewed black braid on this guard and put it around her waist, and said from now on nothing would remove it. "But the nex' day she fever, fever. She go to the lookman and tell him," and he informed her that he knew everything that had happened. "My man came to warn you," he told her, as he gave her a protective treatment. "Now she keep the guard good," taking care to have its strength renewed periodically.

5

Not all ventures require the advice of a lookman. Some are disposed of with the aid of a store of popular knowledge that is the possession of the entire adult community. Certain esoteric practices are typical only of specific families, but this is the result of some special formula, or cure, or interpretation of an omen that had been the exclusive property of the family, and has been passed on from one generation to the next. A knowledge of good and bad days

is general. One building a new house would never start
work on the foundation on a Friday. "Friday is a day of
trouble. Couldn't finish." The good days are Monday
through Thursday, and Saturday. When a marriage is to be
decided, the month when it is to take place is of importance. The favored months are October and December,
but for the day on which it is to be, the almanac is consulted by the girl's mother. Only if there is reason to believe
that there is some disturbing factor in relation to the marriage will a lookman be asked to divine, to determine if a
specific date will be propitious. Friday, as we have seen, is
the day for feeding magical charms.

There are also popular remedies for the prevention and
cure of *maljo,* the evil eye. Persons who have it in them to
give the evil eye may do this unwittingly, giving it to a
child who is found attractive, or a fine hen seen running
about in the yard, or a growing field. "Some people don'
give *maljo* for bad. They like the chil'. They gives it to
stock in the yard. You have a nice fowl' an' it die. It was
maljo."

The manner of diagnosing a child's illness caused by the
evil eye is, apparently, simple. "Chil' don't take breast at
all, and crying, crying. Somebody ripe (mature) come, say,
'Oh, the chil' have *maljo.*' " The child is "flogged" on the
face and head — "Say *maljo* make face stiff, can' cry out,"
— until it "bawls," while Catholic prayers are recited. "If
you don' sanctify, the chil' will die." If while a person com-
pliments a baby, he takes the precaution to pinch it lightly,
no ill effect will result. To protect a child against the evil
eye, or to cure it, indigo blue is rubbed behind the ears, on
the palms of the hands, and the soles of the feet, while in
addition a piece of indigo is sewed into a bit of cloth, to be
worn about the neck on a cord. A serious illness resulting
from the evil eye would require more intricate treatment.
"You take the sick child to some Roman Church person to

say praise. Can be a man or a woman. Then you take candle and light it, and get holy water and bush you call sweet-broom, flog the child with bush."

It is usual to place a guard about the neck of a cow, and especially a calf just born. For this, the individual house-holder has his formula. One way to fashion such a guard is to take a seed called "horse-eye," to pierce it, and put a ribbon through it, fastening this about the calf's neck. "But you put something in when you bore the hole. It black like asafisita (asafoetida), and say, 'I put that there for the ol' mammy and ol' daddy. Nobody to hurt it.' " This is allowed to remain about the neck of the animal until it falls off.

To prevent *maljo* against land being cultivated, "a big thing now, they call *maljo* bean," and "thing you call dragon's blood," are planted along the boundary. Unless there is a poor harvest nothing more need be done, but if the yield is poor, a friend in passing might say, "Me, I look after my fiel' busy," suggesting that his friend had failed in vigilance against the evil eye, or some other enemy power. "I got no money for that business. Me a work my own jungle," is the answer. Nevertheless, he will not fail to take immediate steps to avert a recurrence of a bad harvest. "He bring about nine people now. They cook food — everything that grow, rice, and yam, and potato, and cassava, melon. Kill a fowl, no goat. Kill it on the land, and let the blood run. Then cook all this food. Also parch corn, and grin' it."

Before the food is eaten, three or five of the men go about the field throwing the cooked food, the rum and the *sam-sam,* as the parched corn is called. "Then they dig a place in the center of the land, and throw in the food, say, 'This is for all you especially. Watch my land. Do help me.' " When the men have finished eating they sing, to the ac-companiment of a rhythm played on a box — "They has no drum" — and the striking together of two pieces of iron.

> "Me a go, me a go
> Me a come
> Me a go yonder, yaya.

> "Me a go
> Me a come
> Yaya do
> Papa do
> Uncle do
> When we gone
> Watch de place."

The owner of the field, when he next plants, will also take care to solicit the surveillance of the Saints of the Church by throwing holy water in the field. "On Good Friday, Roman Catholic pries' blesses the cistern. Everybody goes get a bottle. Old members bring a bottle for you" [who are not members of the Roman Church].

Those persons who detect the evil eye, or the presence of bad magic that had entered a house, or that is hovering about a man, are called "people with four eyes." Persons born with a caul have that gift, and certain members of the Shouters groups bring from mournin' groun' gifts that enable them to see things unseen by normal eyes. Should such a one entering a home be heard to exclaim, "A heat here tonight," this would mean that a spirit against whom preventive measures had to be taken immediately was present.

As indicated, dreams are held to contain a message from the spirit world, and therefore they must be interpreted. Not all dreams require professional advice, for there are many whose meanings are popularly known, meanings that, in the main, derive from the principle that significance is the opposite of content. A dream that while walking up a hill one stumbles and falls, crashing down to the foot where stones are lying about, is good. "Some offspring will get rich." To dream about flying is good also. "Persons you see flying will come to some honor or good work, or good business." To dream about getting married is a portent of death in the family. If one dreams of seeing a carriage going by fast, this is a sign that "some quick message go come, good or bad." A big black snake in a dream warns of the approach of an enemy — "big enemy." If the dream of the snake continues, and the person kills it, that tells that the enemy will be conquered. The appearance of a policeman in a dream, if in connection with a quarrel, is evidence of an approaching case in court — "You goin' to have courthouse work." Unwelcome, too, is a dream about having children, for "you wouldn't have any." A dream that one is a member of a large family foretells "famine — hardness — come down on you," while to dream of an approaching boat means good news. "If goin' from you, well, it carryin' away," and, therefore, is not at all a good omen.

Any dream that boded ill fortune would be referred to a lookman. "Have people, not lookman, that are clever and keep dream books, and tell what dreams mean. Lookman, too, have plenty books, big ones about dreams." The professional lookman and obiaman, however, get supplementary information from the spirits, while the Shouters who look get theirs from visions and meditation.

How significant dreams are held to be is illustrated by the following account: "I was pregnant and felt great pain. The doctor said I was making two children, and because I am narrow in the hips, one child was being pushed up." Since the doctor said this woman must have a certain medicine at once, she sent a messenger with two shillings. "But the doctor refused, say it was more money." There was no more money in the house, because pay day was

Monday. "I vex with doctor, say ain' goin' again." That night she had a dream in which she saw two quarreling women standing near the water. One was her mother and the other her aunt. They said to her, "We tell you, go to doctor. Why you no go?" She explained that she had been angered by the doctor's action. Her mother just said, "Huh," but her aunt, "Quarrel, say, 'All right, let she go in the boat.'" The boat was black and white, and many men were there.

She awakened from her dream just as the clock struck twelve. "I 'fraid. Wake my husban' tell him. He take one shilling, go ask man to look. Come back say, 'Was bad. The boat was coffin waitin'.'" The husband borrowed some money and got the medicine for her. "He come back with he pony wet, near dead," but she took the medicine by nine o'clock the next morning. Before the child was born the lookman her husband had consulted gave her three baths. "Was three spirits on me. A Tobago man sen' it. He worked land left to me. . . . After I born child, I say, 'Is land you wan'? All right, keep my land. I here.'"

6

Another power to be guarded against is that of the vampire, the *sukuyan,* and the werewolf, the legarou, or as it is sometimes pronounced, *nigawu* or *legawu* (*loup garou*). The two beings, though not clearly differentiated, are held to be anti-social; their activities are regarded as criminal, and punishable by death. The vampire may be a man or woman, though tales about women are the more common. A male legarou is more difficult to trap, because men have tricks to work for them. But whether men or women, the knowledge how to become a legarou is transmitted in families, and all those of like propensity are friends, and help each other when in trouble.

Children going home from school make crosses in the road with white chalk, or a stick, if they think a sukuyan is going in the same direction as they. "If sukuyan there, can't pass that cross." A useful thing to remember when wishing to be safe from the attack of a vampire is to whisper "Thursday, Friday, Saturday, Sunday," three times, then a person can talk with impunity even about a legarou and name her.

A common practice of these women is to come in the morning and ask for salt or matches. "They not brave at all, but ask in a soft voice. But you mustn't give them, yes? Give them salt and they take it and work on it, then you can't bar them." This is no occasion for indirection, but rather, "You say, 'Thursday, Friday, Saturday, Sunday. You devil, come to suck me las' night, now come for my salt.' " Means must now be found to protect the house against the power of this vampire. The windows and doors are immediately marked with crosses. A pair of scissors and a mirror are fixed above the door, inside the house. "When they come and look in the glass, then they are 'fraid of their disguise. They come 'fraid of their own self."

These tales of catching the vampire follow a consistent pattern. There was once a woman legarou who "did suck she own husban'," so that the man got thinner and thinner. When she was not satisfied with what she got from him, she went elsewhere at night, visiting the homes of other victims. The husband was so ill that he went to a lookman who told him, "Man, you have a wife is a legawu." The lookman gave the husband some medicine, and instructions that he was not to take his habitual nightly cup of tea before bedtime. The lookman said, "Tonight when she give you tea, sit by a window, and don't drink it, but throw it out."

This he did, and he went to bed, feigning to sleep. Then he heard her call,

" 'Kin, 'kin, you no know me?
'Kin, 'kin, you no hear what you mistress say?
'Kin, 'kin, come off, come off!"

She took off the skin and put it behind the large water
barrel. Twice she leaped and then went through the roof.
As the man watched this, he said to himself, "My wife, that
what she do?" The sky seemed afire, and the room was very
light. He salted the inside of the skin thoroughly, then put
it in place behind the water barrel where she had left it.
When she returned before break of day, she tried to get
back into her skin, but could not because the salt burned
her.

" 'Kin, go on.
'Kin, you no know me?
'Kin, you no hear what you mistress say?"

This was repeated three times, and each line was spoken
three times. "Skin squinch, he draw, can't go on, he burnin'
her." So the woman put away the skin, wrapped herself up
in a blanket, and lay down under the bed.

Later in the morning, when the husband called to her,
she answered him from under the bed that she was ill with
fever. When he offered to go for a doctor, she hurriedly
said that the fever was going away. The husband left for
his job, but on the way he told the police and the doctor.
For two days the woman refused to come out, until, "They
sen' off call female nurses with aprons, cyaps." People say,
"Can't understand the freshness. It smell like shark. Mus'
be sukuyan." The bed was finally taken away, and the
woman seized. "Doctor look at her. No nails. He say, 'She's
an old hag, man, you married to, a bad sukuyan.' " So "de
public take her over." They tied her, and took her to the
town hall. She was tried and condemned to death. "They
put her in a big puncheon, tar it inside, put her in a cart,

carry her on a high hill. They put pitch oil in it and light it, and roll it down the hill."

A simple method of insuring a home against an attack by a legarou is to place a broom upside down behind the door. Even if the legarou were inside the house, this would make her powerless to do her work. But if one of them had a trick to facilitate the hated work, the knowledge of a lookman would have to be called upon for stronger protection. This is usually done by setting a trap for the legarou, and giving him several lashes while he is in his nonhuman form. "Lookman spoil him with lash. Keep him till day clean. Then Government take him, burn him in tar barrel." For once the lash of the lookman has come down on the vampire or werewolf, he cannot put off his animal features, and his apprehension is thus not difficult, according to report.

CHAPTER X

THE AVENUES OF SELF-
EXPRESSION

ADJUSTMENT TO LIVING, essential to the individuals who compose any group, lies in balancing attainable goals against frustrations. Where the fulfillment of goals is greatly outweighed by the frustrations, social and psychological tensions appear, and unless compensatory avenues of self-expression are established, serious maladjustments will result. In Toco, though the adjustment of the people to the life they lead has been seen to be an uneasy one, there is nonetheless an adjustment, for avenues of self-expression are present to give a sense of purpose to the life of the individual and stability to the culture of the society.

Some of these compensations have been implicit in the descriptions of various aspects of Toco life. Poverty is widespread, but there is sufficient variation in individual economic status, even on this low level, to permit the play of prestige drives based on competition and display. The institution of the family is not too closely defined, but ties of affection between spouses and between parents and children persist despite broken unions and the absence of broader kinship structures. Counterbalancing lack of fulfillment in the religious experience of members of the established churches is the system of belief that man's destiny can be read by those with "sight," and that through traditional observances, without benefit of clergy, and by means of the control of the forces of magic, men and women are assured a degree of self-determination in their ways of life.

2

Lodges in northeastern Trinidad, as among the Negroes elsewhere in the Island, in addition to providing the social and insurance features for which they are founded, satisfy a desire for ceremonialism and leadership. These associations are, indeed, a primary outlet for the political activity denied this group living under the controls of the colonial system, with the result that the maneuverings within the larger organizations bring forth widespread interest and partisan discussion.

From both the economic and social points of view, lodges are mutual self-help institutions of significance, for lodge-brotherhood entails more than going to meetings and paying dues. If a member is ill, his fellows visit him; if he comes on hard times, they aid him; in disputes they try to arbitrate; and where affiliation with one of the more important groups is involved, the lodge is a principal source of prestige.

At the core of these lodge affiliations lies the need of a socially respected funeral and a proper burial. How important this is to Toco folk has been cited in the discussion of family expenditures where, as we have seen, the item of lodge dues for husband and wife finds a place in the poorest household. The reasons why an acceptable burial is so great a necessity were given in the discussion of death.

Lodges may be divided into two categories, the non-secret mutual aid groups, and the "orders," or secret societies. In Toco, the Rose of Sharon and the Toco Benefit Society are in the first category. A branch of the Star of Bethlehem, and the Northern Star, a local lodge, are in the second. The Mechanics, the Foresters, and the Freemasons are other "orders" established in the area. Certain individuals from Toco and its surrounding region belong to them, but they have no chapters in Toco itself. Catholics are not permitted to join these orders — certainly not the Freemasons — but there is good evidence that the ban is not too well observed. "Pries' don' allow it, so when they joins, they have to hide it." The Anglican minister, on the other hand, holds special services for these orders when they request it, and no other religious group places any bar to membership in them.

The Rose of Sharon society is essentially an insurance organization with social and ritual features. It has chapters over the entire Island. Officers of a chapter are the "legate" ("that's what they call the President"), secretary, treasurer, two trustees, a marshal, and the members of six committees. Both men and women may join, but all officers are men. The treasurer must be known and trusted, and have land or other property to assure his responsibility, and to guarantee the bond he signs when he assumes office. The trustees count the money that has been received and turn it over to the Treasurer, who puts it "in de bank" — the postal savings office — from which it can be withdrawn on three days' notice. The committees bring various proposals to the entire membership, who debate them and vote on their acceptability. The President presides at these meetings, and "has to ring de bell an' knock de hammer" when discussion becomes heated. Measures must have his signature to become "de law," but he "cyan't sign if more is against than for."

The dues for the Rose of Sharon Society are twelve cents a week for adults, one-half that amount for a child until he is about twelve years old. Sick benefits are nine shillings a week for adults, and four shillings sixpence for a child during the first seven weeks of illness, half these amounts for the next seven, then one-fourth for seven more. Each seven weeks the amount received is cut one-half, until a payment of twelve cents per week is reached, at which time, if the member continues ill, this amount goes on until his recovery or death. It is "a pension for life." The society also pays for the doctor, though hospitalization, for which one must be taken to Port-of-Spain, is beyond the Society's resources. In this case "It's government business," and the individual pays a shilling a day unless he has no property — and "you don't tell if you can help it." But at every meeting the officers "beg the members to be careful not to get sick!"

Each member may register his dependents, who receive half the established member benefits. Thus a child, registered as a dependent, could be protected to half the amounts indicated above, while if husband and wife, each a member, registered one another as dependents, and either fell ill, the other would receive one and one-half times the usual benefit. This occurs rarely, however, since members are allowed to register only two dependents each, so that the privilege is reserved for their children.

The death-benefits of this society are twenty-five dollars for an adult member, half that amount for a registered dependent child. This is sufficient to cover funeral expenses, because, it will be remembered, the principal outlay is for the cedar boards needed to make the coffin, and for lining it. Friends "dig de hole," and other friends who are carpenters "make de box." But it is not the obligation of the society to make it possible for the coffin to be covered with cloth, or varnished "to make it nice."

Dues in the Rose of Sharon may be six weeks in arrears without prejudice to the rights of a member, but these rights lapse with the seventh week. If ill, a man borrows enough to reinstate himself, paying the loan with the aid of benefit money, though if he owes too much ("falls in arrea' so he have no benefit"), he merely rejoins. "Call that rein-state." This is done in a special ceremony, with a song for the occasion:

> "I was a wandering sheep,
> Stray away.
> I did not love the fold,
> I did not love my Father's voice,
> I will not be controlled."

They read "de declaration" to him again; then all shake his hand and welcome his return. He pays his fee of two shil-lings, and is admonished to remain in the society and enjoy its benefits. In former years, lodges lent money at low in-terest rates, but during the period of this research continua-tion of this practice had been found impossible.

Like other mutual aid groups and lodges this society attempts to resolve disputes between its members before they reach the court. "Lodge don' like court business for its members." This function goes beyond the settlement of disputes within the membership. "If I'm a lodge member, an' you not, an' we have trouble, the 'legate come to you ask if you would let the lodge judge and settle the matter between you an' me." Intervention of this type was exem-plified in a case which was already before the court. A workman of a Public Works Department gang, in a dis-pute over a relatively small matter with a fellow worker — the amount involved was but forty cents — drew a gun when the other reached for a rock to throw at him. At the next session of court, where the matter was brought by the police, the plaintiff failed to appear, whereupon on the basis of the police charge the one who had aimed the gun was fined ten dollars and bound over to keep the peace. In the meantime, the officers of the lodge to which both be-longed had worked to good purpose to effect a reconcilia-tion and to reduce to proper proportions a quarrel over a minor matter that might have brought serious penalty had the charge been pressed.

The Toco Benefit Society, which is not so large as the Rose of Sharon, makes smaller payments, though the dues are the same. At death, the sum of twenty-four dollars is given for the coffin and related expenses, while sick benefits are eight shillings fourpence, sixteen cents less than that of the other organization. Nonetheless, people join it; for just because it is a local society, contacts are closer and a quality of friendship lacking in the larger group is thought to exist. "You get better fellowlation, so you don' mind less money," was the expression of a member of the Rose of Sharon in discussing the Toco Benefit Society. "It isn't nice in bed sick by yourself all day," she said, "and when you're sick, more people come and see you." In structure, objectives, rituals, and regalia the two groups are about the same; and both are to be differentiated from the secret societies, the "orders."

"Order mean secret," it was asserted. "You mustn't speak the business. If a man talk, they hol' him, flog him. They talks plenty operatics there." Each man who belongs customarily pays seven shillings as initiation fee, "to join." With this money the society buys rum, rice, and other foods. The initiate provides a fowl, and like the other members must furnish a new goblet, plate, spoon, knife, and fork for his use at this and later occasions. To make of the initiation an important event, the order prefers to "join" several persons at the same time. With the members contributing a shilling each, the sum collected makes possible rich fare for the occasion, including cooked pig's head (souse), a favored delicacy. At the feast, there is always a vacant chair — "a comfy one" — before a place set as for a participant. "Even if the society is not an order, they show reverence for those gone before."

All "orders" have the sickness and death benefit aspects

of the lodges. At the death of a member, all the other orders attend "in uniform" — the Masons with their aprons, the Foresters with sprigs of green in their mouths, but at the funerals of lodge members, they do not ordinarily appear in their regalia.

The Masonic order, which holds the greatest prestige of any of these associations, is what is termed "an upstairs society" — the meetings are held on the second floor of a two-story house. "You hear de noise an' don' know a thing about it." Its rituals of death, report has it, are particularly impressive. The wife and children of the dead bid farewell to the corpse before the membership arrives, for when they appear they close the bedroom door and take charge of preparing the body. "They have a big ceremony, make a big noise, sing their own hymns." A man's regalia is placed with him in the coffin — "wrap things in paper and in cloth so it's soft. Then they stand outside the door with crossed swords." If someone tries to look, they "clash their swords," and everyone inside "growls." Those nearby "run away to break de neck."

"Orders" help the family of a dead member as much as they can, though their assistance is dependent upon "how long he was in the order." According to the current report, "Mason have some society dey call Widow an' Orphan." They help educate the son of a deceased member and look forward to having him as a member in his father's place. "Even after the death-benefit is paid, they once gave as much as forty-five dollars to help a widow bring up her children."

One of the things the people of Toco stress about "orders" is the cost of membership. "In orders," said one man, "you always have to give money. The thing they call capital." Or, again, "Everyone cyan't belong to an order. It's that certificate that cost plenty" — this, in addition to continuing expenses. "Big people belong, not poor, because they always have big upkeeping and upstairs."

The password is the important element in the secrecy that is one of the most attractive aspects of the orders. After a person has paid his dues, it is said, "they bring out the password that's sent from America." If a stranger enters and cannot give the password, he is flogged. There is a special knock on the door, and when it is heard, the "legate" orders, "Take his word." "If he don' know it, they say he's a fraud. That's when they flog him. They has plenty ceremony. They eats. They have big dogs that bark, and you meet men with crossed swords if you try to go in." When they initiate, "people plenty in de road, listenin'." The day for this rite becomes common knowledge because provisions for the lavish feast must be bought ahead of time. The only public part of the ceremony occurs when the legate "throws away" food specially cooked without salt, and rum, for the dead members. This, however, happens early in the morning, and only those who stay the entire night see it. "Some sit up to watch till day-clean," it was declared.

Unlike the mutual aid societies, the "orders," except for the Star of Bethlehem, take only men. "Women have too much tongue." But the one Trinidad organization with political aims, the United Negro Association, a branch of the large international society founded by the late Marcus A. Garvey, had no such barriers. There was no chapter in Toco, but persons from the village belonged to the branch at Cumana. "This lodge pay benefit, like others, but don' do much else. Government won't allow Garvey to stay."

The rewards that come from participation in lodge rituals are thus found in the gratification of social and aesthetic drives, in the expression of the leadership impulses within the group, and elation at being the repository of secrets when confronting outsiders. They are also manifest in the fulfillment of the prestige drive as reflected in economic status in belonging to several associations, and in personal self-esteem as being a man of consequence in the community.

3

The effective political controls of Toco life rest entirely outside the hands of the people in the village. There is no mayor or council; the district has no local body which considers problems peculiar to the region. All directives regulating behavior come from the capital, Port-of-Spain; while law enforcement is in the hands of a few police, headed by a sergeant, who are not Toco natives and are a part of a force whose operations cover the entire colony. To what degree this makes for the attrition of any sense of the political realities is illustrated by an incident in the course of this field-work. A petition to the Governor was being circulated asking that the Toco doctor — a government official — be given a telephone, and that the service be extended along the north coast of the Island. It came as a surprise, and as something to be painstakingly explained, that an American citizen could not properly participate in local affairs by signing a petition concerned with the internal arrangements of a British colony!

In general, this situation of outside control is accepted as a regime which has always existed in the experience of the people. Some of its characteristics, such as the old age pensions, the health services, and the Public Works Department, are recognized as bringing obvious benefits. Certain regulations, however, are actively resented, such as those strict laws that had been drawn to suppress the activities of the Shouters — laws whose effects have been discussed, and whose operation will be shown in the description of the trial, shortly to be recounted, of one such group.

Certain stresses in the political situation are rendered the more immediate through the injection of the racial factor. The senior representatives of Government in the district, who regulate the day-to-day existence of the Negro folk of Toco, are almost all white. In 1939, the Warden and the Magistrate who sat in the local court, were white; the head of the Public Works Department, a mulatto, was of predominantly white ancestry; and though the sergeant in charge of the police detachment appeared to be of unmixed African descent, his responsibility to his white superiors was underscored in the minds of the Toco people by the fact that at the time of this investigation the commissioned ranks of the police were closed to Negroes.

With participation in political controls completely absent from the Toco scene, their lives regulated by power in the hands of those of different racial stock and often of foreign cultural background, frustrations arise. At the time of this study, no overt acts of discontent had been committed in Toco. But two years before, strikes had taken place in the oil-fields, and their effect had not yet been dispelled,. as the words of certain calypso songs popular in the area, or even of the semi-ritualistic *bongo* songs, show. The movement headed by Marcus Garvey, which at one time had gained wide popularity, was often commented upon. "He see things too clear. He talked about the first shall be last and the last shall be first." Haile Selassie was a symbol of similar, if not greater import. For though by 1939 the Italo-Ethiopian war was over, and Selassie had suffered defeat and was in exile, all this was either unknown or overlooked. The point was made again and again that he was "fighting the battle of the black people against the whites for the control of Africa." Fortunately, some outlet for the drive for political participation is afforded, as we have seen, in certain of the churches and in the lodges, where position can be objectified through office. The means employed to attain the various posts in these organizations arouse prolonged interest in the community as a whole, while a shift in administration in these groupings is the subject of much discussion and gossip both before and after the event.

4

The one governmental institution where there is direct participation is the court, which has an important place in Toco life. Of significance, from a psychological point of view, is the fact that court sessions give opportunity for self-expression afforded by no other Toco institution. Since the local court is one of first instance, those who appear before it are only rarely represented by counsel. It thus not only becomes a center of Toco activity, and a place where the drama inherent in the public resolution of private disputes and quarrels is to be enjoyed, but also provides a setting for the clever man, where he can establish a reputation for quick thinking and telling retort.

The second court session of June, 1939, was well attended despite the rain. The Magistrate, a young official not too long in the colony, sat on a platform at a table, an open space before him, the witness at his right, those attending court seated on benches that filled the rest of the room. As each case was brought up, witnesses were escorted outside by the policemen on duty, to remain out of earshot until called to the stand. On this day, the first two cases were those of men charged with having unlicensed dogs. They were fined five shillings each on their pleas of guilty, and given fourteen days in which to pay their fines.

Next came a dispute between two men, one of whom had caused a tree to be felled so that it damaged a number of cocoa trees growing on the land of the other. There was obviously bad feeling between them, and the dispute over the testimony was acrimonious. Damages for seven completely destroyed trees and for seven half-destroyed at the rate of a shilling a tree were awarded, plus costs and the expense of clearing the wreckage. After this a larceny case, involving the theft of two chickens, was judged. The accused was adroit, and his questioning of witnesses concerning their ability to identify a red or speckled hen that had no other special traits was sharp, while his discussion of what kind of chicks were hatched from a setting of twenty eggs was ingenious popular genetics. The principal witness against him, his sister-in-law, was motivated by bitter enmity, and this was so skillfully played on by the defendant who, in a dramatic interchange between the two, brought out the fact that he had refused her offer to live with him, that the case was thrown out of court, and the fowls awarded the accused, who was discharged as not guilty. Village gossip agreed that he was guilty of the theft but that the woman's spite had turned the scales in his favor; his tactics, however, were applauded as masterly.

A land ownership case was of particular interest in that it had the unusual feature of involving litigation between a mother and her son. The plaintiff claimed that while serving overseas during the war of 1914–18, he had sent his mother money to buy land for him, which she had done. Since his return, he had been living on half of the ten-acre plot she had purchased; but now she had ordered his eviction. The attitude of the spectators showed plainly how distasteful a quarrel of this kind, between mother and son, was to them — an opinion echoed later in talk about the village. In this instance, no decision was rendered, since the problem was so difficult that the case was remanded to the Supreme Court. In the final case, involving the alleged theft of $1.36 from the purse of a woman who had come to the house where the accused was living, the defendant was found guilty and put under bond to keep the peace for the next two years.

The next session of the court, two weeks later, had a

lean calendar, not unusual in this law-abiding community. The rock-throwing, gun-pulling case referred to in previous pages was first judged. Next was that of a young woman accused of having called another names. Her former keeper took the stand to testify in her behalf, but his testimony was not convincing, and she was fined $1.50 and bound over to keep the peace for a year. Another name-calling complaint followed, but there the facts were not established, and the case was dismissed with some asperity by the magistrate. A civil action involving a debt, when called up, was stated to have been settled out of court, while the final case concerned a three dollar balance owed for some ten months on a suit of clothes made for the defendant by the plaintiff, a tailor. An interpreter had to be called, since the defendant claimed to know only creole; he first offered to pay twelve cents a month, then a shilling, then — too late — fifty cents. He was ordered to pay a dollar a month and, when he declared with passion that "they could put him in jail" before he would meet this charge, to be confined for fourteen days if the payments were not made promptly.

Other sessions of the court offered similar cases, and were disposed of after the same dramatic wrangling of the principals, to the impartial relish of the villagers. These court sessions comprise a cross-section of the life of the region, and repeatedly provided confirmation of statements about Toco ways of life made in conversations but not otherwise susceptible of control.

No point under dispute is small enough to escape being brought to trial — the Magistrate even told of cases where an accused, aged six, was charged with pummeling a defendant, aged five! In one such action brought during the period of this study, the accused was seven years old. When the court had been cleared, a woman swore that the young defendant had "called her names and thrown things at her." The case was dismissed with the recommendation that should it happen again the boy's mother "give him a good hiding." Automobile accidents, the disposal of animals kept for one person by another, assault, quarrels between children that lead to an exchange of blows between their parents — all are actionable, and are threshed out in public. Questioning is done by the principals; witnesses are permitted to tell their stories in their own words; the police are rebuked if their charges are not properly made.

Court procedure, then, serves the Tocoan as a local newspaper, as theatre. Here he may be party to the small dramas of the region, and to the extent that as plaintiff, defendant, or witness he has an opportunity to plead a cause, he experiences a degree of participation in the direction of his own affairs. All these aspects of the place of the court in Toco life, but especially the dramatic aspect, are to be found in the trial of the Shouters who were arrested in Matelot and who were judged as a group.

5

Court day saw a larger crowd than usual when the Shouters' case was called. The accused were placed in a semicircle facing the court, where they were to stand during the long day's proceedings. Of the twenty-four defendants, twenty-two answered to their names when called, while the two who had to come from Port-of-Spain arrived later. At this point they were merely charged; one man, with "carrying on a shouting meeting," one woman with "attending a shouting meeting, having property used for a shouting meeting, and obstructing justice," and the others with "attending a shouting meeting." The plea of each in turn was, "Not guilty."

Three other cases, of the type given in the preceding section, were disposed of before the absent defendants arrived. The atmosphere in the courtroom became tense as the

Sergeant of police, the head of the local detachment who had ordered the raid, read his complaints against the Shouters, and satisfaction was shown by the spectators as he was rebuked by the Magistrate for not wording these properly. The complaints were admitted as amended, and then the Corporal of the local detachment took the stand.

He testified that he, the Sergeant, a constable, and a civilian had, on the previous Saturday night, gone to a place near Sans Souci where, at about 11:15, they had heard "loud and noisy singing," so loud it could be heard a quarter of a mile away. Peering through the window of the house from which this singing came, he heard the principal accused preaching, "Brothers an' Sisters, tonight is the night. Book your passage, the boat will be here soon," with the others responding "Amen!" to each phrase. "If your passage is not booked, you be lef' on the other side of the Jordan. Sisters and Brothers, repent an' be baptized!" Then the people began to sing "Jesus, Lover of My Soul," in a "a sad and mournful voice."

The Corporal described the scene. In the house were benches, and a table with candle, flowers, a Bible, and other books, which were produced in court as evidence. He identified all the defendants, first in a group and then, at the instance of the court, individually. The principal woman accused, he said, was not in the room, but in the kitchen, where were also six persons with their eyes bandaged. As the people in the room started "movin' their heads and swayin' their bodies," she saw him and called "Police! Police!" whereupon people ran until he and the others went inside the room and called out "Not a man move!" There he saw persons with their heads bound, and the table with the various articles already mentioned on it. An interlude that amused the spectators was the passage when the Corporal spoke of the "Sankey" and handed the hymnbook to the Magistrate, who, not knowing what the term meant, thought of it as a "song key," until it was explained to him. Under the table, the Corporal continued, was a stick (a wand), which they called a "rod of light." On being questioned, he explained baptism to the court as "seeing Jesus; keeping behind the teacher." He said that five candidates got away from the kitchen, and that the six with their heads bound who were assisting at the services were aides to the preacher.

Since no one wished to cross-examine him, he gave way to the Constable, who corroborated much of this testimony, except that he reported that all the accused, except one of whose identity he said he was uncertain, were in the house, and also declared that the principal woman defendant was outside the house when she called "Police, police!" as a warning. He added, "I saw one or two people change their attitude by shaking their bodies" — an attempt to reach legal phraseology in describing possession. He was cross-examined by one man about the position of the house, though not to much point, as far as could be seen. The civilian who formed the third member of the raiding party showed no enthusiasm for his role of witness for the prosecution, and merely substantiated the fact that there had been a raid, and that some people, "ran at the sight of the police."

The case of the defendants was drawn with skill. For as the first accused testified, there had been no baptizing, no shouting meeting at all, but they were all attending a "year-night wake" for the mother of the woman who owned the house; that far from preaching, he had been making a little address as chairman. He denied that he was a teacher, or that there was anyone in the kitchen with eyes bound. He also contended that the reason why the women had their heads bound with kerchiefs was merely that the night was cold. When asked about his statement regarding the ship, he replied, "What ship? No ship can come into a house! I wasn't goin' nowhere!" — a reply that was repeated by several others, until the Magistrate told the Sergeant, who was conducting the cross-examination, that the word obviously had been used metaphorically, and it was not necessary to press the point. The next man to take the stand in his defense told the same tale, remarking as to the bound heads, "Females always tie the head, or wear hat." Four more took the stand before the noon adjournment, all telling the same tale, all refusing to identify the wand, or admit there was to have been any baptizing, or that anyone gave an alarm when the police came, or that anyone ran away.

After adjournment, the same procedure continued, each of the twenty-four testifying in his own behalf. The proceedings became more and more tense as the participants grew more tired. The first two to testify were a couple of "traffickers" — that is, peddlers of goods — from Port-of-Spain, who also bought produce to take back, and customarily stayed at this house when in Sans Souci. They declared they had merely been sitting in a corner of the room, since there was nowhere else to go. The others charged were from various localities — Matura, Cumana, Guayamara, Rampanalgas, and Mayaro, and the questioning turned on several vulnerable points in their cases — how long they had known the woman who presumably was giving the "year-night wake," whether or not they had known her mother.

The Magistrate became more and more insistent on the question as to why, if this were a wake, no mention had been made of the mother's name, or why there had been no eulogy. Not knowing local usage, he did not realize that, whether their defense rested on fact or not, what they were describing followed customary procedures since, as we have seen, the dead is eulogized only at the very end of a rite of this kind, and at a more advanced hour than the time of this raid. He questioned each as to his religion, and the defendants gave their religious affiliations as follows: 13 Baptists (two had been Catholics, two Anglicans), 1 Moravian, 7 Catholics, 3 Anglicans. One or two who said they were Catholics were reprimanded, and reminded that they are not permitted to attend services or ceremonies outside their Church.

Two of the men, one from Sans Souci and another from Matura, stated that "the works of Matthew" were being fulfilled in this "persecution for singing hymns." Another, when asked whether the wand was used to light the lamp, looked vaguely about and said, "Light a lamp? No, sir. You cyan't light no light with a stick 'less it got match on the end," a remark that brought forth a call for order. The principal woman defendant denied everything. She said she had not held the wake earlier because she did not have the money for it, and explained the speech heard by the raiders as the first of a series of "heartfelts." One girl said she had just stopped at the house on her way to Matelot to visit, while several woman stressed the fact that they had returned to Sans Souci only to get the change of clothes they had left behind when arrested, when the prosecution was seeking to obtain an admission that the group, after their release on bail, had gone back to the scene to finish their "baptizing."

When the testimony was completed, and the Magistrate had summed up the case, he found that all the defendants were to be judged guilty. Then, amid an impressive silence, he stated that since in the earlier case he had tried the expedient of fining the leaders heavily and dismissing the others, this time he would fine everyone charged and found guilty. The principal male defendant was assessed ten dollars, or twenty-one days in jail, the woman ten dollars plus ten shillings plus two dollars cost, or fourteen days imprisonment; and a penalty of ten shillings fine, or seven days in jail, was imposed on all the others.

There was obvious relief at the amount of the fines, and excited talk as sureties were exacted of all those convicted who were not known to the police. Several elected to serve jail sentences rather than pay fines for what they considered a violation of their right to freedom of religious expression, but except for the woman at whose house the rite was held, all weakened before the end of the day and allowed their fines to be paid for them. The imprisoned woman could be seen working about, under police guard, during the next two weeks. She and the case were the subject of many discussions in the village, and she was kept fully informed of affairs by the simple device of having groups of villagers, their backs to her, loudly discuss current happenings.

6

Recreational opportunities in Toco are those of village life anywhere — an occasional dance, an occasional football game, church socials and festivals, and the cycle of births, confirmations, marriages, wakes, all celebrated as elaborately as means permit. The traditional reels and bele dances for the ancestors occur irregularly, and, as has been commented on, are given quietly and often secretly, in order to avert the public and private chidings of priest and parson. In the years of economic depression all rites were modest.

The week's climax for the younger men and women is the Saturday night dance, when a good share of the earnings of the younger men — "they not thrifty at all, you know" — are spent attending dances in neighboring villages, paying jitney fares, as well as the price of admission. The more provident, however, attend only the local dances. Once there is a family to provide for, the price of admission can seldom be spared, and the dance is watched from the outside.

For the older folk, the important event is the Sunday dinner, spoken of nostalgically by those who, having come on hard times, are compelled to forego the relished foods, and the flow of gossip that follows their enjoyment. For the woman of the household, this repast is of particular importance, and she never speaks of it with understatement; rather does she lavish on the memory of her successes all the fine detail and descriptive exuberance she can command. It is as though the dull weekday meals could be tolerated only in anticipation of the Sunday fare that, with ingenuity, could be contrived to give to the family not only favorite dishes, but a modicum of self-respect, as being the equal of others.

Old and young delight in telling, and hearing told, all the little incidents that go on in the village. To the outsider the speed with which news spread never ceased to be a source of amazement. Equally amazing was the celerity with which a story acquired a texture that made of the commonplace a thing of meaningful or ironic sequences, often going back to relatives long dead, or at the very least recalling to memory some comparable happening that led to unforeseen climaxes. No story was too trivial to stir an active response from the community, and to set in motion the weaving backwards and forwards in time of tales of supernatural deeds, and of retribution. Repudiating the meagerness of his everyday world, the Tocoan draws on tradition and wit to fill a canvas with more than life-size figures — and always there is the humorous detail, the grotesque situation, the incisive comment.

A jitney accident, the death of a destitute man, a raid of a Shouters meeting, are not allowed to rest as events explainable in terms of known causes and known effects. Such incidents at once become plausible results of magic set against a man, or mark the advent of a new jumby to haunt the community that denied him a decent burial, or underscore the punishment of a Shouters teacher for becoming over-bearing in her success and refusing the counsel of the humbler church members. This quality of seeking out the dramatic incident in each occurrence, and of elaborating on it with witticism and ridicule, describes the Tocoan more than any other. It goes far to explain the quarrels over trifles that lead to charges in court, the importance of the diviner who can interpret omen and dream, the role of the old women of the family who can invoke the power of the dead. It explains equally well the sympathy felt for the Shouters' worship, the pleasure of the "spiritual hymn," with the quickening tempo that makes it an exciting dance tune.

We can pass over lightly those traditional songs that punctuate animal tales of the Uncle Remus type — the cycle of Anansi stories — and others of a similar character. For these are told infrequently by adults in this community — at an occasional wake, or to the school children by an old grandmother, on a night of full moon. No conscious desire to have these stories perpetuated was met, even among the old men and woman, but the interest of the children, who know them well, and their eagerness to retell them, keeps their tradition alive.

Not in story telling alone, however, does this dramatic impulse find expression, nor in the detailing of current incident. A favorite method of comment is in song. The form is not one of narrative detail, but of deft allusion, of the suggestive image. The pattern of putting into song important happenings of the day lies deep in the tradition of the group. Improvisation is not considered a specialized gift, a talent of the few, but its molds are at hand for any ready wit, any alert mind. A song may be the collaboration of several persons, and there are, of course, at any given time, some men and women who excel as song makers.

Various molds shape the songs emerging from the local

scene. Some are newly improvised for ritual occasions, like the reel-quadrille cycle of dances given at the conclusion of an important healing rite to honor the ancestors, or the traditional bele dance as a more generalized form of remembering the family dead, or the bongo dances performed at wakes. For each group there are melodies that have come down from one generation to the next. To introduce a new song, an old melody, to which new words are put, might be used, or two melodies might be combined, or a melody might be reworked. There is no copyright to be infringed, and to reshape or rework an old tune is considered not only a valid but a welcome method. Of the well-known copyrighted American popular melody, entitled, "Underneath the Harlem Moon," the young men who gave it explained, "The Toco band invented it, and we catch it from them."

But not all melodies are rephrasings of old ones. Sometimes a tune heard, a European tune, can be "swung" into a desired rhythm, with perhaps a change of a few measures, or no change at all. In this case the words to a traditional song might be joined to the new melody, or a proverb might be used and to it added lines from older songs. Many times this is done half-consciously, or unknowingly. Several young men came forward to claim songs as their own, when, in fact, the songs were but little changed commercial recordings — Trinidad calypsos, and Harlem blues. What is demanded is that the phrase be apt, the rhythm appropriate, and the melody pleasing. It is doubtful that the Tocoan is aware of the consistent conformity to traditional themes of the songs he sings; nevertheless, the mold is there both to guide him and, in a manner of speaking, to limit him.

A scrutiny of some of the themes that underlie the songs that are sung, and some of the songs themselves, will aid in clarifying these points. The pattern of comment on current happenings places emphasis on the humorous, the pretentious, the malicious. An occasional note of pity, or self-pity enters; and the more frequent theme of the braggard, or the strong, boastful fellow; and the love motif. But the principal effect sought for and achieved is laughter.

The song may decry the free and easy manner of the young girls, and tell of the "Bay Road girls" who "have no pride," who neither work nor want, "But cock up their *lala* (dress), to tempt the Bay Road boys"; or as in an old favorite, it may satirize the laws of "government," always being careful to ascribe shortcomings or absurdities to another colony — in this instance Barbados:

> Ba'bados Governor
> Make a new law, say,
> All married men sleep a kitchen,
> All single men sleep a chamber;
> All married men sleep a hashes (ashes)
> All single men sleep on bedstead.

To a Tobago governor a song attributes a law about taking "a rich man powder," with the effect that, "He go swell you belly for nine month"; and the refrain is that the mother and father of the girl are neither to scold nor beat her, "Because me an' de boy know not'ing."

The theme of taunting a rival occurs often. A man is said to be so dark that, as he is told, "You take out you photo in a black burn pan." Congo Justina is apprised that no one will marry her, "For you face like a whale, an' you jus' come from jail." Another woman is admonished as follows:

> Gal, you too rough,
> You're too tough
> You're not enough,
> I wonder who man a go marry to you?

The elderly woman who weds a man much younger than herself is pilloried unmercifully. The one couple of this

kind that lived in the village got on well together, but when
the woman passed, someone was sure to begin whistling or
humming the song about, "Gangan (old lady) who worked
with a Bible, worked with a razor," to get her man. Clemen-
tina, Maria Coolie, and Camille are criticized as bad
women.

> Clementina yo-ho
> Give me back me dolla', gal.
> Oh you mumma jus' dead
> An' you're takin' the men.

Maria Coolie is accused of accepting men's money, and turn-
it over to her own man, while Camille is called "accursed"
and a "beast." A recurring allusion is to the girls who love
not wisely, as in the reference to those who broke their confirmation vows:

> Bishop Bree meet a jetty ge'l,
> All dem ge'l a break their confirm;
> Pa'son Turpin whe' yo' labor gone?
> All dem ge'l a break their confirm.

Variations on the theme of the young girl who finds herself with child are innumerable. No names are mentioned,
but the special point of the renewed popularity of any one
of the variants is that in the soft humming of the women,
and the whistling of the men, it broadcasts through the village streets a recent incident. One can be certain, if the
song is much heard, that this mishap had occurred in a
family of some social pretensions — a property-owning
family, where the children had enjoyed special educational
advantages, or were better dressed than other children, or a
family that numbered some important laymen of the established churches, or an official's family, or of one that had
been heard to lay stress on the married state as against the
keeper relationship. In the rendering of such a song, the

subtly worded satire becomes a vehicle of the broadest farce. Thus, the song would tell,

> Me belly a grow,
> Me mumma no know,
> Poor me wan,
> Wha' me go do?

Or the song may recount that three, four steamers came and there was no letter for the girl. "No quarril Camille, me go min' de baby."

At times a note of pity accompanies criticism of the young girl in trouble, as in the song for 'Ti fille Zutala, who died from the effects of the poisonous bitter cassava root that is used as an abortive, or the woman who tells how, "Dominic' (Dominican) scorpion sting me-o," and that going to the white-man's doctor, or the black-man's doctor was of no avail. The refrain, "Poor me wan, wha' me go do?" appears in song after song. Not only in the instance of the girl who had sought adventure and had come to grief is this heard, but the one whose, "House been bu'n," also interpolates this question.

The love theme may be the appeal to "Mary-Anne" to, "Le' go me man," telling that he is a decent man, and that she loves him; or it may be the gay English tune,

> Pink an' blue, pink an' blue,
> Little do you know what love can do;
> Love can kill, love can cure,
> Love can make a rich man poor.

A man may express his love for a girl by singing to her, "I want a pretty woman, for to sell me groun' provision," though often it is sung as if the suspicion were not far away that a pretty woman was not to be leaned on heavily in matters of economic aspirations.

The bragging, defiant songs are of the *bongo* type, and they affirm that no woman holds sway over the singer, or he may exclaim in a calenda song, "I sell me soul, give the devil." He may boast that he is known everywhere in the Island, that he is a *bongo* terror, that he is a Congo lion, that he had been charged "for murde'," or announce himself as "Lucife', he the son of the man, that never surrender."

An illustration of how innocent-appearing the words to a song may be, is had in the "wata' works" calenda song that originated from the incident of the introduction of a new street-cleaning machine in the capital. This machine had succeeded in cleaning only the middle of the road, calling for the use of men to follow in its wake and sweep the gutters. Its use was discontinued after a short trial:

> Wata' works
> Wata de road-a
> Wata' de yard,
> Wata de house.

The following *bongo* was composed while this investigation was in progress, and throws light on an occurrence that evoked comment in song, and the form this comment took. Village gossip could not fix on its authorship. "The rude boys make it up," was often said, but though the older people spoke deprecating words about its popularity, they could not disguise their enjoyment of the satire. The song refers to the first raid on a Shouters meeting during the summer and, as already discussed, the arrest of its leader and several members of the group. This leader had won a large following, and we need here mention only the fact that when preaching she was wont to exclaim that her faith made her happy, and that she was, "All full of vigor." This phrase became the core of the song, the point of mockery. The melody is traditional.

One for the mornin',
All full of viga',
She bawl for she mother,
They charge she sixty dolla'.

The sum of sixty dollars alluded to represents the fine imposed on her by the Magistrate, and her crying out to her mother mocks her lack of self-possession when she was arrested, and especially when the police removed the sacred bands that had bound the heads of those about to be baptized.

A demonstration was given of how the correct name of a person sung about is changed, and so phrased that some word resembling it is used with a *double entendre*. In the following song the word "trowe" — to throw or cast away — is used as a substitute for a name.

Buku Bay young girl,
Dem so bragging and t'ief,
Me hang me pork on me fireside,
Trowe carry 'im gowe.
Who you think?
Trowe carry 'im gowe.
Who you say?
Trowe carry 'im gowe.

The song given below shows how a proverb and a traditional refrain are joined in a calenda song:

Rollin' stone
Gather no moss,
Moin pas tini mamma (I have no mother),
Moin pas tini papa (I have no father).

The fisherman's song which follows illustrates the same process. Here words are taken from a folk-tale, and to these is added the comment about Bella who is in the yard, with the implication that the work she does may not have social approval.

> Yard-o, yard-o,
> Bella in de yard-o
> If you want to see
> De monkey dance,
> Bus' a pepper in he tail;
> Monkey play de fiddle,
> Baboon play de banjo,
> Yard-o, yard-o,
> Bella in de yard-o
> Master dead, he lef' no money,
> Missus have to work all about.

The Tocoan who gathers for communal labor sings as he works. Any secular tune may be introduced, though the songs most commonly heard are of the calenda, or stick-play group, or the "cheer-up," which is in form very like the calenda, or the carnival melodies, with the "sailor" songs in particular vogue. One of these, sung by the Sailor Band in the carnival of 1939, may be given:

> Texas sailor comin' down,
> You will see dem.
> See we marchin' down de road,
> We comin' to win all de prize
> Oh laws, we comin' down de road,
> Oh laws, we are comin' on parade,
> Oh laws, we comin' to get de prize on de road
> Oh laws, we got de bigges' banner over de town.

A favorite carnival type is the "Yankee." The costume consists of "a black waistcoat and flannel pants, an' a silk shirt, with beaver hat with a feather. Women carry fan, and men guitar. Then the face is black up, and the dance is quick, quick." Two popular Yankee songs follow:

John Gilman want tobacco,
His guitar want a string,
He wants some money
To buy some clothes
To put on his naked skin.
In the worl' the old folks say,
It ain't gonna rain no mo'
Oh, when I am up I am up (hiccough)
Oh, when I am down I am down (hiccough)
When I'm only half-way up,
I am neither up nor down.

*   *   *   *   *

Hippo, my Yankee
Hippo, my Yankee boy
Down de rive', down de rive',
Down de rive' we mus' go
Hippo, my baby
Hippo, my baby girl.

The Tocoan has a name for each song he sings, and each is fitted into a category of dance. There are the reel or qua-drille songs, which include the jig, the maringo and the "passy" or *passé-mazunga,* as it is sometimes called, all of them being figures in the reel cycle. He refers to the bele songs, calling the dance for which they are intended the *belier,* or Congo or *juba* dance as well, and adds, "We dance it because the dead people like it too much." He names the calenda, or stick-play songs, the bongo songs that accom-pany this wake dance, and the cheer-up songs that go with a Grenada dance "near to calenda." There are cocoa-danc-ing and wood-pulling and fishermen tunes in the work-song group, and there are the carnival songs.

There is also the calypso, but calypso is a name not often heard in Toco, except when commercial records are being discussed. "Calipso, or caliso, as old people used to call it, is dancing in carnival," an old man explained, and he added, "Young people today go for creole dances with clarinet work." But the method of an earlier day was to "sing on people," and the creole phrase for it is to *fatigue* someone.

The calypso has been made famous by the recordings that have had wide distribution outside Trinidad. For most white residents of the capital, indeed, this kind of song is the only type thought of when Negro music is mentioned. Many of the problems it raises — the origin of the term, the mode of composition of music and words, the "calypso tent" of carnival time — would be outside the scope of this discussion, even if an excellent analysis of these problems by two Trinidadians, Mr. Charles S. Espinet and Mr. Harry Pitts, had not been available. Other aspects of it treated by these students are also worthy of note — the fertility of the inventive strain shown in the words, the calypso "war," where "calypsonians" meet to exchange personal comment on each other's foibles, or the economic aspect of the calypso bands. Here we can but indicate to what degree the calypso follows a pattern which is fundamental in Trinidad Negro music, a pattern of self-expression achieved through comment and analysis, as demonstrated in the words to other types of songs found in the remote corner of the Island with which we are here primarily concerned.

Even in the commercially recorded calypsos the same themes we have found in the Toco reel and bele, *bongo* and calenda, are to be constantly encountered. The calypsos "Bad woman," and "Matilda," who "t'ief me money, run go Venezuela," employ the motif of the free and easy girl. "Why, why Sofia" plays on the theme of the young woman in trouble, with the comment "Poison is a silly drink," to indicate her way out of her difficulty. "She want to get me in matrimony," is self-explanatory, while "I don' wan' no young gal, I want an ol' lady to marry me," brings in the theme of the elderly woman with a young husband. Topical subjects abound in the calypso, as they do in Toco songs such as the *bongo* that was cited, the difference being that events of the day, no less than local happenings, are seized upon by the calypsonians, so that one can obtain a record such as "Hitler Demands," which in 1939 ended with the prophetic refrain, "We goin' to run y'outa Germany."

The patterns that have been shown to determine the words to types of songs other than the calypso that are heard in Toco, are well phrased by Messrs. Espinet and Pitts, when they state: "The calypso is a form of criticism, a living witty comment on contemporary events. . . . Despite the lightness of the vehicle, the calypso usually contains philosophies of the simple things in everyday life, the words displaying a deepness of thought . . . one would least expect from the singer and the surroundings in which it is sung." That the calypso has become the best known of Trinidad musical forms has no special significance for communities such as Toco, where calypso songs of local origin are part of a broader stream of musical self-expression. Nor does this fact in any sense detract from that quality in the calypsos that has given this song-type its wide popularity, for its vitality is to be ascribed to the very fact that it is part of a larger body of tradition that has lent it the molds of improvisation, a musical idiom, and the thematic devices it so skilfully employs.

CHAPTER XI

RETENTIONS AND REINTER-
PRETATIONS

IN ANALYSING THE CULTURE of the Toco Negroes, we are confronted with an intricate and subtle example of cultural integration. The processes of human civilization in change under contact, operating in terms of the specific historic sequences that stripped the Africans of certain of their aboriginal institutions and made for the kind of adaptation their descendants achieved, have produced the psychological complexities that have been seen to exist behind a façade of cultural simplicity.

Historically considered, the roots of Toco culture lie in Europe and Africa. Yet neither the institutions under which its people live, nor their attitudes toward their ways of life are at any single level in full consonance with either European or African tradition. For where, as in Toco, the power and prestige of the European stock have effectively set the tone of convention in European terms, retentions of African custom in immediately recognizable form are relatively few. The structure of society, its economic base, its political controls, its religious practices have been seen to be in large measure European. The validation of these forms of behavior is at the same time seen to lie in traditions that give to them meanings not shared by Europeans. What has happened is that the African contribution to this culture, functioning beneath the surface, and giving its

287

own significance to European institutions and beliefs has more often been made in terms of reinterpretations of African custom than as full-blown retentions of African ways of life.

We may now look back at this culture in the light of the hypotheses advanced in our opening pages, indicating what of African custom has been retained, how this was integrated with the European conventions that were accepted, and how both these were reinterpreted in terms of one another. In doing this, we shall refer not only to relevant aspects of the cultures of West Africa and the Congo, but also to similar adjustments achieved by Negroes in other New World areas. For only in such terms of reference is it possible to assess the underlying significance of this body of custom in New World Negro culture and, more importantly, in the wider sphere of the processes of change in human civilization as a whole.

2

The division of Toco society into socioeconomic groups, although cast in Euro-American patterns, is in accord with African tradition, and has been reinforced by continued African sanctions. The recognition by Africans of difference in status, and the acceptance of the relationships between members of different social strata, is a phase of African culture that has struck and continues to impress all observers. The principal distinction to be drawn is that in Africa, wealth and high position are equated with political power. But in both areas there is conscious striving to better the status of the individual and his family. Enterprise is valued in Trinidad as in Africa, where tales of commoners rising to the rank of chief are not unusual. The circumstance of slavery acted to reinforce preexisting African recognition of rank and of differing status. When freedom came, the ancestral patterns remained, reinterpreted in terms of New World organization of society.

The diet of the Toco people is marked by certain dishes that came directly from Africa. Here no changes were necessary, for the women, drawing on the resources of a similar tropical environment, merely continued the culinary arts they had been taught by their mothers. Sweet and salt *pemi*, mentioned as a delicacy of the Toco cuisine, are African dishes. *Sansam* is pounded parched corn, mixed with salt or sugar, and eaten dry. Its African character is recognized by the people. "This is African real food," said one. *Cachop*, the "special food of the Yarriba," is also made of cornmeal, like *pemi*, but is baked in a pot rather than boiled. *Calalu* is famous as an African dish over all the New World; a crab and okra stew, with pork-fat and grated coconut, which "they like too bad." *Acra*, boiled salt-fish dipped in flour to which has been added pounded hot peppers, and fried in deep fat, employing coconut oil, is another favorite. "Comes out brown an' pretty." In African fashion, too, we find all these dishes sold in the market places.

Eating habits are African. The "breakfast" at about ten o'clock, with the second principal meal in the late afternoon or early evening, is in essence the schedule of meal times found everywhere in those parts of the continent from which the forebears of the Toco Negroes were brought. Here, too, as in Africa, the man of the family eats apart from the mother and children. "She just give him food," and if friends of his come to have a meal with him, she serves them all. European conventions intrude into this pattern when families visit each other, for then men and women eat together.

The lines of division of labor between men and women, though in general following African custom, are blurred. As there, the men cut the brush and prepare the ground, both men and women plant, and the women do the weeding. Fishing and hunting are for men, housework is for women. Working for wages on the roads or in the estates was, of course, unknown in West Africa and the Congo, and hence few rules of aboriginal practice apply. Yet adaptation of the old pattern to the new scene is indicated, for example, in the coconut industry, when the men gather the nuts while the women take out the meat, or in the case of cocoa when men "brush" and plant while the women weed. Such craftsmen as are found — blacksmiths, tailors, cobblers — are, as in Africa, men, but all needlework, excepting only tailoring for men, has been taken over by women, who thus follow the European tradition.

Building operations are, in Toco, men's work, following African custom. The apprenticing of the young to craftsmen or the informal training in less specialized occupations received by a child at home is African, but it is also in the European pattern, and marked the slave regime as well. The "caretaker" institution — whereby a child is sent to be reared, in return for its services, by a family that can give it advantages it cannot have at home — is, however, an African tradition. This institution has persisted widely among Negroes in the New World as, for example, in the *kweki* custom of Dutch Guiana or the *'ti moun* convention of Haiti.

The *gayap*, whereby men cooperate in performing tasks that benefit from concerted effort, has its counterpart in Africa, though the custom of mutual self-help is far more widely spread than on that continent. The similarity of the *gayap* tradition to that underlying the various "bees" of American frontier days is obvious. The *gayap*, nevertheless, examined in all its features, is seen as the lineal descendant of such an institution as the Dahomean *dokpwe*; in Haiti one finds the *combite* as its equivalent, or in northern Brazil, the custom of *troca dia,* or "exchange of day's (work)." Here is an example of the retention of a custom which was immediately applicable to the requirements of the slave system, where gang labor was the fundamental technique employed in working the estates. Under freedom, the older custom merely reasserted itself, to obtain results that were beyond individual effort.

Maize came to West Africa from the New World. There it was adapted to the practice of planting yams in rows, and with it, in the same pattern, were planted vines that used the corn-stalks to support them, and others that trailed along the ground between the rows. This complex, when brought by the Negroes to the New World, met that which the Europeans had taken over from the Indians. Thus, as one gardener in Toco stated, "Beans with melons, pumpkins and cucumbers are planted with corn, and that makes a crop." Congenial, too, to the Africans must have been the rotation of dry and rainy seasons, since for the cultivation of their gardens this entailed no change in established procedures.

The supernatural sanctions of farming represent one phase of culture wherein retentions of Africanisms are found in greatest number. The sacredness of the silk-cotton tree and the need to determine whether it can be felled or not, the offerings given such spirits as are believed to dwell in it, the determination if the brook flowing through the field has a *mâit' source* and the manner of placating this spirit, are all quite African. Planting in accordance with the phases of the moon is, however, as prevalent in European lore as in African. The Church harvest festivals are European, but the "throwing away" of first fruits for the ancestral dead is continued in African manner, though with all care to secrecy.

In a similar way, the charms used by hunters and fishermen, the dangers of whose callings are emphasized as in Africa, are immediately comparable to their African equivalents. The concept of the *papa-bois* is of special interest, for it is the Trinidad manifestation of a West African category of supernatural beings known as the "little people" of the forest — the *ijimere* of the Yoruba, the *mmoatia* of the Ashanti, the *azizan* of Dahomey; or the Guiana *apuku,* the Brazilian *'saci,* and other "little folk" who are found in the Negro lore of all parts of the New World.

Within the sphere of woman's work, the phase most characteristically African is not that the women sell in the market, but that their earnings are their own. This follows African custom, where the economic position of woman has always been high. Here, as in Africa, she enjoys that degree of economic independence which reserves to her the decision whether she will spend what she earns to buy food for her household, clothing for her children or, in a household of higher economic position, if she wishes to please her husband, perhaps for some enterprise for which he requires money, or some gift for him.

A final African element in the Toco economic system, retained without even a change of its Yoruban name, is the savings device called *susu.* The Yoruban word is *esusu,* and persons from Barbados and Guiana who live in Toco told of its form in their homes, where it is known as "a meeting" and "boxi money," respectively. Its function has been explained; that it should have persisted so strongly in Trinidad as to be finally recognized in the laws of the colony, testifies to its tenaciousness and to its usefulness as an institution for the new regions where it had been preserved.

These Africanisms, nonetheless, when examined in the light of the whole range of Toco economic life, should be recognized as the minor retentions or reinterpretations of African forms they actually are. The clothing that is worn, the utensils employed are all imported. Little or nothing of the technological skills that make the African native self-sufficient remain. Here the suppression of Africanisms has been most complete, as will be apparent when we analyze their incidence in other aspects of Toco culture.

3

It has been shown that both legal marriage and the informal union termed "keepers" share in the formation of the Toco family; that both these enjoy social sanction, though they are endowed with differing degrees of prestige; and that in terms of the patterns of Toco conventions there thus is in this dual system nothing reprehensible. We are, indeed, here faced with one of the most interesting series of reinterpretations to be found in the entire range of Toco or, for that matter, of New World Negro custom. For here is a translation, in terms of the monogamic pattern of European mating, of basic West African forms that operate within a polygynous frame.

In West Africa and the Congo, where the children born of a mating belong to the man's family, and are under his control, certain ritually decreed fees must be paid to a prospective bride's family, and certain tasks must be performed for her father and mother. Should the girl merely join the man and form a union, living together without his paying these fees and discharging these obligations, children born to the couple remain under the control of the woman, or her family, no matter how enduring the match.

In Trinidad, practices governing the payment of fees, or the control of children have disappeared. What is left is the classification of unions into marriage and keeper types, the looseness of the bonds that bind a man and woman in a union — here applying to both classes of matings — and the attitudes derived from the existence, in Africa and later under slavery, of the nucleus of mother and children as the basis of the family structure.

The substance, if not the form of the obligations of a suitor toward the parents of the girl he wishes to marry are to be discerned in legal marriage. The formal letter, which under the law carries contractual force, is the reinterpretation of what, in Africa, are addresses to the parents of the girl made through an elder member of the family acting as an intermediary, and the contractual nature of betrothal; in Haiti, it is known as the *lettre de demande*. The investigation of the family of the young man by that of the girl, and of her family background by his, is similarly fundamental in African practice. The informal convention that a young man work for a few days during the planting season in the garden of his girl's father is a truncated expression of the African requirement that he prepare a field for his prospective father-in-law; though there, unlike Toco, he continues to do this or a comparable task periodically after his marriage. The contributions of food given if a close relative of a fiancé or spouse dies, not mandatory in Toco, is one of the most rigorously observed requirements of a man or woman in West Africa. The need to obtain the consent of the ancestors to the match, by holding a reel dance and giving the *sakara* sacrifice, is entirely African, deriving from the sanctions of the ancestral cult which, in uninstitutionalized form, are represented in Toco by the beliefs in the power of the dead members of the family that, as has been seen, function widely there.

It would be expected that with the disappearance of the sib, and the tradition of counting descent on only one side of the family, African patterns of exogamy would also disappear. In Toco, all that remains of this is a feeling on the part of the old people that one should not marry a second cousin, though even this rule is being dismissed with the dictum, "Second cousin no family." Only fragmentary, also, are the retentions of West African traditions of the sororate and levirate. There, when a man dies, his brothers and sons customarily marry his wives, and among some West African peoples, when a wife dies, the widower takes one of her sisters. In Toco, however, such marriages are sanctioned only if the original mating produced no offspring.

In all matings, the importance of "having the family behind you" is to be looked on as the retention of a complex of attitudes and relationships so deeply rooted in African culture that not even the experience of slavery could change it. Europeans also have family ties that strike deep, yet the quality of this feeling is one which, in kind and degree, is quite different from that of Europe. One recalls the shocked reactions in the courtroom when a mother and son bitterly contested the ownership of a plot of ground. A woman does everything she can to obtain the consent of her parents before entering into a marriage or a "keepers" relationship of which they are inclined to disapprove; a wayward daughter is brought under control by a rite denouncing her conduct to the ancestors. All this is a part of the pattern which, with the sanctions imposed and guardianship granted by the spirits of the family dead, gives stability to family life in full African fashion, even where unions often do not endure.

This also explains the importance of the household in the rearing and training of children. In essence, this is based on the retention in Toco of the nucleus of African kinship structures which, as explained, consists of a mother and her children living in a hut within her husband's compound, also inhabited by her co-wives and their children. That this nuclear unit has evolved into such a household as the one headed by the elderly woman, previously described in detail, where her grown daughters are still more or less under her direction and some of their children entirely given over to her care, merely represents in one respect the logical development of this African institution under the influence of slavery and of the particular socioeconomic position of the Negroes after slavery was abolished.

Further examination of this household reveals attitudes that are to be ascribed to other reinterpretations of African custom. We have seen that in this grouping, since the father assumed financial responsibility for a daughter and subsequently for her first child, these two members remained under his guardianship. Unlike the case in West Africa, in Toco the concept of the children "belonging" to a man has neither ritual nor economic import. Nevertheless, whenever the man provides the support of children born to him, his authority over them is recognized. Of equal significance is the attitude of the woman who heads this household toward the grandchild she has supported from infancy. She had been given no contributions towards the child's rearing, and therefore the child's mother could make no claim to it.

Thus in considering the forms taken by the family and the behavior associated with it, we are faced with a retention of African custom that has been reinterpreted so drastically as to make the resulting institutions not only susceptible of description as pathological manifestations of the European family but ones which, in fact, have been frequently so described. Nevertheless, as we have seen, these forms of the family are not pathological at all, but rather demonstrate how tenaciously a tradition can be held to, and how the process of reinterpretation can give to custom resilience and malleability in the face of new circumstances.

In examining the customs surrounding birth and training of children during the first years of their lives we shall find it useful again to recall our hypothesis that in the New World the process of stripping from the Africans the larger institutions in their culture left them only the more intimate aspects of earlier ways of life, for here retentions of this order abound. That abortion is held socially repugnant and must be practiced, if at all, in secrecy, is not particularly restricted to Africa; but that the enforcing sanction is in the fear that the ancestors, in their resentment, will cause barrenness is African. Another Africanism is found in the fact that a diviner is consulted when a woman has a first pregnancy, or has experienced miscarriages, or her previous children have died.

Notifying the family dead that a first child has been conceived, and asking their aid and that of the saints — transmuted from the African deities, although here European belief enters as well — for a good parturition or, should there have been a series of still-births, for the survival of the infant, is similarly in accordance with African custom. The measures taken by the lookman to counteract the evil magic that, in Toco, is believed to have "tied the baby" in the womb of the mother, or where a woman is held to have a "jumby belly," represent retentions of African belief and behavior in forms but little changed.

Toco has carried over from Africa many of the practices surrounding childbirth, and many of the beliefs concerning the significance of various characteristics of the newly born child. Depositing the umbilical cord in a hole over which a fruit-bearing tree is planted is found in many parts of Africa, though there the tree usually becomes the property of the child. In Africa, as in Toco, it is held that a baby with extra fingers or toes will be lucky, and that an infant born feet foremost is a dangerous being. The custom of giving a child born after a series of miscarriages a "funny" name, acting toward it as though it were disliked, dressing it poorly, taking precautions to nullify the magic that had caused the previous still-births, and vowing the child to a saint — reinterpreted from African deities — all constitute a complex widely spread among those who live in the areas from which the African ancestors of the Toco Negroes were obtained.

The African derivation of the cult of twins can be localized, for its form indicates the influence of the "Yarriba" component in the Trinidad Negro population. The fact that twins are held to bring good luck, the elaborateness of the rite of emergence from the house held for them, as compared to that for ordinary infants, their being taken to nearby houses to receive gifts that must be given in two equal parts, and the customs that follow the death of one of the pair are all variants of the Yoruban-Dahomean tradition, even to some of their details. These customs are also found in Brazil, Guiana, Haiti, Cuba, and elsewhere in the New World in similar specific form, where twins are given either their Yoruban or Dahomean designations *ibeji* or *hohovi*. In the Gold Coast, the Ashanti regarded twins as so important that, if they were girls, they became wives of the king, if boys, his servitors; and they were brought to him in a golden bowl. But eastward of the Yoruba, twins are destroyed at birth, for the respect in which the more westerly peoples hold them, because of the supernatural power they are believed to wield, turns to fear.

Other Africanisms found in the care of infants and rearing of children, in addition to the rite of emergence of mother and child from the house nine days after birth, as already mentioned in the case of twins, can be reviewed briefly. Baptism is a Christian rite, but the interpretation of its need to keep the child from joining the spirits of the forest is African; while the one baptismal name that in Toco is held secret is the counterpart of the "real" name given an infant in Africa, a name whose use exposes him to the force of any magic set against him. That an infant must never be left alone or, if this is unavoidable, must have magical or supernatural protection is a tenet of belief found everywhere in West Africa, its reinterpretation in Toco being manifested in placing an open Bible or prayer book at the side of the child whose mother is urgently called away from it, and has no one with whom to leave it.

The convention of giving an infant a gift when the first tooth appears, and the little ceremony performed when the first deciduous tooth falls out, come directly from Africa. In Dahomey as in Toco, this first tooth is thrown on the roof of the house — though by the child rather than the mother — and a little dance is held by its playmates, who sing,

> "I don't want the teeth of a pig,
>   They're big!
> I want the teeth of a goat,
>   They're small!"

The experiences — almost inevitably, it would seem, traumatic in effect — of those who soil the sleeping-mat are paralleled in West Africa, even to attaching a live frog to the offender, and sending the child out in the street to be shamed by the taunting songs of its playmates.

Other aspects of growing up which are African either in form or sanction include the manner in which a child is trained in household duties or in working the field, the importance for black magic of a girl's first menstrual cloth, the punishment of wayward children by the ancestors. But most important, to return to the household as a unit, are the attitudes toward father or mother. Here we must once again refer to the hypothesis advanced in the first chapter of this work, since the instances of the relationships within the household that were given show how, in the lower socioeconomic strata of Toco society at least, the father, as in Africa, remains on the periphery of the nucleus constituting the household, whose center is the mother, a grandmother, an aunt.

4

The role played by the spirits of the dead has been shown in these pages to be of great importance. In enforcing ethical and moral strictures, in aiding descendants when in difficulty, in sanctioning marriages, in keeping away evil magic and assuring safety in parturition, the influence exerted by the ancestors is impressive. This complex of beliefs is to be regarded as a retention of the African ancestral cult which in Africa is the most important single sanctioning force for the social system and the codes of behavior that underlie it. These manifestations in Toco are on a far smaller scale than in Africa. But the sanctions imposed by the dead are no less effective in the mind of the Toco Negro than they were for his African forebears, and from this fact the need for proper burial rites derives.

In Toco, as in Africa, the funeral and the rituals accessory to the final disposition of the spirit of the dead must be adequate in terms of the standards of the community. The tale of the anger manifested against the children of the village by the ghost of the pauper who was slighted in death can be matched in the many stories of this kind recounted in West Africa. The reinterpretation of respect due the dead in terms of the European patterns of wearing distinctive mourning clothing, and the penalties assessed, often on a child or grandchild of the delinquent one, are also found in many parts of the New World, as, for example, in Haiti.

In the funeral rituals details of African practice can be seen to have been interwoven with the canons of Christian burial to make up the body of Toco mortuary custom. To wash a corpse is common practice in human society, but the "plugging" of the body orifices, the tying of the chin with white cotton lest the mouth open, the fact that the eyes must be closed else "he's looking back for somebody," the care that is taken to see that no one obtains any of the body fluids with which to work evil magic, and the placing of whips with the body of a man suspected of having been done to death, are all specifically African. The displeasure of a dead parent, shown when "the box" becomes "heavy on the son's side," or the passing a child over the coffin three times and bathing it in the water used to wash the corpse in order to protect it against evil magic, are also directly from Africa.

The feeling that the body on the way to the grave should not rest on the ground is found, in somewhat different form, in African rites of death. The rituals of the churches were unknown in Africa, but the prominent role of the lodges is paralleled in African custom by the place of the societies to which a dead person belonged and, more especially, those of his children and their spouses. Placing of lodge regalia, of membership cards, baptismal certificates, and other honorific documents in the coffin is also a reinterpretation of African custom.

The complex of commemorative rites, which includes the wake, merits some attention. Wakes, once again, are common over the world, but many aspects of the Toco wake, especially the dances and those elements of the rites not generally witnessed, stem from Africa. These include addressing the dead with candor, as though he were present, pouring water about the house, and in front of the coffin, the *bongo* dance and the story-telling and game-playing sessions and, at the "forty-days," the offerings for the other ancestral dead of the family. The mock quarrel between chairman and assistant has its parallels in African custom, where the goal is to amuse the dead at his last visits among the living. The "heart-felts," in their competitive aspects, also resemble the manner in which sons and sons-in-law of the dead in Africa compete with eulogies of the departed.

More important, however, is the reinterpretation of the

"forty-days" ritual in terms of the pattern of partial and definitive burial found in all West Africa. Among some peoples, such as the Ashanti, it takes the form of commemorative rites about forty days after death, elsewhere it involves an actual exhumation of a corpse and its reburial; everywhere its object is to permit the surviving family to amass whatever is deemed necessary to pay the dead proper respect in terms of lavishness of outlay. It exists in other areas of the New World as, for example, in the United States, where a funeral may be held many months after burial, or multiple funerals may be given for a person, such as a preacher, who ministered to several communities. The African ceremonies for the dead at various anniversaries of death, also found in Brazil and Haiti, are present only sparsely in Toco, however, except for such rites as the "feeding" of the "yard spirit" and other family dead on All Souls Day. But the function of the "forty-days" as the occasion on which the spirit of the dead is finally sent forth, remains to fulfill the function of the African definitive burial, despite hymn-singing and other non-African aspects.

The concepts of soul, spirit, shadow, and jumby also fall in the realm of transmuted belief. For although these are conceived in the light of Christian doctrine, they are nonetheless effective retentions of the multiple-soul concept found in all West Africa and the Congo. Toco Negroes, it will be recalled, feel that on death the soul, which is the essence of the living being, passes to God. When the dead is entrapped and put to the uses of a practitioner of magic, the "spirit" becomes the "good or bad workman" that carries beneficial or harmful power. The soul is therefore the essence of the individual, while his spirit is that which becomes the ghost or jumby. His shadow, on the other hand, sometimes identified with the spirit, goes about when a person sleeps, and has the adventures which he experiences in dreams. And it is during these escapades that it can be called forth and "captured." In this event, the individual falls ill, and in the African manner is to be cured by a dance given for the spirits of his ancestors who, it is hoped, will rescue the entrapped spirit and restore it to its owner.

The inconsistencies in these beliefs, the inability of the Tocoan to give any commonly accepted version of the meaning of soul, spirit, shadow in relation to each other, in no way invalidates their significance for him. This is merely an expression of the incomplete nature of the retention of a systematic African body of concepts regarding the souls of men, in their integration into the system of Christian doctrines.

5

At a given period in the history of any people, certain aspects of their culture seem to have more relevance for the integration of their aspirations and goals than do others. Such highlighting of interest has in our initial discussion been termed cultural focus. For the Africans of the Guinea Coast and the Congo, this focus lies in the realm of supernatural sanctions. This explains why the ancestral cult in Africa is so important a factor in stabilizing kinship structures, and why other elements of the world-view of the West Africans have proliferated into complex systems of theological concept and ritual expression of belief.

Toco culture corroborates the findings in New World Negro cultures everywhere that Africanisms have persisted more in the religious life of the people than in any other aspect, save only folklore and music, which were favored by the indifference of the slave-owner to their continuing expression. But the history of the New World religious experience of Negro peoples shows no dearth of direction from the Europeans. From the first, the Africans were proselytized. They were baptized on their arrival in the New

World, and ministers and priests of the churches in each region used all zeal to convert them. In Catholic countries, such as Cuba and Brazil and Haiti and in early Trinidad, adaptation to this proselytizing was simple. The Negroes became converts of the Church and lived in the faith, achieving this without inner conflict by identifying the Saints with their African gods through a process of simple syncretism. Where Protestantism prevailed, however, reinterpretations of necessity were of a less direct and more subtle character. In Toco, as in all Trinidad, except where the Shango cult prevails, we must consider reinterpretations arising out of the demands of adjustment to patterns of Protestant worship.

In this process, the role of the established denominations must not be dismissed as of little significance, even though they fail to meet the need for mediation in the personal, intimate affairs of living, or afford but a meagre outlet for emotional and psychological participation. The Tocoan is no religious dissenter. The impulse to "belong" reinforces the deeply imbedded tradition of the need for security in matters of a supernatural order. Moreover, the sense of dependence on the rites of the conventional churches is strongest in relation to christening and death, rather than marriage, let us say, or confirmation, which are valued chiefly as prestige-giving ceremonials. Analysis discloses that in this differentiated response to Church sanctions is found a reinterpretation of first significance. For with the stripping of the ancestral traditions in the New World, those facets of religious organization that in Africa pertained to the tribal deities, and were conducted in cult-centers by cult-heads, have in Toco been transferred to the domain of the established denominations. At the same time, those practices, again of a more intimate nature, that impinged on the activities of households — divining in relation to personal fortunes, magic practices bearing on individual motivation for

the enhancement of individual aspirations, or the thwart-
ing of enemy well being — continued outside the churches.

But even though cognizance has been taken of the reinterpretation of ancestral tradition that has delegated to the
approved churches collective worship, still to be considered
is the Shango cult, which though having no establishment
in Toco, figures in the religious thinking of the people; and
similarly, the Shouters, who though few in number and
poor in resources, are mentioned with such frequency when
matters of religion are under discussion.

The Shouters, indeed, represent a series of reinterpretations to Protestant patterns of African religious experience
that are typical of those made by Negro religious groups
everywhere in New World Protestant countries where white
supervision has not been too stringently imposed. As will be
seen later, this sect represents a point of transition between
African religion, represented in Trinidad by the Shango
cult, and undiluted European forms of worship, as found
in the Church of England, among the Moravians, and, to a
lesser extent, the Seventh Day Adventists and the Baptists.
When the Shouters are compared to other groups in Toco,
they are equated not so much with churches as with
"orders"; and they are often referred to as a lodge. This is
done for several reasons, some of the more obvious being
the internal organization, the intense feeling of unity within
the group, the canons of mutual aid that regulate the relations of the members to each other, the discipline exacted
of members, the ritual handshake, and the ways in which,
at funerals of adherents, the group takes charge.

All this represents a reinterpretation of African cult-or-
ganization and cult-belief within the framework of Protestantism. The head of the Shouters group, the "teacher" or
"leader," who has the highest degree of spiritual power and
control, is the equivalent of the African cult-head, the
priest. The more important church officials correspond to

the principal assistants of such a cult-head, who in Africa are initiates of long standing and of proved capacity. In West Africa, initiates receive their gods who, like the Holy Spirit of the Shouters, possess them so that they dance and sing, in rhythms comparable to those in Trinidad Shouters' "temples." Each African god gives his devotee a function to perform, and these functions are like those conferred on a Shouters initiate by his "gift." More important is the fact that each brings from his baptism "a hymn, a psalm and a chapter that is his" — the parallel, in Protestant terms, of the specific songs and drum rhythms and modes of speech which, in both the Shango cult of Trinidad and in West Africa itself, cause the particular devotee "to receive the spirit."

Some of the terms used for officials of the church are indicative of retentions of African usage. "Father" and "mother," for leaders, is equivalent to the Yoruban or Dahomean word for priest — *babalorisha* or *vodunon*, literally "father of the gods," a "possessor of the gods." The role of the "judge" who tests leaders and settles disputes within the group, or of the "surveyra," who finds the four corners within which worship is carried on, or of the "diver" who brings back the spirit of those possessed, or of the "prophet," are all found in African cult-groups. The "watchman" and "prover," who seek out evil-doers and test the rectitude of members have their African counterparts, while the fact that the spirit will come to a Shouter, who then testifies concerning misdeeds of members of the group, is a common practice in Africa and among New World African cults, though in these latter cases the one who testifies does so while possessed by his particular deity. The importance of the central post in the Shouters "temple" is West African; the chalk-marks on the floor, though in detail influenced by books of magic dating back to the Middle Ages, correspond to the *verver* markings in the *vodun* cult of Haiti; while poles with cloths of various colors attached will be seen everywhere in sacred localities of Africa and the New World.

The vision-experience of a Shouter, as earlier recounted, describes the manner in which the African gods often come to those they desire for their worshippers, except that the vision of the Shouter was of Jesus. The service he rendered the "teacher" who baptized him and instructed him is not unlike the obligations of the African novitiate toward his priest — discharged there, however, more often by his family than by the one undergoing initiation.

Instruction before baptism, revelation of the hymn, psalm, and chapter, binding the eyes of the novitiate, baptism in "living" water and the ensuing possession by "de Holy Ghos' " is comparable in New World practice to the preinitiation African custom of washing the head to dedicate it to the god, without, however, making of the individual a full-fledged cult-member. In Africa, after the deity signifies his desire for the one he has selected to be trained to his service, the initiation, once begun, must continue until completed, though it may be deferred until the family has resources adequate to support the cost of induction into the cult. In a sense, the time between baptism and mourning can be correlated with this interval.

The rites of the mourning ground hold many resemblances to initiation into the African cult-groups. There is a period of seclusion which, though not so long in Trinidad as in Africa — or for that matter in Brazil — is as long as the time during which the person being inducted into the *vodun* cult of Haiti is kept from the outside world. The fact that the novitiate is reborn and, as a child, has all his wants cared for, that muscles, tired from holding a single position over long periods, are massaged; the fact that inattention is punished by the spirit, and that one learns to "talk language" — these are all details to be found in the initiatory rites not only in West Africa, but, like the preceding examples, in the African cults of Brazil and Haiti and, in all likelihood, in Cuba as well.

Other details are that one takes a new name after mourning, and that at the ritual which marks the emergence of a group from their initiatory experience, each novitiate demonstrates his spiritual power and ability. In Africa and the New World countries mentioned, like in the Trinidad Shango cult, this takes the form of performance in the dance. That in the Shouters temples it is expressed in testimony given, or in a spiritual hymn that has been revealed only to the initiate, indicates the form that this particular reinterpretation of aboriginal custom has taken under Protestant concepts of the Universe and Protestant modes of worship.

One striking correspondence that represents a retention of African custom in Shouters' post-mourning practice is the need for one who has returned from mourning ground to remain in seclusion for a few days. The African theory, blurred in its retention here, is that the spiritual experience has been such as to wipe out earlier training; that the initiate is a child, and must relearn secular tasks, such as the use of tools and utensils and the performance of skills associated with everyday living, so as to execute them with effectiveness and without personal hurt. The phrasing of the Shouters, that care must be taken lest the spiritual quality of the gift gained in the mourning ground be impaired by too abrupt contact with the workaday world, shows solicitude for the power rather than the individual to whom it has been vouchsafed. But the statement that, "they mustn't handle a knife or cutlash or handle money," is too much like the symbolic reintegration of the initiate into the daily round, found in West Africa and among Afro-Brazilians, to be fortuitous.

In the Shouters' services that have been described, a number of African retentions, some in quite unaltered form, may be named. The transmuted Sankeys, formed into Shouts, and the "spiritual hymns," are from the point of view of their rhythms, their accompaniment of hand-clapping and patting of the feet, and the motor-behavior that marks their singing, fully in the African pattern, as is the belief that the god himself improvises in song. The African character of the possession experience is self-evident, not alone as concerns the theory of possession, but also in the bodily movements of those possessed. The white dresses worn by the women initiates, the informality of children's behavior at services, the pouring of water three times at each corner of the "temple" and at the central post, and "talking in tongues" — such unrelated details are all African. The need to permit one to whom the spirit has come to finish his possession no matter what the urgency to end the rite — as occurred at the Sunday evening service that was described, where the ten o'clock rule was being violated and the danger of arrest thus increased — is another such detail. For in African and in Afroamerican cults where the drums bring on possession, stopping the rhythms abruptly before the god "leaves the head" of his devotee is dangerous for the one possessed.

The use of the shepherd's crook by the "teacher" in a Shouting group is a reinterpretation that once again underscores the importance of the Shouters as a kind of half-way stage between African and Protestant forms of worship. The image of the congregation as a flock led by a shepherd is common to Christian teaching, as is the designation of Jesus as "the good shepherd." But the leader of the Shango group also carried a shepherd's crook when possessed by his African deity, Shango, the God of Thunder. In Yoruban-Dahomean theology, Thunder charges through the sky as the ram, and the animal sacred to this god is the sheep. Here the process of identification is not difficult to follow, and illustrates, with clarity, the way in which retentions of African customs were achieved through the process of reinterpretation.

The question may well be posed why the Tocoan is not content to leave to the established churches the rites that see to the welfare of the community and certain other ceremonies that touch the individual in relation to the larger groupings, while caring for his personal religious safeguards through the avenues of divination and magic; or else adopt the Shango worship which stands at the other end of the scale. Here we are, in reality, confronted with two antithetical factors that operate to give the Shouters their importance in Toco life.

On the one hand is the pull of African-derived traditions that, comprehending fulfillment in the present, in earthly well being if the gods are properly worshipped, make difficult a harmonious syncretism with the Christian doctrines of sin and punishment, and other-worldly reward. We have but to recall the affirmation the Shouter senses in having a "gift" that is evidence of active participation in the Eternal scheme, the stress Shouters repeatedly place on the exaltation in being "filled with joy," or the importance they lay on "rejoicing," as the dance of the entire congregation about the central post is called, to perceive how this sect satisfies those traditional African values to be looked for in man's relations to the supernatural.

The second factor is the reaction against tradition, as shown in the desire to throw off older practices which are the active expression of ancestral belief and stand in the way of the urge to acquire the European idiom, with its palpable rewards, in totality. This is the reason young men say, "Baptis' don' shed blood. Say Jesus shed his blood. Don' have to kill animal now," when they state their preference for Shouter as against Shango worship. But the end result of these two drives is the same. For both the pull of

traditional values and the reaction against them give meaning and worth to the Shouter complex of belief and ritual,
and thus, through integration reached by means of reinterpretation manifest in these diverse approaches, validate the
place this complex has attained in this society.

6

There are two explanations why it was easier for the African under slavery to retain his beliefs in divination and
magic, and in the practices associated with them, and to
pass them on to his descendants, than to continue his aboriginal forms of worship. In the first place, these are matters
that involve no public rituals and can therefore be carried
out in the privacy of a cabin, or in an isolated spot in the
open country-side. More than this, however, is the fact that
the forms of African magic and European magic — and the
general concept that it is possible to foretell coming events
— differ only in detail. That this unconscious recognition
of affinity was present among Europeans as well as Africans
is illustrated by the well-documented fear slave-owners had
of the magic powers of their slaves.

Digression at this point to analyse the phenomenon of
the Old World Cultural Province is not feasible, but it is
of value to indicate that this similarity between European
and African practices, found as well in certain other aspects
of culture, notably folklore, is explainable by the fact that
both continents form part of an area over which have been
diffused, through centuries of contact, certain elements that
have become common to the entire vast region. Thus, although the European and African streams diverged in detail, when they came together again, as in Trinidad and
elsewhere in the New World, they merged as easily as the
waters of two rivers which meet to form a third.

Striking evidence of this is had in the way in which the

obiamen and lookmen turn to mediaeval books of magic, such as Albertus Magnus, for formulae with which to actuate their powers. Even more striking is the eagerness of these men to obtain the mail-order catalogue of the Chicago house of de Laurence, a man renowned throughout the West Indies as a worker of magic, whose charms and roots, divining rods, and crystal balls are believed to possess great power to operate in this realm of the unknown. These objects are sought because they are set in a pattern which, though European in origin, is also that of the ancestors of the Toco, Trinidad, and other New World Negro diviners and workers of magic.

Among certain African emphases to be discerned in the beliefs concerning the ability of workers in magic to mobilize supernatural forces is the view that every power for ill can also be employed for good, and conversely, that a good charm can have its evil complementary role. We see in this a refusal to accept the European dichotomy between good and evil. In West Africa, among Europeanized natives, as in the syncretisms of African cults of the New World, the trickster Legba or Eshu is identified with the Devil. But the Devil with whom this trickster is identified is not the embodiment of evil found in Christian theology, but rather the Devil as he is envisaged by the Tocoans — and as Legba or Eshu is thought of in Africa — as one who can help as well as harm. "Even Jesus used Beelzebub, you know," is a quotation that may be recalled here. This attitude also extends to the jumbies employed by workers of magic as their "messengers," usually, but by no means exclusively, bent on evil errands.

Toco also emphasizes the African aspect of this Old World pattern by attaching extreme importance to divination. Divination is by no means absent from Euro-American culture, even to the present, but the extent to which the Tocoan feels it necessary to consult his lookman far

transcends European practice in this respect. In Toco these
occasions are to be counted in terms of the number of difficult or critical situations faced by an individual in his adult
life. The absence of skepticism is like that of Africa, where
magic and divination are living beliefs, and not, as in
Europe and America today, furtive survivals of earlier conviction. The explanation of failure to achieve desired results framed in terms of misuse of the lookman's power also
stems from this firmness of belief.

In the idea that the obiaman works with the "soul of a
person cast out," a jumby, we find a reinterpretation in
terms of Christian concept of the standard African belief in
the use, by the worker of magic, of a captured soul as his
"messenger." But that two obiamen should pit their powers
against each other in a contest between two jumbies controlled by them is entirely African. The fact that an obiaman exacts a large payment for his services, while the remuneration of the "teacher," who is concerned only with
good, is what the client desires to give, is the local version of
a familiar African theme. Of African character are many of
the techniques of "looking," and the "tricks" or other
charms or medicines used in achieving magic ends, such as
the employment of "thunder-stones," or the grouping of
poison with supernatural devices in the general category of
evil magic.

The use of a chicken whose feathers stand erect — a
"sensa-fowl" — to detect any charm set against its owner is
likewise African, for in Africa, as in Negro rural communities from southern United States to Brazil, fowls of this sort
are to be found scratching about in many a yard as a protection against evil. That the power of a charm can be vitiated
by failure to observe the taboos its ownership imposes, and
that this power must be periodically renewed, is also common African belief and procedure.

On the other hand, it would be impossible to indicate

either African or European provenience for such concepts as those of the evil eye or the legawu, a combination of the French *loup garou* and the West African vampire. The ways of tricking these beings into capture is present in the folk-tales of all the Old World province. To put salt on the skin of such a being when the skin is cast off, or to set a broom upside down near the door, are only two of a number of devices — which, perhaps there as elsewhere, include putting in front of the doorway grains of cereal to be counted, or leaving a needle with a broken eye to be threaded, tasks that occupy the creature until dawn, when it is caught.

7

The means of self-expression open to the Toco Negroes, except for their aesthetic manifestations, are European in their derived forms. Lodges and orders tend to carry on the secret society tradition of West Africa, assure proper burial to members, and pay respect at their feasts to their dead by setting a place for them. Other than this, there is little in them not to be found in the general patterns that orient such organizations wherever Euro-American culture holds sway. The same is true of the courts, which are organized and conducted by the Colonial government, and operate in terms of English law and procedure. Here, too, all that is African is the delight in the well-turned phrase, the interest in the situations of human conflict interpreted in subsequent gossip as being caused by supernatural or magical forces, and the pattern of eloquence in advancing an argument — all phenomena so general in nature as to make specific reference to African practice quite impossible.

In story and dance and song, however, the matter is quite different, for here West African forms as well as sanctions are present. The Anansi tales, though today relegated to the place of children's stories, are nonetheless the same accounts of the exploits of the spider, whose name is given to this category of tale, that are told in the place of its origin, the Gold Coast, by the people of the Ashanti and the Fanti tribes. In Africa, these animal tales, which set forth the trickery of the principal character — who always prevails by guile, since he is small and powerless against the strength of the larger beasts — have among other uses their employment as allusions in divining sessions, or play a part in the education of the young. In Toco the telling of them is not widespread; this reflects the degree to which this culture has over the years moved toward the European side of the cultural balance.

African riddles and proverbs are heard in Toco, but again, only occasionally. Children in their story-telling sessions enjoy riddling, but unlike in Africa, one rarely hears a riddle on the lips of their elders. Proverbs, too, are strangely absent from the conversation of Toco folk — strangely, that is, because among most Negro peoples in the New World no less than in Africa, proverbs are introduced continuously to punctuate, illustrate, and moralize upon all situations that confront human beings. When an attempt was made to collect proverbs, to facilitate a colleague's comparative study of Antillean folklore, it was necessary to illustrate with proverbs collected from neighboring islands before anything but European aphorisms could be obtained; and those who remembered the sayings typical of African and New World Negro cultures were elderly folk, who themselves had lost the habit of using them in everyday speech.

Dancing shows a range of styles from the purely African, as in the *bongo,* to European and American social dances, of both more and less recent vogue. Certain older European dance-forms have received frequent mention in the preceding pages — the reel, the jig, the quadrille, the passé. These are carry-overs from the early days of Negro-white contact, as are the tunes to which these dances are danced, many of which are of familiar Scotch-Irish derivation. How readily elements in differing traditions can be combined is once more exemplified in the use of these tunes and old-fashioned dances as integral parts of the rites of those aspects of the African ancestral cult that have been retained in Trinidad. For the reel and bele are danced when the ancestors are called to cure an illness or assent to a wedding or for similar occasions — a curing rite, as has been seen, being actually called a "reel." The reason for this is that unlike the gods, the worship of the ancestors is by means of secular dances in Africa as well. And since, to gain the favor of the dead, what they had enjoyed in life is offered them, what the "old people liked too much," is danced. The *bongo* is the dance reserved for wakes, both on the night preceding burial, and at the commemorations of the ninth and fortieth day after death, and any subsequent anniversary rites.

Musical forms vary from the European reel and quadrille songs to the preponderantly African Shango-cult music. Detailed musicological descriptions cannot be given here, but an analysis of the large collection of songs made during this study shows that despite the influence of European musical style, there is, on the whole, more of Africa than of Europe in this music. Some of these African characteristics are the emphasis on rhythm, the tendency, in rhythmic accompaniment of the melodic line to introduce and maintain polyrhythms, the antiphony between leader and chorus in singing, and the employment of intervals characteristic of African music.

Motor behavior while singing, such as swaying of the body, and the manner in which handclapping is done with cupped hands rather than with flattened palms, is likewise African. Shango cult-music is accompanied by a battery of drums, with the words to the songs in Nago, the language of the Yoruba, as were the songs recorded by the "Yarriba" woman of whom mention was made in the first chapter. The "Shouts" which develop out of "Sankeys," and the "spiritual hymns" may be regarded as marking a half-way point between the two styles that are employed with such catholicity of taste and adaptability in rendition by the folk of Toco and of Trinidad.

As has been indicated, the calypso, best known of Trinidad song types, represents a traditional use of song to comment on current happenings, to phrase social criticism, to convey innuendo. The verses of almost all the song types of Toco, except those hymns to which the words are set by the song books, have been seen to be cast in this tradition, which is entirely African, even to the impromptu character of improvised comment on a theme of current interest. Such a song was "All full of vigor" that had to do with the arrested Shouters teacher; such are the improvisations of the calypso tent where the leaders of Port-of-Spain bands who make commercial recordings and appear on the radio, comment on the foibles of each other in friendly contest. This is the pattern by which, in West Africa, a song that names no names is made up to castigate an enemy, and sung in ancestral rites, or in the market place, or by a wife as she works about the compound to express her displeasure with some act of her co-wife. Even though some of the music is cast in the mold of European folk tunes, and the words are in English, nothing of African purport or intent has been erased. For despite its non-African form, this musical complex can be regarded as nothing less than a retention of the purest type.

APPENDICES

NOTES ON SHANGO WORSHIP

SHANGO, the God of Thunder of the Yoruban people of Nigeria, gives his name in Trinidad to the complex of African worship found there. The Island has several Shango groups, each with mutually exclusive membership, the members of each group profuse in their praise of their own cult-head. They tell of his or her healing gifts, of the African esoteric knowledge he or she commands, and at the same time affirm that certain African gods that in their own cult-center are sent away as undesirable are welcomed in other "houses." We shall see later what manner of gods these are.

How does one become affiliated with the Shango cult? In Toco, in answer to inquiries regarding what was known there of this worship, it was asserted that the Shango people form healing and dancing groups, and that those who belong have African spirits. Such a definition explains the place of this worship in popular thought. An individual, let us say, who visits a Shango cult-head because of some malady, and feels that he has benefited from this consultation, will emerge with an interest in the worship conducted by the cult-head. It may happen, further, that such an individual will be told by the cult-head that some African god desires to be worshipped actively by him; that this illness has disclosed the impatience of the god with him whom he had chosen to be a devotee. After a treatment that involves propitiatory offerings, such a person is encouraged to con-

tinue visiting the public rites of this group, until such time
as the god demonstrates that he will countenance no further delay in having him prepare himself for formal
worship.

Another might be attracted to the activities of the group
by an interest in the dancing phase of this worship. After
frequent visits to the cult-center, he would receive a direct
or indirect suggestion that a consultation be had with the
priest or priestess, to determine if this interest had not been
dictated by a god who had chosen this means of leading the
individual to undertake his worship. Some minor offerings
would then be given to the god to enhance the fortunes of
the individual, and in time, following pressure from the
god — which might be expressed in some distressing occurrence, or ill-health — would lead to the rites that would
make of the individual a cult member.

Such examples do not include the important group of
memberships that are passed on in families. These do not
necessarily descend from parent to child, but rather from
one kindred to another — often going from a grandmother
or great grandmother to a male or female grandchild. The
inheritance of such a god may be revealed by divination to
ascertain the cause of some illness in the immediate family
of the person who has been elected to succeed to the spirit,
or the successor herself may fall ill, or the fact may be indicated in a dream. But the most common method by which
the desire of the god is told is in the sudden possession of a
younger member of the family by the ancestral spirit.

The group with which we are concerned demands no
formal initiation. "We has no mournin'," said the priestess,
using the Shouters' word for the period of retreat that is
called for in the acquisition of supernatural "gifts." The
rite that is exacted is the ceremonial washing of the head
to dedicate it to the deity. For when possession occurs, the
god is conceived to be taking control of the individual by

entering his head, and displacing the awareness of the every-day world with an awareness of a supernatural order. This new awareness interprets the will of the god, who dictates bodily posture, type of dancing, songs sung, word ejaculations, or the more sustained phases of prophecy.

"Before we wash the head," said the priestess, "they must fall." This act of "falling" is construed as the culminating gesture of the god in demanding worship. When this occurs, the individual lies unconscious, or later, regaining partial consciousness, mutters unintelligible syllables while rolling on the ground or foaming at the mouth or wishing to do violence to himself or others. "A person can fall anywhere, but it mostly happen in she own house," it was said. A member of the family then comes to the priestess of his acquaintance to tell what had occurred, and at a time agreed upon, the one who had "fallen" has this rite of head-washing performed. He thus comes under the tutelage and professional care of this cult-head, and in turn assumes the obligation of formal worship of the god.

It was made clear that not everyone who uses the services of the cult-heads of the Shango groups acquires a god, or needs to engage in the active worship of one. If the "fall" occurs to a person who has not frequented any special group, the choice of the house with which to be affiliated is determined by the family; but if the "fall" takes place at a cult-center, then it is recognized as the god's own choice of place of worship. Moreover, the identification of the god that seeks to be worshipped is made self-evident when this occurs, for in the *chapelle* where the one who has "fallen" is taken to be brought out of possession, he crawls toward the chromolithograph of the Saint who corresponds to his god, and lies there face downward. "If you fall under St. Anne's picture, we know is St. Anne who ride you."

For the rite of head-washing, the worshipper himself, or his family, will pay to "make the massage with leaves and other things." A goat is furnished as an offering to the god, and a large kerchief in the color sacred to him, which is either worn about the waist or about the neck. The comb and basin that must also be provided for the washing ceremony may henceforth be used by no one else. "After the head is washed, don' let anybody to play in the head. Don' let anybody touch the head. That is why you binds it. If anybody strike the head after it is washed, then the person will fall down." This renewed "fall" will repeat the behavior of the first fall, for the head will have been desecrated, and the god will require propitiation before he is quieted. To emphasize the importance of keeping the head, which now belongs to the deity, from profane contact, the priestess added, "Anyone touch my head, I go bite off he hand!"

A devotee takes the name of his god, adding the suffix –*si* to it to designate the relationship. *Si* in the language of Dahomey has the literal meaning of "wife," but by extension is applied to any worshipper of a god. In Trinidad the designation is employed in the same context as in Dahomey, Ogunsi, Oyasi, Shangosi, Yemanjasi becoming the names of those whether men or women, who are consecrated to these respective gods.

After the head has been consecrated to the god, instruction follows in the manner of his worship. The day of the week sacred to him must be observed. The devotee must bathe that day, and put on clean clothes. Whenever possible the new worshipper should "go to praise" — prayer-meeting or mass — on that day. Sexual continence must be observed that night. At home, a small table is placed against a wall, and over it a chromolithograph of the Saint who corresponds to this African god is hung. A candle must be placed underneath it in a holder, flowers, and a dish with *obi*, the sacred kola nuts. If the god is Shango, a thunder stone is put there on a dish; if Ogun, something of iron, for he is god of metals and of war. For the water goddess Oshun, there is an anchor, which is her emblem; for Yemanja, also goddess of the water, a stone shaped to suggest a fish. All these must be especially consecrated by the cult-head. "Each Saint have his own goblet," the priestess continued, meaning by this the brown pottery jug which holds water sacred to the god. "So we make a little *chapelle*," she concluded, using the créole word for chapel.

In answer to the query whether a single individual can be possessed by more than one god, the reply was unhesitating. "Is only one for each person. Sometimes a Saint come for a dance when another have paid passage, but he comin' for a little pleasure." Thus a worshipper of Yemanja can dance along with Oshun, and Oya and Ogun, but "only Yemanja will *ride* she." The idiom "to ride" is used to express the concept that when the deity enters into the head of a devotee he becomes master of the body of the worshipper, and uses it as a vehicle. If at a given time a person who had been prepared for the worship of a god does not wish to dance for him at a ceremony at which the gods will be called, he may take two pins and cross them in fastening the undershirt, or the shirt. "That tie him. Then he don' come," the priestess declared. But her son interrupted with the cynical observation, "Sometimes he come anyway. Come strong."

Once the individual is dedicated to a god, and has established that god in its little *chapelle*, he has but to observe at home the day sacred to the deity, and to speak certain invocations when asking for good health and well being, or for some special favor when about to engage in a new undertaking. The principal rites for the god will take place at the cult-center once a year, or preferably, if means permit, twice a year. This requires offerings to the god, and a ceremony directed by the cult-head during that period of the year set aside for the cycle of rituals that honor the gods of all the worshippers of the group, when the important public dances are held. Here, the recognizable signs of those who are offering sacrifices to their gods is in their dress. For this rite, women wear a *driette,* a long dress that has a wide skirt of ankle length and longer, and a tight bodice, with a kerchief to match the print of the dress. "Don' always tie kerchief aroun' wais', but wear it." Men wear a kerchief in the color of the god.

2

The complex of houses which constitute the cult-center of one Shango group is perched high on a hill above the capital, on a street that is but a short distance from a main road. To the west can be seen the city, the harbor, and the distant Venezuelan Andes. The compound is surrounded by a fence, the lower part of which is crudely made of flattened gasoline tins, topped with the round ends of the metal casks in which pitch is stored.

There are several houses in this compound, the first, reached by a series of uneven steps, being the dwelling of the priestess and her husband, an old man, who rules with an iron hand. Next to it is another dwelling, and then facing it, but sloping downhill, is the "tent," as the open shelter, roofed with galvanized iron where the dancing takes place, is called. Directly in front of this, but on posts some twenty-five feet away, is the *chapelle,* while flanking it is the cook-house. Pigeons circle about the yard continuously, and sensa-fowls are underfoot. It will be recalled that these are the fowls — in appearance like feather dusters because of the feathers that stand up, erect, and with necks so innocent of plumage that they have a naked look — that dig up any evil magic that may be buried about the grounds. Several dogs come in and out of the yard, and a large, friendly cat makes herself at home near the cooking shelter.

The *chapelle* and the "tent" — which, incidently, are in a sense connected by a thatched passageway — are the important ceremonial units of the compound. The first is barely more than six feet by ten, and curtains over the doorway in the sacred colors of Shango screen the *chapelle* from view when the wooden door is open. The "tent" has benches about its four sides for the cult participants, while the drummers' places are arranged to face the *chapelle*. At one side there is a clothes-rack for the convenience of the players, who hang their coats on its pegs while taking over at a ceremony.

Suspended from the roof of the "tent" are eight drums of various sizes, from which are selected the three required to form the battery for any ceremony. These drums are headed on both sides, and are rather more like the European type than the African hollow-log form, though they are played in African fashion. The two largest drums speak to the gods. "One is for Saint Michael and the other Saint John the Baptist," the old man explained, employing the Catholic identifications for Ogun and Shango. Of the three smallest drums, one was for Ogun, and two were Congo drums; the three medium-sized ones were called *omele*. All the drums are played with sticks, but whereas a drummer playing the large one always uses two of them, the medium and small ones may be played either with one stick and one hand, or two sticks. Of the large drum, the old man said, "It be the one that roll and cut."

In the *chapelle*, there was first of all a table near the door to the right for Yemanja, the god of the priestess, whose blue and white colors were in evidence. Above the table hung a large chromolithograph of Saint Anne, with whom this deity is identified. On the table in a dish lay an oil-saturated stone of a shape resembling a fish. This the priestess referred to as "Mother." Another dish with flat, nut-like objects, the priestess called *après Dieu*, and explained,

"This is the watchman for the table." There were small lithographs of Saint Cyprian, whom she called Saint "Ci-pari," one she said represented "The Lord when He come from tomb," one of the Sacred Heart of Jesus, which she said was for the Yoruban god Asharoko, one she described as being for "the Lord Himself," and one which she said was for "Shango — Saint John the Baptist." At the side of the lithograph of Saint John was a tall shepherd's crook, of beautifully polished wood. "When you see a crook, it always be for Shango." Nearby affixed to the wall was a flat wooden cross with each end carved; this was said to be for Saint Thomas. "He doesn't dance yet. The girl who dance for him did not come," said the priestess, adding that she could not remember the "African saint" for him, though earlier she had equated Dada with the cross.

Next to the Yemanja table was the one for Shango. This time Shango held secondary rank, since as the god of the priestess' husband, who was second in command of the cult-group, he had to yield precedence to the goddess of the principal member. On the wall above the table were grouped chromolithographs: the largest that of Saint John the Baptist as a youth, then another of "The Lord Himself," then Saint Joseph, then one of the Infant Jesus and Mary. One was of Saint Philomène, who is identified with Oshun: "She always have anchor in the sea, and she have a crown," the priestess told. The next lithograph was said to be for Da Luwa, who was also called Saint John, then one of the Sacred Heart of Jesus, here again equated with Asharoko, then one of Saint John baptizing in the Jordan. There was another of Saint Catherine, the goddess Oya, one of Saint Anthony, here identified with Dada, though earlier this saint was equated with Abakoso; one of Saint Michael with sword and scales, called "Ogun — St. Michael," and one named "Saint Antoine and Jesus," using the créole term. "The Lord with crown of Thorns, who be Zewo," came next, and finally one of "Saint" Jonah, holding a harpoon, and equated with Ajaja. On the table itself were paper flowers, kola nuts, and a candle in a holder.

Near the ground was a rack for the ceremonial paraphernalia used by possessed dancers. These included a stick for Zewo, an axe for Shango — "That be he battle axe" — an anchor for Oshun, a red and white stick with an arrow point representing the harpoon which the dancer for Ajaja uses, and two shepherd's crooks for Shango, one for "Shango the Rider," and another one for "Shango, the man without the head," Saint John the Baptist.

The third table in the room was said to be "for everything." It held various sacred objects, and was in honor of deities that did not belong to the categories just listed. There was a dish of kola on the table, "carbide for light," conch shells "to warn the gods of trouble," and stones sacred to various deities, candles, and paper flowers. Above it hung a "guard" to see that no evil power entered the place of worship. On top of a nearby shelf was a bell for Bozuwa, a god that goes with Minana, "the mother of all the saints," who is also accompanied by Parara, said to be a brother of Bozuwa, and Ogun, who "they say he is father." "She does a lot of praying," the priestess observed of Minana.

3

The designations for the chromolithographs in the *chapelle* that were furnished by the priestess and her entourage made clear how complete was the identification of African gods with the saints of the Church. By citing direct quotation in several instances, it has been possible to indicate how often the names were given in a hyphenated form, like Shango-Saint John, or Ogun-Saint Michael. Equally evident is the fact that the usage is also interchangeable. The large drums were described as being for Saint Michael and Saint

John, while a chromolithograph of Saint John the Baptist was designated as "Shango." In order to make valid the correspondence of Ajaja, a god of the sea, with Jonah, sainthood was conferred on Jonah, for the concept of god and saint are one, and to have conceived of Jonah as a lesser being would have disqualified him for such identification.

The phenomenon illustrated is the one called syncretism, observed and reported upon especially from many parts of the New World, where Africans have translated their aboriginal religious structure into the patterns of worship of their new environment. Such renderings of belief and worship have proved both simplest and most felicitous when the accommodation was made to a pattern of Catholicism, since its multiplicity of saints made feasible parallelisms to a multiplicity of nature deities. But though syncretism occurs in many parts of the New World where Negroes live, the same identifications are not always made.

The table that follows includes alternate pronunciations heard, the sacrifices acceptable to each god, the day and color sacred to each, as well as the paraphernalia associated with each in the dance. It will be seen that the concept of individualizing each deity not only according to powers and function, but according to personality type, which lies at the core of African worship, also finds expression in this New World center where African religious practices are maintained, though here, as elsewhere in the New World, this is rarely as finely drawn, or is as complex in its differentiation.

The gods are said to go in threes — the phrase is "Saints have three voices" — and as an example the following groupings were given. In the Thunder group, with Shango, are Dada, whose Catholic symbol is the cross, and Aba Koso, who corresponds to Saint Anthony. These three are said to be brothers. Ogun is visualized either as having three at-

African God	Catholic Saint	Day Worshipped	Sacred Color	Food Eaten	Paraphernalia
Shango	Saint John the Baptist	Friday	red & white	sheep, cock, rum	shepherd's crook
Dada	The Cross	not given	red & white	sheep, cock, rum	——
Aba Koso	Saint Anthony	not given	red & white	sheep, cock, honey & milk	——
Ogun	Saint Michael Saint Raphael Saint Michel (Fr.)	Thursday	red & blue	red cock, goat (must not be black), rum	"sword"
Zewo (Ozewo)	"The Lord Himself"	not given	orange	pigeons	stick
Asharoko (Oshoroko)	"The Sacred Heart"	Saturday	brown & white (green)	land turtle & guinea bird, rum	——
Ajaja	"Saint Jonah"	not given	red & white	red cock, land turtle, guinea bird, rum	"harpoon"
Da Aluwa	Saint John	Wednesday	red & white	cock, goat, cattle	——
Bozu-a (Bozuwa)	could not recall	Wednesday	red & white	goat, pigeon, land turtle	——
Minana	could not recall	not given	white, with orange band	goat, fowl	——
Yemanja (Emanja) (Amanja)	Saint Anne	Tuesday	blue	goat, fowl, a little rum	——
Oya	Saint Catherine	Wednesday	green	female goat, chicken of any color, except black	——
Oshun (Osho)	Saint Philomène	Wednesday	lt. blue (green)	goat, fowl	——
Eshu	The Devil	not given	not given	not given	——

tributes, or as being the surname of three brothers, each one of whom is identified with a Catholic saint. Thus what quality of Ogun which is "the war man" is identified with Saint Michael, Ogun the iron worker with Saint Raphael, while that manifestation of Ogun which cures and gives the protective guards is equated with Saint Michel, differentiated from Saint Michael when the name is pronounced créole fashion. Again, the goddesses, Oya, the wind — 'She's a bright spirit, the wind be everywhere" — Yemanja (or Amanja, as the pronunciation often heard designates her), and Oshun [the latter two, both goddesses of the water] are sisters. The correspondences are Saint Catherine, Saint Anne, and Saint Philomène, respectively. In the group of "goblets" in the *chapelle* were four for Shango, one of them called "Shango the Rider," three for Bozuwa, three for Oshun, two for Yemanja, two for Ajaja, and one each for Zewo, Ogun, Asharoko, and Minana. The colors and day of worship and food were the same for all the three "qualities" of Ogun, and for the triad Dada, Shango, and Aba Koso, though the latter prefers honey and milk to rum. No African god parallels the "Souls in Purgatory" who are worshipped on Monday, and it is interesting that no Catholic saint was named for either Bozuwa, or Minana.

Other gods that were named and described were at this time not worshipped by the cult-group we are considering, either because none who were possessed by these gods were members of this group, or they were disliked. Not represented in the *chapelle* because they had no worshippers were Batala, worshipped on Wednesday; Osa, identified with Saint Francis, and described as "a doctor"; Parara, a brother of Bozuwa, and a son of Minana by Ogun. Of those not acceptable to this group, the foremost was Shakponon, the Yoruba god of the earth who punishes by giving skindiseases, among which is smallpox. Another was Osain, in the Yoruba country god of leaves. Here it was said, "He is a devil. He sen' plenty trouble. He is a brother to Eshu."

The sex and habitat of the gods and the order in which they are called will next be tabulated, together with whatever comment was made on each:

Name and sex	*Habitat*	*Characterization*
Eshu (m.)	"Lives everywhere"	"We drive him away. He is always in mischief."
Ogun (m.)	——	"He works iron; he is a war man, and he cures, because there are three Ogun brothers."
Bozuwa (m.)	"Lives above"	"He is a ruler, too. He takes messages from Ogun."
Shango (m.)	"Lives above"	"He gives thunder, lightning, and sunlight."
Asharoko (m.)	Unknown	"He is a very great man."

Name and sex	Habitat	Characterization
Ajaja (m.)	In the sea	"He is a king." "He is a big man."
Da Aluwa (m.)	In the sea	"He is a king."
Oya (f.)	In the air	"She is the wind."
Yemanja (f.)	"More in the river"	——
Oshun (f.)	In river and sea	——
Minana (f.)	Unknown	"She gives grace, and likes praying."

One young man brought up the name of Agwe Woyo (the Dahomean god of the sea) as an African "Saint," but another demurred, "That is no Saint. That is a wake hymn." Except for the African gods enumerated in the order of summoning, which are the ones worshipped at this center, it was evident that the priestess, as well as the members of her group, was more at home with the names of the Saints. Similarly, it was remarked that though Shakponon was not worshipped by the group, the cactus plant sacred to him and his pantheon was found in the yard.

4

When a dance is in progress, the door to the *chapelle* is left open, so the gods may be free to leave the shrine where they had been called by invocation, and "possess" their devotees. The drummers are seated behind the battery of the three ritual drums, the small Ogun, one of the medium-sized *omele* drums, and the large talking drum, the Shango or Ogun, depending upon the god who is to be given pre-eminence that day. Seated nearby, and standing about the seated drummers, are the men who will replace those at the drums, and those others, the young boys who are fascinated with the drums, but are not as yet skilled enough to play at a principal rite. On the floor, in front of the drums, is a lighted candle, which is extinguished by each devotee who in the first throes of possession comes to address in pantomime the drums that sound the rhythms of his god. This is relighted each time by the priestess, her husband, or some other cult-member of experience.

Water is poured three times in front of each newly possessed person, and anyone whom the priestess, or one of those experiencing possession, wishes to be possessed as well. Several of those possessed will take this water and drink it, thus calming the intensity of initial possession, and leaving them sufficiently eased to continue dancing without violence, but with a skill and control that marks this cult group as one where excellence in dancing is valued. This was made evident when the priestess herself became possessed. Though a large woman, she danced with consummate artistry, an artistry, in fact, characteristic of these large women, who astonish the more by their lightness of foot, and their supple use of body.

Despite the violence of some of the possessions, all the dancers demonstrated a high degree of skill and discipline in the ceremonies that were witnessed. The singing, similarly, was not only enthusiastic, but showed training. Several times, the husband of the priestess would cup his ear to shut out the volume of sound from the drums, and listen for the trueness of the melodic pattern, meanwhile with his own strong voice bringing the chorus into pleasing unison.

The early part of one dance, in accordance with customary practice, was devoted to minor healing rites. The priestess to whose head Ogun had come was pacing back and forth, and scowling at the women on the bench in front of her. She talked in *patois,* and interspersed her comments with grunts, giving commands to her assistants to bring her various things from the *chapelle.* She finally called one of the seated women to her, and gave her a treatment. Holding a broom-like switch, she took the woman's head between her two hands, and began butting her forehead with considerable force against the forehead of the patient. Then she ran her hands down the arms of the woman, down her legs, and finally put her head against the woman's abdomen. This she pressed so hard that the woman grimaced with pain, and cried out "Oh, laws!" The priestess next picked up her grandson, who was less than a year old, threw him up in the air, caught him, and swung him by one arm. Then she shook him, and carried him about by his legs, holding him upside down. The child's shrieks were partially drowned out by the drums, but this treatment was continued for several minutes, until she placed him astride her back, the little legs resting on her hips, and danced with him. When she handed him back to his mother the child was quite calmed.

The priestess next observed an elderly man who had been walking about, showing signs of oncoming possession. Both she and her husband worked on him, but there was no response stronger than the swaying back and forth in place, with his eyes shut. They took off his shoes, and rolled back his trouser-legs so that he might be free to dance when the spirit finally did seize him, but still no possession ensued. The priestess thereupon signalled for her long "switch broom," and with this in hand, she took a backward step and began to lash the man vigorously over head and shoulders and back and arms. Still the god refused to come, and the man walked away, reappearing some time later, relaxed, with his clothing in order.

By this time the "tent" showed filled benches. Many spectators crowded against the railing, peering over the heads of those in front of them in order to follow the proceedings. Among those seated inside the enclosure, and those standing about, it was evident from the perceptible "freezing" of the muscles of the face, the sightless stare, the twitching of shoulders and shaking of the knees, that the gods were not far away. Soft whistling was heard from a boy among the spectators, and the priest called out sharply in rebuke. Whistling may bring the dead to the ceremony, and the gods and the dead must not come together. He also corrected those who sat with crossed legs, for anything "crossed" will keep the "saints" away.

The priestess was now possessed by "Amanja," her own god, and therefore the ruling deity of the *chapelle*. Noticing that a candle was lighted in the *chapelle,* she objected that only Ogun's altar had been given a light, whereupon the Yemanja and Shango tables were lighted, too. She danced toward the drums, and then circled about the dancing space, being joined by her husband who had come down from the house to correct the singing, but had also become possessed.

He danced opposite the priestess for a little, disappearing, and reappearing shortly from the *chapelle* with a red kerchief tied about his head, and two sashes hanging diagonally across chest and back, a red one over the left shoulder, looped over his right hip, and a white one over his right, fastened over the left hip. In his left hand he carried a tall shepherd's crook, raised above his head, and from it, too, streamers in the colors of his god, Shango, were fastened.

One drummer quickly surrendered his drum to another, and remained standing uneasily until, of a sudden, he was possessed by the goddess Oshun. He was given a green kerchief to replace the red he was wearing, and danced energetically after the initial swooning. He went about the ring of singers and spectators pressing their heads, but after a time, merely walked restlessly about the dancing space.

A woman in pink became possessed, and so strong was her seizure that it took several people to restrain her sufficiently to get a red band for Shango about her. She dashed into the *chapelle* and came back, to dance before the drums in a manner which those about characterized with approbation as "strong." She became somewhat quieted only after she had thrown herself into the arms of the priestess, after which she made a tour of the dancing space, greeting those seated in the name of her god. While this was in progress, there was another possession by Shango. The young man, in his early twenties, leaped high into the air, and came down on his head in the muddy puddle where the sacred water for each possession had been poured. Supported by several cult members, he remained in this position, legs waving in the air, until the priestess got him to his feet, when he joined her and the woman in pink in the dancing. At this time, and throughout the night, the priestess danced toward each of those possessed, fixing them with her eyes, and touching them gently in a caress.

The next one possessed was a woman, another "strong" dancer, who signalled for something which she described in gestures. A goblet with a green ribbon about its neck was brought to her, and this she placed on her head and began to dance. Without a head-pad to steady it, and without spilling any of its contents she danced vigorously for thirty-five minutes. Opposite each of the possessed men, then toward the four corners of the "tent," back into the center again, and repeating the dance to the four corners, she continued, with only short interludes of pacing about the dancing space. It was evident that among both cult members and spectators there was admiration for this performance of Asharoko, who chose to manifest himself so exuberantly that night.

During this time still another young man became possessed, this time for Ajaja. He went to the *chapelle* and returned with a wooden harpoon, the end of which was whitened, and which he used as a wand when he danced. Going counter-clockwise about the dancing space, he touched with his "harpoon" the heads of all those who were inside the railing. When he stood before a woman dressed in a white figured silk dress, whose head was bound with a towel, he took her by the hand and urged her with gestures to follow him to the *chapelle*. It was not possible to observe what was taking place inside, but the priestess, who was seated, happening to glance in that direction, jumped to her feet, and ran toward the shrine. It was not long before the woman with the covered head returned to the "tent," and the man followed, now free of his possession. Although it cannot be stated what the priestess had seen there, the incident is nevertheless of interest as showing the surveillance over what goes on, and the prompt checking of what is considered unseemly.

One of the drummers began to complain that his arms were tired. From the expression of his eyes, it was evident that he was approaching possession. He walked about, moving his arms, and then for a few moments stood still before the drums. Suddenly the god came, and he sprinted across the dancing space from one end to the other, until he was calmed with the ceremonial pouring of the water, the extinguishing of the candle, and the little ritualistic acts that fix the attention of the possessed. The dancing that followed held participants and onlookers tense with appreciation, for this drummer was indeed the darling of his god, Ogun. He was possessed of a voice of great beauty, he was a superb drummer; and now in his dance he showed that he was equally endowed as a dancer.

Meanwhile the man who had been possessed by Ajaja was trying to "bring the god" to the heads of several women. He stood before a well-dressed young girl and brought her to her feet, leading her to dance with him. He then went to another and tried to induce possession in her, but the priestess intervened, "Don' force it. Let the Saints come as they want to." She led the young woman away, still "with a clear eye." The well-dressed girl, however, stood to one side, and moved uneasily from one foot to the other, until standing tall and statuesque, she made her way to the *chapelle*. While she was gone, the possessed Ogun and Asharoko went about the dancing space greeting everybody.

But soon the statuesque woman came from the *chapelle*,

brandishing a wooden sword. Taking Ogun's red scarf from his neck, she tied it about her as a sash. Twirling her weapon recklessly in the faces of those she came to, whether standing or seated, she danced backwards and forwards toward the drums. Then she executed the most intricate steps, as she charged the four corners, thrusting with her "sword" in every direction. Cult members, whether possessed or not, moved back, and kept well out of range as she wielded the weapon. She next got the drummer who played the small Ogun drum to place it on her head and to follow her as she danced, beating its rhythm while it rested there.

Now those first possessed were beginning to regain consciousness. They danced in subdued fashion until, turning from the drums, they remained standing in one place, their eyes glued to the doorway of the *chapelle*. Suddenly on a dead run, they would make their way toward it, leaping in the air as they approached the steps, and hurling themselves in a kind of dive onto the floor, to lie prostrate in the small shrine, with their feet projecting from the doorway. One succeeded the other in this rite of emerging from possession. Only the woman Ogun, the last possessed, continued dancing with her sword. But her manner, too, became quiet, and soon she was ready to go among the participants to greet them in the name of her god by touching their heads with the flat edge of the sword. When her possession was over, the dance was ended.

OFFICIAL DOCUMENTS BEARING ON TRINIDAD NEGRO CUSTOMS

THE FOLLOWING DOCUMENTS, taken from official sources, have bearing on three elements in Trinidad Negro culture that have figured prominently in the discussions of this book. They concern the Shouters sect, the practice of obeah, or magic, and drumming and the *bongo* dance.

1. SHOUTERS

The Ordinance under which the prosecutions of Shouters in Toco Court were carried on is phrased in these terms: *

An Ordinance to render Illegal Indulgence in the Practices of the Body known as the Shouters
(28 November, 1917)

1. This Ordinance may be cited as the Shouters Prohibition Ordinance.

2. (1) A "Shouters' meeting" means a meeting or gathering of two or more persons, whether indoors or in the open air, at which the customs and practices of the body known as Shouters (hereafter in this Ordinance referred to as "the Shouters")

* *The Laws of Trinidad and Tobago . . .* in force on the 30th day of June, 1925. Revised edition, London, Waterlow and Sons, 1925. Title III (ii) , Chap. 27, "Shouters Prohibition," pp. 362–364.

are indulged in. The decision of any Magistrate in any case brought under this Ordinance as to whether the customs and practices are those of the Shouters shall be final whether the persons indulging in such customs or practices call themselves Shouters or by any other name.

(2) A "Shouters' house" means any house or building or room in any house or building which is used for the purpose of holding Shouters' meetings, or any house or building or room in any house or building which is used for the purpose of initiating any person into the ceremonies of the Shouters. The decision of any Magistrate in any case brought under this Ordinance as to whether a house or building or room in any house or building is a Shouters' house shall be final.

(3) The term "Manager" includes any person having control over or charge of any estate or land whatsoever in the Colony.

3. It shall be an offense against this Ordinance for any person to hold or to take part in or to attend any Shouters' meeting to be held in any part of the Colony indoors or in the open air at any time of the day or night.

4. It shall be an offense against this Ordinance to erect or to maintain any Shouters' house or to shut up any person in any Shouters' house for the purpose of initiating such person into the ceremonies of the Shouters.

5. (1) If it shall come to the knowledge of the owner or manager of any estate or land in the Colony that a Shouters' house is being erected or maintained, or that Shouters' meetings are being held, on the estate or land over which such owner or manager has control, he shall forthwith notify the non-commissioned officer in charge of the Constabulary Station nearest to such house, estate, or land of the erection or maintenance of such Shouters' house or of the locality or place at which such Shouters' meetings are being held.

(2) The manager or owner of any estate or land in the Colony who fails so to notify such non-commissioned officer as aforesaid, or who knowingly permits the erection or maintenance of any Shouters' house or the holding of Shouters' meetings on any estate or land over which he has control, shall be guilty of an offense against this Ordinance.

6. It shall be an offense against this Ordinance for any person at or in the vicinity of any Shouters' meeting to commit or

cause to be committed or to induce or to persuade to be committed any act of indecency.

7. (1) It shall be lawful for any party of members of the Constabulary Force, of whom one shall be a commissioned or non-commissioned officer, without a warrant to enter at any time of the day or night any house, estate, land, or place in or on which such commissioned or non-commissioned officer may have good ground to believe or suspect that a Shouters' meeting is being held or where he may have good ground to believe or suspect that any person or persons is or are being kept for the purpose of initiation into the ceremonies of the Shouters, and to take the names and addresses of all persons present at such Shouters' meeting or Shouters' house.

(2) It shall also be lawful for any member of the Constabulary Force to demand the names and addresses of any person taking part in any meeting in the open air which he has good reason to believe is a Shouters' meeting.

(3) Any person refusing to give his name and address to any member of the Constabulary Force when asked to do so under the authority of this section shall be liable to be arrested and detained at a Constabulary Station until his identity can be established.

8. Any person guilty of an offense against this Ordinance shall be liable, on summary conviction before a Magistrate, to a penalty not exceeding fifty pounds.

The discussion by the Attorney-General that preceded the adaptation of this Ordinance throws light on the derivation of the Trinidad Shouters, and gives the official reasons for the presentation of this measure by Government: *

Shouters Prohibition Ordinance, 1917

The Attorney-General: The next bill for the consideration of the house is one of an altogether exceptional character. As perhaps the House will realize, it is very far indeed from the desire of the Government to do anything which interferes with

* *Debates in the Legislative Council of Trinidad and Tobago,* January–December, 1917. Trinidad, Government Printing Office, Port-of-Spain, 1918. Session of 16 Nov., 1917, pp. 349–351.

the liberty of the subject and the right of the individual to choose the way in which he should worship. But, unfortunately, a condition of affairs has arisen in the colony by reason of the practice of a sect or body calling itself the Shouters which has, so far as the Government sees, made it necessary to come to this House and submit proposals for interference in the practices of that body. Apparently the Shouters have had a somewhat stormy history from all I have been able to learn regarding them. They seem, if they did not arise there, to have flourished exceedingly in St. Vincent, and to have made themselves such an unmitigated nuisance that they had to be legislated out of existence. They then came to Trinidad and continual complaints have been received by the Government for some time past as to their practices. Apparently, the neighbourhood in which a Shouters meeting takes place is made almost impossible for residential occupation. I understand there is or was one meeting place in Belmont at which their meetings were conducted with such fervour that the shouting and the singing and the noise generally could be heard somewhere about the Transfer Station. It is not only the inconvenience caused by the noise which they make that has given rise to this legislation, but also the fact that from the information that has been received, the practices which are indulged in are not such as should be tolerated in a well-conducted community. I say that this legislation is exceptional in character, but it is submitted to this House that exceptional circumstances call for it. The effect of this bill, if passed, will be that attendance at Shouters' meetings will be made by Section 3 of the bill unlawful. Now it is always difficult in preparing a bill of this kind to define the class of person whom you wish to reach. At present they are called Shouters, but if this House merely said that Shouters were to be prohibited from holding meetings, the question might very well soon arise as to whether a new body called Shriekers were Shouters. The result is that Section 2 defines what a Shouter is or what is a Shouters meeting in very wide terms, and gives a wide discretion to the Magistrate to decide whether a body or members of a body brought before him are Shouters or something else. I may say that in a large measure the provisions of this Ordinance have been adapted from an existing law in St. Vincent. I quite freely admit that the powers conferred upon the Magistrate are very considerable under

Section 2, but, personally, I have been unable to devise any better scheme of dealing with the trouble which is sought to be met by the provisions of this Ordinance. Other provisions of the bill provide for entry by the Police on premises where Shouters' meetings are being held. It throws a duty on all owners or managers of land to inform the Police that Shouters' meetings are taking place on their estates, and it also, under Section 6, prohibits the committing of acts of indecency or immorality in the neighborhood of Shouters' meeting places. The need of the latter clause is due to the fact that certain of the initiatory ceremonies necessary to be gone through before you can bcome a Shouter are of a kind to which the term "indecent" or "immoral" can alone be applied. I move the second reading of the bill. . . .

Clause 6

The Hon. Dr. Prada: What does that really mean?

The Inspector-General of Constabulary: There is a building in connection with this ceremony which is called the "Mourner's House." In this those being initiated are placed and are not allowed to come out for a considerable time. They are not supposed to speak during this period, and when they do come out they, generally, are very emaciated. That is one of the practices.

The Hon. Dr. Prada: That is hardly indecent.

The Inspector-General of Constabulary: At the meeting they take their clothing off and commit all sorts of indecent acts when they get shaking.

The provisions in the Constabulary Manual which govern the actions of the police in making arrests under the Ordinance, and which afford a useful definition of the practices which define Shouters activities, can also be given: *

Shouters

The Shouters Prohibition Ordinance makes illegal the practices of the body known as "Shouters," and its provisions should be rigidly enforced by the Constabulary.

* *Trinidad Constabulary Manual,* compiled by W. E. Power. Trinidad, Government Printing Office, Port-of-Spain, 1936. p. 175.

The question as to whether the customs and practices complained of in any instance are those of the Shouters is one for the Magistrate to decide, and, as his decision as to this is final, in all prosecutions the complainant himself or his witnesses should be able and prepared to give evidence of the practices, etc., of these people.

These practices include as follows:

    (a) Binding the head with white cloth.
    (b) Holding of lighted candles in the hands.
    (c) Ringing of a bell at intervals during meetings.
    (d) Violent shaking of the body and limbs.
    (e) Shouting and grunting.
    (f) Flowers held in the hands of persons present.
    (g) White chalk marks about the floor.

The Ordinance must be referred to as regards the right and powers of the Constabulary in this connection.

2. OBEAH

The prohibition of obeah, or the working of magic, is enforced under the Summary Conviction Offenses Ordinance, 19 May, 1921. In it, the proscribed practice of magic is thus defined:

"Obeah" signifies every pretended assumption of supernatural power of knowledge whatever for fraudulent or illicit purposes or for gain or for the injury of any person. . . ." *

The relevant paragraphs are as follows: †

Superstitious Devices

48. Every person who, by the practice of obeah, or by any occult means, or by an assumption of supernatural power or knowledge, shall intimidate or attempt to intimidate any person, or shall obtain or endeavour to obtain any chattel, money, or valuable security from any other person, or shall pretend to discover any treasure or any lost or stolen goods, or the person who stole the same, or to inflict any disease, loss, damage, or

---

* *Laws of Trinidad and Tobago,* Chap. 25, par. 2, p. 317.
† *Ibid.,* pp. 333–334.

personal injury to or upon any other person, or to restore any other person to health, and every person who shall procure, counsel, induce, or persuade or endeavour to persuade any other person to commit any such offense, shall, on conviction before a Magistrate be imprisoned, with or without hard labour, for any term not exceeding six months, and, if a male, may be sentenced to undergo corporal punishment, and if a female, may during such imprisonment, be kept in solitary confinement not exceeding three days at any one time and not exceeding one month in the whole, as such Magistrate shall direct.

49. If it shall be shewn, upon the oath of a creditable witness that there is reasonable cause to suspect that any person is in possession of any article or thing used by him in the practice of obeah or witchcraft, it shall be lawful for any Justice, by warrant under his hand, to cause any place whatsoever belonging to or under the control of such person to be searched, either in the day or in the night, and, if any such article shall be found in any place so searched, to cause the same to be seized and brought before him or some other Justice, who shall cause the same to be secured for the purpose of being produced in evidence in any case in which it may be required.

The explanation of this Ordinance in the *Police Manual,* and the procedures to be employed in enforcing its mandate, are these: *

Obeah

Superstition, in spite of the advance of education, is still very prevalent in the Colony, and is not as might be thought by some, confined entirely to the lower and more ignorant classes.

"Obeah" is defined as every pretended assumption of supernatural power or knowledge whatever for fraudulent or illicit purposes or for gain or for injury to any person.

It is almost always necessary to employ "Police Spies" in order to detect and prosecute to conviction persons charged with the practice of Obeah, and, invariably in these cases it is suggested by the defense that the case for the prosecution is a tissue of lies, and that if anyone should be punished it is the com-

* *Laws of Trinidad and Tobago,* pp. 67–68.

plaintant or the "Spy" for procuring or inciting the defendant to commit the offense.

Power is given under the Ordinance to any Justice, on the oath of a credible witness, to issue a Warrant, which may be executed at any time in the day or in the night, to search premises belonging to or under the control of a suspected person and to seize all articles used in practice of Obeah and found therein.

There is, however, no authority under this Warrant to apprehend the suspected person and it is, therefore, well in such cases to so arrange that the person suspected may be detected in the act of committing the offense so that he may, by virtue of the Constable's general power of arrest on view, be apprehended on the spot, and, along with any articles found, be taken before a Magistrate.

A "Police Spy" or a person used for the purpose of entrapping an offender is not an accomplice and does not need corroboration. — R. *v.* Beckley, 73 J. P. 239; R. *v.* Hensur, 6 Cr. App. R. 76; R. *v.* Mullins, 3 Cox 526.

There is no need to prove an intent to defraud or deceive in cases of this kind. Alexander v. Butler, Trinidad Appeal Court Decision reported in *Port-of-Spain Gazette* of 16th December, 1931.

Occult practices referred to in the section of the Summary Conviction Offenses Ordinance dealing with this class of offense were referred to and defined in the case of Figaro *v.* Mollineaux, which came before the Trinidad Court of Appeal on the 22nd November, 1938. *Vide Port-of-Spain Gazette* of the 23rd November, 1928.

The cases of Landeau *v.* Alexander, Trinidad L. R. Volume 2, page 376 and Deval *v.* Lambert, Trinidad L. R. Volume 4, page 104 should be referred to in this connection.

3. DRUMMING, AND DANCING BONGO

The limit of ten o'clock for gatherings where drums and other percussion instruments are employed, and prohibition of the *bongo* dance, are laid down in another section of the Summary Conviction Offenses Ordinance: *

* *Laws of Trinidad and Tobago,* Chap. 25, p. 345.

Playing Drums, Dancing, etc.

80. Every person or occupier of any house, building, yard, or other place who shall —
    (1) without license under the hand of a commissioned officer of Constabulary, permit any persons to assemble and play or dance therein to any drums, gong, tambour, bangée, chac-chac, or other similar instrument of music, at any time between the hour of ten o'clock in the evening of one day, and the hour of six o'clock in the morning of the next day; or
    (2) permit any persons to assemble and dance therein the dance known as "bungo" or any similar dance,
shall, on conviction before a Magistrate, be liable to a penalty not exceeding ten pounds, and it shall be lawful for any constable, with such assistants as he may take to his aid, to enter any house, building, yard or place where any persons may be so assembled, and stop such dance or seize and carry away all such drums, gongs, tambours, bangées, chac-chacs, or other instruments of music, and the same shall be forfeited.

Instructions to the police for enforcing this measure are: *

Playing Drums, etc., during Prohibited Hours and Dancing the Bongo Dance

The drums should be seized and the owner or occupier of the premises in which the playing, etc., took place should be prosecuted.

It will be noted that no provision is made in the Ordinance for the punishment of persons other than the owners and occupiers and, therefore, the persons present and actually playing the drums, or otherwise taking part in the dancing, etc., must be proceeded against as aiders and abettors.

* *Constabulary Manual,* p. 213.

REFERENCES

THOUGH a considerable list of books wherein some information on Trinidad is to be found might be given here, we shall restrict ourselves to those works which contain data bearing on the past and present of the Negro population.

For historical materials, these three volumes are basic:

JOSEPH, E. L., *History of Trinidad,* Trinidad, 1840

DE VERTEUIL, L. A. A., *Trinidad, its Geography, Natural Resources, Administration, Present Condition and Prospects,* London, Paris and New York, 1884 (2nd ed.)

It is from this volume that the early census data given on p. 22 are taken (p. 158), the quotation on the "Yarribas" on pp. 28–29 (pp. 158–9), and the citation concerning the early people of Trinidad on p. 18 (p. 438).

BORDE, P. G. L., *Histoire de l'Isle de la Trinidad sous le Gouvernement Espagnol.* Paris, vol. i, 1876, vol. ii, 1882

A useful summary of information about Trinidad, its history, resources and population is to be found in the *Enciclopedia Espanole* (s. v. "Trinidad"), while equally useful discussions are contained in the relevant passages of a secondary school text-book by E. W. Daniel entitled *West Indian Histories. Book III, Story of the West Indian Colonies* (London, n. d.). Demographic and other statistical materials are in the *Statesman's Yearbook,* 1944, and in the *Encyclopaedia Brittanica World Atlas.* The work on the calypso to which we refer and from which we quote on pp. 285–286, is by Charles S. Espinet and Harry Pitts, and is entitled *Land of the Calypso* (Port-of-Spain, 1944).

Books written by contemporary travellers about Trinidad

are not many, but those we cite give vivid pictures of early life on the Island. The best we found were:

CARMICHAEL, MRS. A., *Domestic Manners and Social Condition of the White, Colored, and Negro Population in the West Indies*, London, 1833 (2 vols.)

DAY, C. W., *Five Years' Residence in the West Indies*, London, 1852 (2 vols.)

KINGSLEY, CHARLES, *At Last: A Christmas in the West Indies*, New York, 1871

Our citation on p. 19 about the early reaction of Negroes and "Coolies" to each other is from Kingsley (p. 148).

No references will be given here to the various recent reports by Commissions of the Colonial Office in London and by the Anglo-American Caribbean Commission, since they deal primarily with pressing problems that demand melioration. For an overall picture of social and economic conditions in the West Indies during the middle thirties, wherein Trinidad receives predominant consideration, the work by W. M. Macmillan, *Warning from the West Indies* (Penguin Books, London, 2nd ed., revised, 1938) is recommended, especially since its findings did no little to stimulate later enquiries.

The "Sankey," "Jesus, Lover of My Soul," transcribed in Chapter VIII, is No. 58B1 of the collection we recorded during this field-work. The songs whose words are given in Chapter X are also from this collection. These records, having three hundred Trinidad songs, have been deposited in the Laboratory of Comparative Musicology, Department of Anthropology, Northwestern University; while copies have been placed in the Archive of American Folk-Song, Music Division, Library of Congress.

Commercial recordings of calypsos cited in Chapter X include the following:

"Bad Woman" Herbert Raphael Charles (The Lion) and Raymond Quevedo (Attila the Hun). Melotone, No. M12963

"Matilda" King Radio accompanied by Cyril Montrose Orchestra. Decca, No. 17410–A

"Sofia" Belasco Orchestra. Victor, No. 81501–B

"She Want to Get Me in Matrimony" Lord Beginner, with Bert McLean's Jazz Hounds. Bluebird, No. B–4572–A

"I Don't Want no Young Gal" Lord Ziegfield and Bert McLean's Jazz Hounds. Bluebird, No. B–4593–B

* * *

For the cultures of Africa from which the ancestors of the Trinidad Negroes were in large measure derived, the following titles may be consulted:

RATTRAY, R. S. *Ashanti,* Oxford, 1923
Religion and Art in Ashanti, Oxford, 1927
HERSKOVITS, M. J. *Dahomey, an Ancient West African Kingdom,* New York, 1938 (2 vols.)
BASCOM, WILLIAM R., *The Sociological Role of the Yoruba Cult-Group.* (Memoir 63, American Anthropological Ass'n.) , Menasha, Wis., 1944
NADEL, F. S., *A Black Byzantium,* London, 1945
HARRIS, J. S. "The Position of Women in a Nigerian Society," *Transactions,* New York Acad. of Sciences, Ser. II, vol. ii (1940) , pp. 141–148
"Some Aspects of the Economics of Sixteen Ibo Individuals." *Africa,* vol. xiv (1944) , pp. 302–335

Other New World Negro cultures have been described in these books:

RAMOS, A. *The Negro in Brazil,* Washington, 1939
PIERSON, D., *Negroes in Brazil,* Chicago, 1942
HERSKOVITS, M. J. AND F. S., *Rebel Destiny, among the Bush Negroes of Dutch Guiana,* New York, 1934
Suriname Folklore, New York, 1936
BECKWITH, M. *Black Roadways, a Study in Jamaican Folk Life,* Chapel Hill, 1929.
HERSKOVITS, M. J., *Life in a Haitian Valley,* New York, 1937
CAMPBELL, A. A. "St. Thomas Negroes — A Study in Personality and Culture," *Psychological Monographs,* vol. lv, no. 5 (1943)

The setting of this book in the larger problem is indicated in the following volume, which also has a discussion of where in Africa New World Negroes in general were derived, and a sketch of the underlying patterns common to all the cultures from which they came:

HERSKOVITS, M. J. *The Myth of the Negro Past,* New York, 1941

INDEX

i